"This carefully researched, well-organized, and clearly written volume sheds light on Andrew Fuller's theological approach to spiritual renewal. It sets it in historical and theological context, clarifies it against some alternative views, and applies it to related topics. Ryan Rindels is to be commended for this fine contribution to the growing literature on Fuller."

—Christopher W. Morgan
California Baptist University, Riverside

"In the middle of the long eighteenth century, far too many English Particular Baptist communities were locked into a cycle of decline. Their great need was revival.... Drawing heavily on the master thinker about revival in this period, namely, Jonathan Edwards, Andrew Fuller both crafted a theology of revival and actively sought to promote it throughout his busy life. Ryan Rindels has taken for his subject of this monograph this vital aspect of Fuller's life and helpfully delineated its variegated contours in Fuller's thinking and doing. A fine study."

—Michael A. G. Haykin
The Andrew Fuller Center for Baptist Studies
and Southern Baptist Theological Seminary

"Andrew Fuller was at the center of a revival movement among the English Particular Baptists that led to a missionary awakening across the English-speaking world. In this important study, Ryan Rindels ably demonstrates that Fuller's theology of revival was an extension of his larger theological vision for reconciling divine sovereignty and human responsibility. This is a needed contribution to Fuller studies."

—Nathan A. Finn
North Greenville University

"It is positive indeed that Andrew Fuller's importance as a theologian and missiologist is now being recognized, with a growing body of secondary literature examining various aspects of his considerable legacy. This new study, which offers a lucid and satisfying analysis of Fuller's theology of revival, is one of the best to appear in recent years. . . . Historians, theologians, and thoughtful pastors will all benefit from it. It shines a light on the past and also has the potential to illuminate current debates."

—Peter Morden
Author of *The Life and Thought of Andrew Fuller (1754–1815)*

"Scholars have long associated Andrew Fuller with the evangelical revival. Fuller's ministry-focused theology and warm-hearted piety allowed him to incorporate that revival into Particular Baptist life. Rindels offers a helpful examination of Fuller's theology of revival, and by doing so makes a helpful contribution to Fuller studies."

—David Rathel
Gateway Seminary

Andrew Fuller's Theology of Revival

Monographs in Baptist History

VOLUME 18

SERIES EDITOR
Michael A. G. Haykin, The Southern Baptist Theological Seminary

EDITORIAL BOARD
Matthew Barrett, California Baptist University
Peter Beck, Charleston Southern University
Anthony L. Chute, California Baptist University
Jason G. Duesing, Midwest Baptist Theological Seminary
Nathan A. Finn, Union University
Crawford Gribben, Queen's University, Belfast
Gordon L. Heath, McMaster Divinity College
Barry Howson, Heritage Theological Seminary
Jason K. Lee, Cedarville University
Thomas J. Nettles, The Southern Baptist Theological Seminary, retired
James A. Patterson, Union University
James M. Renihan, Institute of Reformed Baptist Studies
Jeffrey P. Straub, Central Seminary
Brian R. Talbot, Broughty Ferry Baptist Church, Scotland
Malcolm B. Yarnell III, Southwestern Baptist Theological Seminary

Ours is a day in which not only the gaze of western culture but also increasingly that of Evangelicals is riveted to the present. The past seems to be nowhere in view and hence it is disparagingly dismissed as being of little value for our rapidly changing world. Such historical amnesia is fatal for any culture, but particularly so for Christian communities whose identity is profoundly bound up with their history. The goal of this new series of monographs, Studies in Baptist History, seeks to provide one of these Christian communities, that of evangelical Baptists, with reasons and resources for remembering the past. The editors are deeply convinced that Baptist history contains rich resources of theological reflection, praxis and spirituality that can help Baptists, as well as other Christians, live more Christianly in the present. The monographs in this series will therefore aim at illuminating various aspects of the Baptist tradition and in the process provide Baptists with a usable past.

Andrew Fuller's Theology of Revival

Divine Sovereignty and Human Responsibility in Spiritual Renewal

Ryan Rindels

Foreword by
Chris Chun

◥PICKWICK *Publications* • Eugene, Oregon

ANDREW FULLER'S THEOLOGY OF REVIVAL
Divine Sovereignty and Human Responsibility in Spiritual Renewal

Monographs in Baptist History 18

Copyright © 2021 Ryan Rindels. All rights reserved. Except for brief quotations in critical publications or reviews, no part of this book may be reproduced in any manner without prior written permission from the publisher. Write: Permissions, Wipf and Stock Publishers, 199 W. 8th Ave., Suite 3, Eugene, OR 97401.

Pickwick Publications
An Imprint of Wipf and Stock Publishers
199 W. 8th Ave., Suite 3
Eugene, OR 97401

www.wipfandstock.com

PAPERBACK ISBN: 978-1-7252-8286-5
HARDCOVER ISBN: 978-1-7252-8287-2
EBOOK ISBN: 978-1-7252-8288-9

Cataloguing-in-Publication data:

Names: Rindels, Ryan, author. | Chun, Chris, foreword.

Title: Andrew Fuller's theology of revival : divine sovereignty and human responsibility in spiritual renewal / by Ryan Rindels; foreword by Chris Chun.

Description: Eugene, OR: Pickwick Publications, 2021 | Monographs in Baptist History 18 | Includes bibliographical references.

Identifiers: ISBN 978-1-7252-8286-5 (paperback) | ISBN 978-1-7252-8287-2 (hardcover) | ISBN 978-1-7252-8288-9 (ebook)

Subjects: LCSH: Fuller, Andrew, 1754–1815. | Spiritual life—Christianity. | Church renewal. | Providence and government of God—Christianity. | Theological anthropology—Christianity.

Classification: BX6331.2 .B29 2021 (paperback) | BX6331.2.B29 (ebook)

Manufactured in the U.S.A.　　　　　　　　　　　　　　　01/21/21

To Janai, for your patience, steadfastness and encouragement during this project, and the grace shown in every sacrifice made as a wife and mother. You are my beloved and my friend.

Contents

Foreword by Chris Chun | ix
Abbreviations | xi
Acknowledgments | xiii

Introduction | 1
    History of Research | 1
    Importance of the Study | 3
    Definitions | 4
    Methodology | 12
    Structure | 13

Chapter One: "Panting After The Spirit": Patterns of English Puritan Spiritual Renewal | 16
    John Owen | 17
    John Howe | 24
    Abraham Cheare | 31
    Conclusion | 38

Chapter Two: "The Spirit has Departed": Dissents' Declension and its Relationship to the Evangelical Revivals | 40
    High Calvinism and Declension among Particular Baptists | 45
    Dissenting Voices for Revival: Philip Doddridge and Isaac Watts | 54
    Evangelical Revivals and Particular Baptist Reception | 68
    Conclusion | 73

Chapter Three: Andrew Fuller and Revival | 75
    Biographical Background | 75
    Formative Influences | 78
    Andrew Fuller's Definition of Revival | 91
    Andrew Fuller's Perspective on Revival in his Historical Context | 94
    Conclusion | 103

Chapter Four: "Use of Means": Fuller and The Fruit of Revival | 105
    Circular Letter: Causes of Declension in Religion and Means of Revival | 106
    On Spiritual Declension and the Means of Revival | 118
    Conclusion | 127

Chapter Five: "The Promised Spirit": Fuller on The Work of The Holy Spirit in Revival | 129
    Jonathan Edwards, The Concert of Prayer, and *Humble Attempt* | 130
    Reception of *Humble Attempt* by Northamptonshire Association | 137
    Circular Letter: On the Promise of the Spirit | 139
    Sermon: *A Few Persuasives for the Revival of Religion* | 143
    Eschatological Optimism: An Impetus for Pursuing Revival | 150
    Conclusion | 153

Conclusion | 154

Bibliography | 159

Foreword

ANDREW FULLER, PREACHER, PASTOR, scholar, missionary statesman, apologist, polemicist, puritan-evangelical, and revival leader, lived from 1754-1815. He was a self-taught farmer's son in England who later became one the foremost theologians in all of baptist history. Fuller's contribution as the theologian behind the missionary activism of William Carey (1761-1834) and the modern missionary movement has been heralded by many. It's no wonder Charles Spurgeon (1834-1892) referred to Fuller as "the greatest theologian" of his century. The recent renaissance in Fuller studies has unearthed many of these impulses, and the role that Fuller played in the Particular Baptist revival. Despite these growing interests, no book-length treatment of Fuller's theology of revival has ever been written, much less published. Ryan Rindels's work fills this much needed scholarly lacuna.

Even before exploring the causes of declension among English Dissenting congregations during the eighteenth century, Rindels frames his monograph in seventeenth-century patterns of spiritual renewal in Puritan divines such as John Owen (1616-1683), Abraham Cheare (1628-1668) and John Howe (1630-1705). He also underscores other dissenting voices for revival during the first half of the eighteenth century, like those of Isaac Watts (1674-1748) and Philip Doddridge (1702-1751). These revivalistic patterns, Rindels argues, laid the foundation for the evangelical renewal in Fuller's time. Rindels then outlines Fuller's Particular Baptist upbringing, where high Calvinism led to a neglect of evangelism and was a hindrance to growth. This personal and theological development provided the context out of which Fuller came to understand revival. Having been influenced by American Congregationalist, Jonathan Edwards (1703-1758), and with the help of the transatlantic Edwardsean network as well as events surrounding his involvement with the Northamptonshire Association, the Prayer call of 1784, and the formation of the Baptist Missionary Society (BMS), Fuller rose to become the theological architect that revitalized Particular Baptist life in the eighteenth and nineteenth centuries. This movement ultimately gave birth to modern missions. While Fuller's contribution to the BMS has been applauded by many historians, Rindels asserts that Fuller was the link between BMS's theology of revival and global expansion. This legacy, of course, still reverberates in our time.

Ryan Rindels's original research has not only demonstrated a comprehensive knowledge of the long eighteenth-century, but his extensive treatment of its Puritan predecessors also makes this a fascinating volume. The readers of this book will reap great benefit from learning how Fuller's theology profoundly impacted the American landscape and played a seminal role in the transatlantic evangelical resurgence. This monograph is a compelling account of Fuller's theology of revival that will help to evaluate the nature and pattern of later Awakenings and even serve to assess spiritual movements of today.

Chris Chun,
Professor of Church History
Director of Jonathan Edwards Center
Gateway Seminary, Ontario, California

Abbreviations

Collected Works

WJE	The Works of Jonathan Edwards
WJO	The Works of John Owen
WJW	The Works of John Wesley
WAF	The Complete Works of Andrew Fuller (1845 Belcher Edition)

Journals

ABQ	American Baptist Quarterly
BQ	Baptist Quarterly
BHH	Baptist History and Heritage
CHRC	Church History and Religious Culture
CHST	Congregational Historical Society Transactions
DBSJ	Detroit Baptist Seminary Journal
EQ	Evangelical Quarterly
FJ	Founders Journal
HTR	Harvard Theological Review
JEBS	Journal of European Baptist Studies
JEH	Journal of Evangelical History
JETS	Journal of the Evangelical Historical Society
JHS	Journal of the Historical Society
JRT	Journal of Reformed Theology
JTS	Journal of Theological Studies

JURCHS	Journal of the United Reformed Church History Society
ICJ	International Congregational Journal
MBH	Monographs in Baptist History
NAVK	Nederlands Archief Voor Kerkgeschiedenis
NTT	Nederlands Theologisch Tijdshrift
PC	Philosophia Christi
PRJ	Puritan Reformed Journal
RE	Review and Expositor
SBJT	The Southern Baptist Journal of Theology
TBHS	Transactions of the Baptist Historical Society
SBHT	Studies in Baptist History and Thought
SCHT	Studies in Christian History and Thought
SEHT	Studies in Evangelical History and Thought
SWJT	Southwestern Journal of Theology
RT	Reformation Today

Acknowledgments

I WANT TO THANK my doctoral supervisor, Chris Chun, for his warm friendship coupled with scholarly rigor, without which I would not be the person I am today, much less the author of this book.

I would also like to acknowledge Michael Haykin for his invaluable guidance, the time spent in answering questions electronically and in person during the last five years, and his assistance in arranging for my dissertation to be published in this series. Michael's personal devotion and academic excellence exemplify the best of Christian scholarship.

Introduction

History of Research

Two centuries after his death, growing scholarly interest in Andrew Fuller has substantiated Baptist scholar Michael A. G. Haykin's judgment that a modest Fuller studies renaissance is at hand.[1] Though some works on Fuller were published in the first half of the twentieth century,[2] E.F. Clipsham's article, "Andrew Fuller and Fullerism: A Study in Evangelical Calvinism," is generally accepted as the origin of the current resurgence.[3] The 1980s saw publication of several dissertations[4] on Fuller's public ministry

---

1. The most comprehensive overview of Fuller studies with an extensive bibliography to the year 2013 is found in Finn, "Renaissance in Andrew Fuller Studies," 44–61. Fuller studies have paralleled a renewed appreciation for Reformed theology among evangelicals that began in the 1950s. Cited in Gribben, "Evangelical Eschatology and 'The Puritan Hope,'" in Haykin, *Emergence of Evangelicalism*, 375.

2. Dissertations include Duncan, "Influence of Andrew Fuller on Calvinism"; Kirkby, "Theology of Andrew Fuller"; Eddins, "Andrew Fuller's Theology of Grace"; Reed, "Historical Study of Three Baptist Doctrines of Atonement"; Clipsham, "Andrew Fuller's Doctrine of Salvation." Articles include Kirkby, "Andrew Fuller, Evangelical Calvinist," 195–202; Payne, "Andrew Fuller as Letter Writer," 290–99. Laws, *Andrew Fuller*, though being the first twentieth-century biography on Fuller it was not widely published and is therefore difficult to access.

3. The article was first in a series on Fuller. See *BQ* 20, 1–4 (1967): "1: The Development of Doctrine," "2: Fuller and John Calvin," "3: The Gospel Worthy of All Acceptation," "4: Fuller as a theologian," 99–114, 147–54, 214–25, 269–76.

4. Young, "Place of Andrew Fuller in the Developing Modern Missions Movement"; Oliver, "Emergence of a Strict and Particular Baptist Community"; Ascol, "Doctrine of Grace"; South, "Response of Andrew Fuller." I included South's dissertation as it is the

and theology with modest attention in secondary sources,[5] while the 1990s were increasingly fruitful with several works on Fuller and his contemporaries.[6] The twenty-first century has surpassed the production of two previous decades in dissertations,[7] secondary works,[8] journal articles,[9] and scholarly monographs.[10] Notable indicators demonstrate wide admiration for Fuller in Britain and North America.[11] Several popular-level works have

---

only one written in the 1990s.

5. "On the Road Again," in Nettles, *By His Grace and for His Glory*, 108–30; Nettles, "Andrew Fuller and Free Grace," 6–14; Milner, "Andrew Fuller," 18–29.

6. George, *Faithful Witness*; Roberts, "Andrew Fuller," 34–51; Ella, *Law and Gospel*; "Sutcliff's Friends," in Haykin, *One Heart and One Soul*, 133–52. It should be noted that Haykin's literary output is too extensive to list all his works on Fuller. I refer a reader to Finn's endnotes in "Renaissance in Andrew Fuller Studies," 54–61.

7. Brewster, "Andrew Fuller"; Box, "Atonement in the Thought of Andrew Fuller"; Wheeler, "'Eminent Spirituality and Eminent Usefulness.'"

8. Morden, *Offering Christ*; Haykin, *Armies of the Lamb*. Several chapters within a large book include: Priest, "Andrew Fuller, Hyper-Calvinism," 43–73; Daniel, "Fuller and Antinomianism," 74–82; Sheehan, "Great and Sovereign Grace," 83–120; Haykin, "'Oracles of God,'" 122–37; Nettles, "Christianity Pure and Simple," 139–73; Howson, "Fuller and Universalism," 174–202; Oliver, "Andrew Fuller and Abraham Booth," 203–22; Haykin, "Fuller and the Sandemanian Controversy," 223–36. Mauldin, *Fullerism as Opposed to Calvinism*. Naylor, "Andrew Fuller," 205–17; Haykin, "Eighteenth-Century Baptists," 264–78; Sell, "the Gospel its Own Witness," 111–43; Sell, "Fuller and Socinians," 119–37.

9. Nettles, "Edwards," 1–18; Haykin, "Andrew Fuller," 29–32; Priest, "Andrew Fuller's Response," 45–73; Young, "Andrew Fuller and the Modern Missionary Movement," 17–27; Morden, "Andrew Fuller and Baptist Missionary Society," 134–57; Chun, "Mainspring of Missionary Thought," 335–55. In 2008, Eusebia: The Bulletin of the Andrew Fuller Center for Baptist Studies published *Reading Andrew Fuller*, a series of articles presented at the Andrew Fuller Center conference in 2007, including: Haykin, "'Great Thirst for Reading,'" 5–25; Jue, "Fuller," 27–52; Trueman, "John Owen and Andrew Fuller," 53–69; Howson, "Fuller's Reading of John Gill," 71–95; Nettles, "Influence of Edwards on Fuller," 97–116; Chun, "'Sense of the Heart,'" 117–34; Pittsley, "Christ's Absolute Determination," 135–66; Wheeler, "Fuller's Ordination Sermons," 167–82. A two-part series, "The Life and Ministry of Andrew Fuller," can be found at *SBJT* 17 (2013). Spencer, "Fuller and the Doctrine of Revelation," 207–26; Morden, "Fullerism," 140–52; Haykin, "Defense of Trinitarian Communities," 258–78; Haykin, "Historical and Biblical Root," 165–76; Haykin, "'Honour of the Spirit's Work,'" 152–61; Haykin, "'Glorious Work of Reformation,'" 127–37.

10. Chun, *Legacy of Edwards in the Theology of Fuller*, a publication of the author's 2008 thesis, traces Fuller's deep theological indebtedness to Edwards.

11. In 2007, the Southern Baptist Theological Seminary opened the Andrew Fuller Center for Baptist Studies: www.andrewfullercenter.org. The Fuller Center website contains a variety of book reviews, study guides, audio sermons, journal articles, and unpublished essays. The center also hosts regular conferences. The *Founders Journal* a consortium of Calvinistic Southern Baptists—though a minority in the SBC—has continued publishing articles on Fuller. Moreover, The *Reformation Today* magazine,

piqued interest among pastors, seminarians, and academically-inclined laypersons.[12] To date, Peter Morden's critical biography on Fuller is the most definitive work,[13] while John Ryland Jr.'s biography is the earliest and most comprehensive nineteenth-century source, though other publications are duly cited by scholars.[14] Perhaps the strongest indicator of a Fuller renaissance is the ongoing publication of a critical edition of Fuller's *Complete Works*.[15] A recent academic work, a Th.M. thesis by Ryan Hoselton focuses on Fuller's theology of virtue.[16] While dissertations, articles, and various secondary works have addressed a diversity of theological and practical subjects, no publication to date has examined Andrew Fuller's theology of revival.[17]

Importance of the Study

Several considerations warrant an exploration of Andrew Fuller's theology of revival. First, evangelicalism, though originally an Anglo-Protestant movement, is now global, with rapid growth coming from the two-third's majority world. That Fuller's contributions to the Baptist Missionary Society were crucial for sending William Carey to India in 1792, renders a genetic link between his theology and ministry and Baptist expansion in the global south. Second, a growing interest in evangelical Calvinism among

---

committed to the 1689 London Confession of Faith, has helpful articles on Fuller. Paternoster has published in their ongoing series Studies in Baptist History and Thought works on Fuller and others in the Particular Baptist tradition. Broadman and Holman Academic's publication of Paul Brewster's book on Fuller is indicative of growing readership.

12. Brewster, *Andrew Fuller*; Grant, *Andrew Fuller*; Piper, *Holy Faith*.

13. Morden, *Life and Thought of Fuller*.

14. Ryland, *Work of Faith*, referred to throughout as *Fuller*; Morris, *Memoirs*; Fuller, *Men Worth Remembering*.

15. At the time of this writing, three of seventeen volumes from a critical edition, published by De Gruyter have been released. See *Diary of Andrew Fuller* in Fuller, *Complete Works of Andrew Fuller Volume 5*; Haykin, *Memoirs of Pearce* in Fuller, *Complete Works of Andrew Fuller Volume 4*; and Finn, *Sandemanianism* in Fuller, *Complete Works of Andrew Fuller Volume 4*.

16. Hoselton, *Love of God*.

17. The closest treatment being by Yong, "Tending to Love." Yong's thesis has some parallels to my proposal, but his work does not deal with Fuller's theology of revival proper. Yong's thesis seeks to demonstrate how Fuller stressed the need for love to bring about local church revival. Two articles by Brewster, "Out in the Journeys Part I," 5–11; Brewster, "Out in the Journeys Part II," 5–14. A search among the ProQuest Dissertations and Theses Global, and Center for Research Libraries databases yielded no relevant results for this topic and Andrew Fuller.

Baptists, and especially in the last two decades, has drawn attention to Andrew Fuller's thought. Thus, his theological assessment of revival merits attention. Moreover, as Fuller was situated in a unique era, deeply affected by the evangelical revivals, his understanding and interpretation of these events would shape the Particular Baptist denomination he influenced.[18] As Baptist identity, particularly in the American south, has been associated historically with revival, practical and theological assessment is pertinent.

Lastly, as Baptists flourished in the decades after Fuller's death, particularly in North America, revivals profoundly impacted the American landscape, leading to exponential growth. Fuller's theology of revival would serve to evaluate the nature and pattern of later Awakenings with their increasingly Arminian emphases. Whether Fuller's understanding of revival could accept or accommodate American revivalism is certainly worthy of scholarly attention, and may provide a paradigm for evaluating, and assessing future Awakenings around the globe.[19]

The thesis of this monograph is that Andrew Fuller's theology of revival was constructed, and methodologically applied, within a Reformed framework of compatibility between divine sovereignty and human responsibility. As abundant reference in sermons, letters, and essays attest, revival was a salient feature in Andrew Fuller's ministry, and no less crucial, his historical context. Fuller was also a Calvinist, who identified with the theological consensus among Particular Baptists of his day. Hence, the perennial debate in Christian theology over the relationship between the divine sovereignty and human agency is applied to the arena of revival. How Fuller navigates the tension between what many claimed as a work of God, but whose activity has appeared anthropocentric will reflect his lifelong pursuit of balancing the razor's edge between high Calvinism and Arminianism.

Definitions

Regarding the proposed thesis, several questions warrant clarification. First, the term "Calvinism," like its cousin "Puritan," does not enjoy scholarly consensus as to a precise definition. What constitutes Calvinism, and who qualifies as a Calvinist are unavoidably complex questions and

---

18. Mark Noll's observation that for evangelicalism to take root, "the longing for revival was more important than a revival itself," is a certainly descriptive of Fuller's theology and ministry. See *Rise of Evangelicalism*, 137.

19. See McLoughlin, *Modern Revivalism*; "Issues and Explanations in Revivalism," in McClymond, *Embodying the Spirit*, 1–46.

historiographical fallacies are easily committed without careful qualification and nuanced terminology.[20] Given that this monograph begins with Puritan figures, and subsequent generations of British Protestants who admired their ministries, and drew deeply from their theology, a satisfactory answer is requisite.

Contemporary historiographic discussions have centered on the broader historical boundaries of the Reformed tradition including the enduring usefulness of Calvin's name. Debate over the nature of continuity between the Calvin and his successors is ongoing and cannot be discussed adequately here.[21] Carl Trueman proposes a mediating position between disjunction and continuity of Calvin and Calvinism that derives from the observation that Christian theology's communal nature precludes ascribing exclusive originality to a single theologian apart from indisputable evidence of uniqueness.[22]

---

20. The most common being reification, anachronism, and generalization. Abraham Kuyper discussed the nature of Calvinism as a "life-system," emphasizing God's sovereignty in all spheres of human existence in his famous 1898 Stone Lectures at Princeton. See "Calvinism a Life-System," in Kuyper, *Lectures on Calvinism*, 7–25. Cf. his quip that Calvinism is, "neither Lutheran, nor Anabaptist, nor Socinian," 9. B. B. Warfield wrote that Calvinism, ". . .means utter dependence on God for salvation. It implies, therefore, need of salvation and a profound sense of need, along with an equally profound sense of helplessness in the presence of this need, and utter dependence on God for its satisfaction." Trueman suggests "Reformed Orthodoxy," as a better designation. Throughout the book, I will use "Reformed," and "Calvinism," synonymously. For further discussion, see Stewart, *Ten Myths about Calvinism*; Muller, *After Calvin*; Muller, *Calvin and the Reformed Tradition*; Crisp, *Deviant Calvinism*, 235–40.

21. An earlier generation of historians made extensive efforts to contrast the thought of Calvin with theological formulations in the seventeenth century, notably, canons of the Synod of Dort (1618–19) and writings of Francis Turretin (1623–87). Their conclusions were that several doctrines in the Reformed tradition were distinct, even divergent from Calvin's own views. In recent decades, a new generation of scholars has sought to mend the breach between Calvin and Reformed scholasticism. What has become termed "the continuity thesis," also called the "Muller thesis" after Richard Mueller's proposals in *Post-Reformation Reformed Dogmatics*, it has nonetheless received critique in contemporary Reformed historiography. Cf. Van Asselt, *Federal Theology of Cocceius*. The continuity thesis broke with an older generation of scholars who insisted on a fundamental break between Calvin and the pre-Tridentine Reformers and later confessional Reformation theologians. These historical insights are drawn from Trueman, "Reception of Calvin," 19–27.

22. Trueman, "Reception of Calvin," 24. Thus, strictly speaking, John Calvin was an orthodox theologian who made minimal contributions in terms of raw content, and by his own testimony had no intention of being a theological innovator. Trueman, "Reception of Calvin," 27. In his 1536 prefatory address to Francis I in the *Institutes of the Christian Religion*, Calvin rebuts charge of teaching novel doctrine, averring that, "in calling it new, they are exceedingly injurious to God, whose sacred word deserved

To avoid the anachronistic fallacy of pitting Calvin versus Calvinism, Trueman proposes approaching texts as historical actions, rather than seeking to answer questions of continuity and discontinuity. Such an understanding leads to consideration of context as a conventional framework, namely diachronic and synchronic dimensions.[23] Whereas the "continuity thesis," has put exclusive focus on the synchronic aspect, a diachronic reading to the topic poses the question of reception of Calvin by later generations not as:

> Does this or that idea, expression, argument, or text stand in continuity with Calvin's thought?" bur rather, for example, "Does the reading of Calvin impact the way this writer reads this biblical text?" and "How is this writer using this idea or text of Calvin in his own situation.?[24]

While this proposal avoids the pitfalls of dichotomist readings, and allows for a fluid reception of contributions by earlier authors, it does not alleviate all difficulties for defining Calvinism in a theological tradition that is far from monolithic.[25] It should suffice to accept Andrew Fuller's self-identify as a Calvinist, which he held throughout his life, presenting theological arguments against incredulous opponents who judged the designation ill-fitting.[26]

---

not to be charged with novelty. To them, indeed, I very little doubt it is new, as Christ is new, and that the Gospel new; but those who are acquainted with the old saying of Paul that Christ Jesus 'died for our sins, and rose again for our justification (Rom. iv. 25) will not detect any novelty in us." See *Institutes*, 8. In the 1559 edition, Calvin reiterates that, ". . .since I began to discharge the office of teacher in the Church, my only object has been to do good to the Church, by maintaining the pure doctrine of godliness. . .," 25.

23. Trueman attributes this insight to Cambridge historian Quentin Skinner's *Visions of Politics I*, and derivatively, Skinner's application of the speech-act theory of J. L. Austin and John Searle. The diachronic-synchronic dialectic, widely used in theological and biblical studies, is drawn from the seminal work by Saussure, *Courses in General Linguistics*.

24. Trueman, "Reception of Calvin," 21.

25. Cf. Coffey's provocative "Rival Reformed theologies," in place of a singular, "Calvinism." See "Puritanism," 263. Cf. Wallace, *Puritans and Predestination*. Mark Noll proposes an inclusive, if vague description: "A traditional religion of traditional European Christendom," in *Rise of Evangelicalism*, 49.

26. Fuller identifies theologically as a "strict" Calvinist as distinct from high or, "moderate" Calvinist, which he describes as, "one that really holds to the system of Calvin." He adds, however, the following caveat: "I do not believe everything Calvin taught, nor any thing, because he taught it; but I reckon strict Calvinism to be my own system." See, "Conversation on Doctrine," in Ryland, *Fuller*, 346. In another letter, Fuller explicitly mentions the canons of Dort as expressive of his own theology, particularly their statements on the extent of the atonement. See *Calvinism*, in *WAF*, 2:711–14. In his *Letters on Systematic Divinity*, Fuller lists three leading doctrines of the gospel as

Revival

"Revival," like the terms previously noted, evades technical definition, and though its etymology is intuitively suggestive, it remains ambiguous.[27] The concept implies regaining what was once lost, of restoring what has become adulterated.[28] Conversely, it points to something new and fresh. As Bruce Hindmarsh observes, "Revival (re-*vivere*) was a matter of both animation and reclamation."[29] Revival also carries baggage due to its variegated appropriation by various Protestant traditions, particularly of the last two centuries.[30]

Continuity from Calvinism to Puritanism faces the subsequent question of historical succession from Puritanism to evangelicalism. David Bebbington has argued for evangelicalism's novelty and hard break with Puritanism, while Mark Noll holds to soft discontinuity. Others, such as John Coffey, Thomas Kidd see greater affinity between the two.[31] Although the word "revival" is rare in Puritan[32] writings, some have described

---

election, the atonement, and the influence of the Holy Spirit. See *Letter II*, in *WAF*, 1:685. For further discussion see Sheehan, "Great and Sovereign Grace," 85–87. Kirkby contended that, "Fuller was entirely justified in claiming that his system of theology was Calvinist after the pattern of the man of Geneva," in "Andrew Fuller," 197. Kirkby lists five evidences for this assertion: i. Fuller does not object to the label "Calvinist" ii. He defends Calvin and Calvinism and treats the Genevan reformer as authoritative iii. Calvin's writings are quoted. iv. His words are frequently echoed and v. his leading doctrines are expounded and defended.

27. For discussions of the meaning of the term and development see Kent, *Holding the Fort*, ch. 1; McLoughlin, *Modern Revivalism*; McLoughlin, *Revivals Awakenings and Reform*, xiii; Carwardine, *Transatlantic Revivalism*. Frederick Copleston notes that in speaking of any historical "decline," one begins speaking as a philosopher, and not as a historian, yet, "if one is to discern an intelligible pattern. . .one must have a principle of selection and to that extent at least one must be a philosopher" (*History of Philosophy*, 2:9).

28. Rack writes that revival possesses a, "certain air of nostalgia, a touch of myth of the golden age" (*Reasonable Enthusiast*, 158).

29. Hindmarsh, *Spirit of Early Evangelicalism*, 69.

30. Distinction between revival and "revivalism," is argued by Murray in *Revival and Revivalism*, to distinguish between the awakenings in New England during the years 1734–1735; 1740–1741, and the distinctive American phenomenon in the first half of the nineteenth century, the so-called Second Great Awakening.

31. See Stewart, "Did Evangelicalism Pre-Date the Eighteenth-Century?" 135–54. Cf. Walsh, "Origins of the Evangelical Revival," 132, 154. Fuller scholar Peter Morden concurs with Bebbington that evangelicalism was a distinctly new entity that began in the eighteenth century. See *Life and Thought of Andrew Fuller*, 25n77.

32. The tenets of Puritanism, identification of its adherents, and even chronology is notoriously difficult, with no definitive scholarly consensus on the subject. "Puritan," was first a contemptuous term of abuse given to five overlapping groups who sought

Puritanism itself as a *revival movement*.[33] J.I. Packer argues this on basis of three considerations. First, Puritans repeatedly used terms like *reform*, *reformation*, and *reformed* to express inward renewal of the heart and life they sought to promote.[34] Second, "personal revival was a central theme of Puritan devotional literature,"[35] and lastly, "the ministry of Puritan pastors under God brought revival."[36]

---

renewal and reform within the Church of England between 1564–1642. See Hall, "Puritanism," 283–96. Nuttall describes it as a movement with porous boundaries and internal tensions in, *Holy Spirit in Puritan Faith and Experience*, 28. Trueman cites the semi-Arian Christology of John Milton and the Arminianism of John Goodwin as indicative of the spectrum's inclusive extent. John Coffey and Paul Chang-Ha give the following definition: "the name we give to a distinctive and particularly intense variety of early modern Reformed Protestantism which originated with the unique context of the church of England but spilled out beyond it." See "Introduction," 1–7. Spurr defines the essence of Puritanism as stemming from a person's conviction that they are saved by God, elected to salvation by a merciful God for no merit of their own; and that as a consequence of this election they must lead a life of visible piety, must be a member of a church modeled on the pattern of the New Testament, and must work to make their community and nation a model Christian society. See *English Puritanism*, 5. For a further list of sources on Puritanism's history see Trueman, "Puritanism as Ecumenical Theology," 327n4.

33. Packer, "Puritanism as a Revival Movement," 2–16. Packer gives a brief and accessible definition of revival as, "a work of God by his Spirit through his word bringing the spiritually dead to living faith in Christ and renewing the inner life of Christians who have grown slack and sleepy," 3. Murray in *Pentecost Today?* places revival into three distinct categories. The first view understands revival as begun at Pentecost and ongoing, being the essence of the New Testament age. This view is advocated by Abraham Kuyper. See *Work of the Holy Spirit*, 127. The second renders revival as, "virtually the same thing as a period of energetic evangelistic activity." The third view has most affinity to Fuller's thought and understands revival as a sovereign outpouring of the Holy Spirit that is greater in measure than is normally the case—difference is in degree, not kind. See Murray, *Revival and Revivalism*, 23. Cf. Beeke, "Age of the Spirit and Revival," 30–49.

34. Packer, "Puritanism as a Revival Movement," 5.

35. Packer, "Puritanism as a Revival Movement," 5.

36. Packer, "Puritanism as a Revival Movement," 42–43. Packer provides the example of Richard Baxter's ministry in which close to 2,000 individuals were converted in Kidderminster and notes the stated purpose for writing the *Reformed Pastor* was that ministers be, "renewed in vigour, zeal and purpose, in other words revived." *Reliquiae Baxterianae*, first pagination, p. 115. Thomas Kidd traces the origins of revival in the American colonies to the seventeenth-century Massachusetts pastor Samuel Torrey, whom he suggests, "might be the first evangelical in New England." Kidd bases this claim on the evangelical preacher Thomas Prince Jr.'s 1757 assessment of Torrey's ministry, of whom the former judged as the first, "instances of the transient revival of religion." Torrey preached a series of election sermons, *Man's Extremity, God's Opportunity* (1695), among which were his greatest revival messages. See *The Great Awakening*, 1–12. Other noteworthy proto-revivals include the, "Sixemile revival at Antrim," in the 1620s. See Hamilton, *History of the Irish Presbyterian Church*, 42–44. In

Though not the first instance of revival denoting a type of spiritual awakening,[37] Isaac Watts's 1731 publication, *An Humble Attempt toward the Revival of Practical Religion Among Christians* is seminal for its proximity to the evangelical revivals, and its author's relationship to its most influential participants. In the treatise, Watts counsels his readers that, "when true Religion falls under a general and remarkable decay, 'tis time for all that are concerned to awake and rouse themselves to fresh vigour and activity in their several posts of service."[38] The following exhortation by Watts reflects a passion and urgency all too rare in the early eighteenth century.

> O let us stir up our hearts, and all that is within us, and strive mightily in prayer and preaching to revive the work of God, and beg earnestly that God by a fresh and abundant effusion of his own spirit would revive his own works among us.[39]

As early as January 1739, the Welsh evangelist Howell Harris was using the word revival along with terms *awakening*, and *reformation* interchangeably.[40] Each was intended to convey, in the words of Eifon Evans, "God's visitation of a community with unusual power attending gospel preaching and resulting in conversions over a wide area, giving sustained reforming effects on a personal and social level."[41] Though revival leaders in the middle third of the eighteenth century communicated a belief that such spiritual stirrings were unprecedented, many scholars suggest that the evangelical revivals should not be regarded, "as a new departure after generations of religious deadness," but rather as, "continuations of [the] seventeenth-century...revival of spirituality," among the Puritans.[42] Assuming a diachronic-

Germany, an "effusion," of the Holy Spirit came at Zinzendorf's Berthelsodorf church in a 1727 communion service that united the settlers of Herrnhut and invigorated the Moravian church. See Hindmarsh, *Spirit of Evangelicalism*, 101.

37. As early as 1674, Torrey would claim, "If God make this Ministry a Converting Ministry, the Work of Reformation will be revived." See Torrey, *An Exhortation Unto Reformation*, 10, 34. As Kidd observes, for the Massachusetts pastor, the work of Reformation began with conversion. Cited in *Great Awakening*, 2. See 327n2.

38. Watts, *Humble Attempt*, 1.

39. Watts, *Humble Attempt*, 125.

40. This was found in Harris's reply to a letter from George Whitefield in which Harris mentions a, "great revival in Cardiganshire..." See Harris, *Brief Account of the Life of Howell Harris*, 113. Cited in Haykin, *Pentecostal Outpourings*, 7. Cf. Nuttall, *Howell Harris*.

41. Evans, "Power of Heaven," 7.

42. Wallace, *Spirituality of the Later English Puritans*, xii, cited in Kapic and Gleason, *Devoted Life*, 31. Evidence of novelty by participants in the evangelical revivals include: Jonathan Edwards self-descriptive, *A Surprising Work of God*, Yale Rector Elisha Williams's judgment that the awakening in the Connecticut River valley of 1734–35

synchronic reading, the works of later Puritans and Georgian figures such as Philip Doddridge and Isaac Watts will be considered as thematically anticipating the revivals that began in the 1730s. Furthermore, Andrew Fuller's understanding of revival, whether it shares direct or indirect theological and/or methodological motifs with the selected individuals, and the nature of the relationship, will be the task of this monograph.[43]

Compatibilism

Historically, the Reformed theological tradition has argued that, first, compatibility exists between actions, including choices, being determined by antecedent causes and/or state of affairs, and second, that human possess free agency in a significant moral sense with respect to at least some acts, including choices.[44] A survey of influential Reformed Confessions of Faith including the *Second London Confession*, suggest a harmonious, albeit mysterious relationship between divine and human wills.[45] "Substantive" or "soft" compatibilism has been the technical modern philosophical definition; its antithesis being libertarianism.[46] The theological task of reconcil-

---

was, "a remarkable revival of religion," and Scotsman James Robe's *Faithful Narrative of the Extraordinary Work. . .at Kilsyth*. Whitefield considered the revivals, "as such as we nor our fathers have heard of." Wesley could write, "This I term *a great work of God*; so great as I have not read of for several ages" (Hindmarsh, *Spirit of Evangelicalism*, 58).

43. That this book begins with seventeenth-century Puritan figures discloses the author's opinion that there is greater degree continuity than discontinuity between Puritanism and evangelicalism. See Coffey, "Puritanism, Evangelicalism and the Evangelical Protestant Tradition," 252–77.

44. See Van Asselt et al., *Reformed Thought on Freedom*, 71–96. See Schreiner and Ware, *Still Sovereign*; Helm, "'Structural Indifference' and Compatibilism," 184–205; Helm, "Synchronic Contingency," 207–22.

45. The *Second Helvetic Confession*, *Synod of Dort*, and *Westminster Confession of Faith*, reject any who believe God's immutable eternal decrees vitiate moral responsibility by disavowing, "the impious speeches of some who say, 'I know not whether I am among the number of the few, I will enjoy myself.'" *Helv* II 10.6. The canons of the Synod of Dort, though it creedaly affirms predestination, rejects antinomianism, stating, "This is far from saying this this teaching concerning election, and reflection upon it, make God's children lax in observing his commandments or carnally self-assured." *Dort* 1.1.13. The third chapter of the *Westminster Confession*, 3.1, though it maintains that, "God from all eternity did. . .unchangeably ordain whatsoever comes to pass," immediately adds, "neither is God the author of sin" and continues, "nor is violence offered to the will of the creatures, nor is the liberty or contingency of second cause taken away, but rather is established." The *Second London Confession*, 3.1 repeats the Westminster Confession verbatim. See Lumpkin, *Baptist Confessions*, 254.

46. Libertarianism is equally nuanced with a diverse spectrum, among which includes advocates for versions that are arguably consistent within the tradition.

ing the diverse array of texts that pertain respectively to divine sovereignty and human responsibility suggests a compatibilist schema. Consequently, canonical texts provide the raw data that serve to ground theological compatibilism. Philosophy, though providing crucial insight and clarification, plays a subsidiary role.[47]

Historian David Bebbington observes that a Christian outlook on history itself involves recognition of a "fundamental tension—an antinomy—between divine sovereignty and human responsibility," and that secular thought cannot avoid that same tension without falling into irrationalism. Therefore, "Christianity adopts a reasonable position in discerning an antinomy between determinism and free will."[48] Moreover, several major theological categories suggest a compatibilist scheme.[49]

"Free Will" (free agency), taken psychologically and morally as, ". . .the power of unconstrained, spontaneous, voluntary, and therefore, responsible, choice," had been judged unacceptable for Calvinists like Fuller who believed it undermined the sovereignty of God. It was the task of Jonathan Edwards in *Freedom of the Will* to discount an incompatibilist libertarianism scheme he deemed, "Arminian."[50] Though Edwards denied a creature's possessing, "absolute power to the contrary," human responsibility was affirmed through his novel distinction between, "natural," and "moral,"

These include two nineteenth-century theologians, Cunningham, "Calvinism and the Doctrine of Philosophical Necessity," and Giradeau, *Will in its Theological Relations*, 401–9.

47. Compatibilism is a minority position among philosophers. Hence, Walls, "No Classical Theist," 75–104. Antony Flew, in a 1954 essay, "Divine Omnipotence and Human Freedom," made a distinction between *determinism* and *predestination*, claiming the former is compatible with human freedom, while the latter is not. Flew suggests dropping the notion of omnipotence altogether but admits this view will be unacceptable to the orthodox believer. See Flew and MacIntyre, *New Essays in Philosophical Theology*. Most Reformed theologians, on scriptural bases, necessarily affirm the personality of God and predestination. Consequently, any determinism is necessarily theological in nature, and philosophers within the tradition continue to defend compatibilism.

48. Bebbington, *Patterns in History*, 166. For a contemporary defense of libertarian free will, see Kane, *Significance of Free Will*; Tempe, *Free Will*; Swinburne, *Mind, Brain, and Free Will*; Plantinga, *God, Freedom, and Evil*.

49. Carson argues that in the person of Christ the very embodiment of the sovereignty-responsibility tension exists. See *Divine Sovereignty*, 207. The notion of verbal plenary inspiration of the Christian Scriptures entails the text being both the words of God and man.

50. Carson, *Divine Sovereignty*, 207. For discussion on the nuances among philosophers and theologians for the terms "compatibilist" "determinism" etc. see Van Horn, "On Incorporating Middle Knowledge," 807–27. See Muller, "Jonathan Edwards and the Absence of Free Choice."

inability.⁵¹ In fact, Edwards averred that if human acts were not necessitated by prior beliefs and desires, such acts would not, properly speaking, be free. Rather, such actions would be arbitrary, random, even outside of one's control. Such compatibilism, a distinctively theological type, believes not only that freedom is compatible with determinism, but that freedom requires determinism.⁵² Edwards's understanding of God's sovereignty and human agency was thoroughly satisfactory for navigating what stood among Andrew Fuller's chief soteriological concerns.⁵³

---

51. It should be noted that among many philosophers, "determinism," is a thesis about the relation between natural laws and states of the world and is therefore, naturalistic and atheological. See Vihvelin, "Arguments for Incompatibilism." A working definition of "theological determinism" is intended here, defined by Pereboom as "[T]he position that God is the sufficient active cause of everything in creation, whether directly, or by way of secondary causes such as human agents," in "Theological Determinism and Divine Providence," 262.

52. See Van Horn, "On Incorporating Middle Knowledge," 819. For a contemporary defense of compatibilism see Wingard Jr., "Confession of a Reformed Philosopher," 263–84. For an up-to-date overview of the contemporary philosophical literature on this subject see Timpe, *Free Will*. Crisp comments that compatibilists believe moral agents could be morally responsible for acts they commit ever if they have no alternative open them. See *Deviant Calvinism*, 168. In contemporary philosophy, this view has been labeled by van Inwagen as, "the *Mind* argument." See *Essay on Free Will*, 126–50. Advocates for theological determinism within the Calvinist tradition include Tiessen, *Providence and Prayer*, 312–14; Ware, *God's Greater Glory*, 85–88 and Feinberg, "God Ordains All Things," 35–37. Interestingly, in the relatively recent past, philosophers such as Harry Frankfurt have made noteworthy non-theological compatibilist proposals, analysis of moral responsibility absent a principle of alternate possibilities. Harry Frankfurt, "Alternate Possibilities and Moral Responsibility," 829–39; also, *Importance of What We Care About*. Frankfurt argues against the idea that free will requires the ability to act otherwise at the moment of choice. He distinguishes between first and second-order judgments that form a hierarchy in which a person who acts according to a desire that is properly ordered acts *whoheartedly*. I am indebted to Crisp for these insights in *Deviant Calvinism*, 203–5. John Fischer and Mark Ravizza offer a semi-compatibilist account of moral responsibility. These authors agree with Frankfurt's premise that alternate possibilities are irrelevant to maintaining moral responsibility, yet they propose what Fischer calls "guidance control"—something issued from the human agent themselves. Unlike Frankfurt, the Fischer-Ravizza proposal allows the source of the desires that inform choice be relevant to the question of moral responsibility. See *Responsibility and Control*, 291.

53. The chief concerns being man's responsibility and divine sovereignty, which Tom Ascol argues is ". . .adequately accommodated in that [Federalist] construct. See "Doctrine of Grace," 264.

Methodology

This monograph will employ traditional methods of historical research drawing on primary source documents such as letters, sermon, essays, and polemical treatises from the period supported by pertinent secondary sources. Andrew Fuller's theology will be framed in its historical context with focus on doctrinal developments and patterns among seventeenth-century Puritans, Separatists, and Dissenters, including early Baptists. Written works frequently cited by Fuller, and others to which he attributes a theological shift, will be given due attention, as will formative events in his life. Writings in Fuller's corpus with exclusive focus on revival will constitute major sections of the monograph.

A broad spectrum of Fuller's publications will be drawn primarily from the Sprinkle edition of his *Complete Works*, and the critical edition when pertinent, to highlight aspects of his theology in support of the author's thesis.[54] An additional dimension will consider the application of Andrew Fuller's theology of revival in late eighteenth and early nineteenth-century Particular Baptist life. Denominational trends, numerical growth, and documentation such as circular letters will disclose how Fuller's views on revival were first implanted, then applied in his lifetime. In evaluating Fuller's legacy among Particular Baptists as a revival-oriented evangelical Calvinist, his theological imprint should be detected among the writings of contemporaries within the Particular Baptist denomination.[55]

Structure

This monograph divides into five chapters, beginning with three later Puritan figures, John Owen, John Howe, and Abraham Cheare, whose selected writings touch on pneumatological themes, and therefore typify approaches to revival among successors within English Dissent. Included among these is a desire for a powerful, "outpouring of the Spirit," to enliven

---

54. *The Complete Works of Andrew Fuller*. Henceforth, abbreviated as *WAF*. This book utilizes extracted writings of Fuller from Ryland, *Fuller*; Morris, *Memoirs;* Gunton Fuller, *Memoir*, in *WAF*, 1:1–41. It also employs various Fuller Mss. from the Angus Library at Oxford University; Beincke Rare Books, manuscripts at Yale University, and the "Heritage Room," at Fuller Baptist Church, Kettering. A one-volume nineteenth-century American edition was published in 2007 by Banner of Truth. See Haykin, *Works of Andrew Fuller*. Unfortunately, the three current volumes of the critical edition, excepting some diary extracts, do not contain pertinent material on revival.

55. Andrew Fuller's impact on subsequent generations of Baptist in Britain and North America will not be examined in this monograph, though it would be a fruitful subject for future research.

their churches. In the case of John Howe, commencement of the millennial reign of Christ leads to a distinctive optimism concerning Christianity's future. Owen's seminal treatise *Pneumatologia*, provides a framework from which Fuller would draw various theological concepts found throughout his revival writings. Consequently, primary concern in Fuller's thought is seeking to harmonize God's sovereign freedom to pour and his Spirit, and believers' responsibility for preparation, and pursuit of it.

Chapter Two traces the historical development of high Calvinism in the Particular Baptist denomination and the consequent declension among its churches in the first half of the eighteenth century. Exceptions to the insular, and theologically frigid pattern among Calvinistic British Baptists, including Benjamin Francis, and Andrew Gifford are noted. Two Congregational ministers, Isaac Watts and Philip Doddridge, were significant for their experience of religious languor early in the century that was eclipsed by revival fervor of the 1730s. Watts and Doddridge wrote and preached passionately, maintaining a moderate Calvinism that did not preclude gospel offers and that prefigured evangelical Calvinism embodied in Andrew Fuller.

Chapter Three gives a biographical summary of Fuller's life, influences, and theological development. Included among these is Fuller's experiences in a high Calvinist milieu, the pastors of the Northamptonshire Baptist Association, and the New England theologian Jonathan Edwards. Discussion on Andrew Fuller's definition of revival and experiences of revival among contemporaries is included. Lastly, the 1784 Prayer Call, and the establishment of the Baptist Missionary Society is noted as the enduring legacy of Fuller's concerted pursuit of revival.

Chapter Four, devoted to Fuller's understanding of "means," and their relationship to revival, examines two writings composed to this end: a 1785 circular letter, and a series of five essays, each of which address causes of declension with extensive remedial measures. The nature of such means, and their relationship to genuine revival that Fuller insisted was always a sovereign work of God, will be examined and evaluated.

Chapter Five explores Fuller's pneumatology, particularly the Holy Spirit's relationship to revival. This includes examining Jonathan Edwards's *Humble Attempt to Extraordinary Prayer*, its impact on the Northamptonshire Baptist Association, and Fuller's own theology. Included is expectation that the millennial reign of Christ on earth was imminent, a view shared by Fuller and his pastor friends. Two sermons, emphasizing the fulfillment of Old Testament prophesy and the consequent confidence that revival would commence, led to greater zeal in prayer, evangelism, and missionary efforts. For such reasons, we see the certitude by which

Fuller judged biblical revelation as compatible with human response that anticipated and prepared for promised revival.

As the second decade of the twenty first century nears its completion, evangelicalism continues geographical expansion with attendant ethnic diversity, a development of which the Northamptonshire Baptist Association could only dream when they instituted monthly prayer meetings in 1784. If he were alive today, Andrew Fuller would likely express concern over the waning of Calvinistic orthodoxy in Baptist circles. He would however, recognize the longing for revival among its churches. Although various theological developments over the last two centuries have adversely affected revival's reputation, Andrew Fuller's theology of revival may offer a robust understanding of spiritual renewal that is faithful to the dual Scriptural emphases of God's sovereign activity and obedient human response. Perhaps, by understanding Fuller's vision of revival, the church militant might also come to share his passion.

Chapter One

"Panting After The Spirit"
Patterns of English Puritan Spiritual Renewal

To evaluate Andrew Fuller as an eighteenth-century Baptist theologian seeking to understand and assess revival, historical consideration of English Dissent is requisite.[1] The evangelical revivals that began in the 1730s, two decades before Fuller's birth, and whose effects reverberated through his lifetime, were preceded by Puritan voices in the seventeenth century calling for spiritual renewal among their own churches.[2] A diversity of media including sermons, treatises, and books, expressed concern over a waning religious zeal that contrasted with the passion of their forbearers. Among several shared motifs in these discourses and compositions was the desire for a fresh and profound invigoration by the Holy Spirit—an "outpouring" or "effusion."[3] Representatives from several groups within late Stuart Dissent including Congregationalist, Presbyterian, Independent, and Baptist, advised leaders and congregants to seek this very end in hope of revival.[4]

---

1. Watts dates the genesis of Dissent in the years 1532–1640. See *Dissenters*, 1–72. Cf. Burrage, *Early English Dissenters*; White, *English Separatist Tradition*.

2. On the evangelical revivals' debt to Puritanism see introduction.

3. Other themes frequently cited include the well-being of "zion," denoting the Protestant church's typological connection to ancient Israel, and the fall of "Babylon," and/or the antichrist, which in much of Puritan literature referred respectively, to the Roman Catholic Church and the pope. See Christianson, *Reformers and Babylon*.

4. See Nuttall, *Holy Spirit in Puritan*. Packer, *Among God's Giants*. I've included "Independent," since John Owen has been identified as such. Additionally, John Howe has been claimed by Presbyterians and Congregationalists alike. Though Independent and Congregationalist were generally used synonymously, the former applied only to those churches in England and Wales, not America. See Walker, *Creeds and Platforms*.

This chapter will focus on three men who composed writings to this purpose: John Owen (1616–1683), Abraham Cheare (1628–1668) and John Howe (1630–1702). These specific Puritans were chosen for sequential chronology, their impact on successive generations of Particular Baptists, including Fuller, and his denominational predecessors by thematic parallel or direct literary dependence. The selected figures fit broadly within the British Reformed tradition, and accepted the designation, "Calvinist." As the sovereignty of God undergirded their theology, any prescription for human action would need account for the primacy of the divine will. This supposition and its attendant theological implications would undergird their understanding of preaching, evangelism, petitionary prayer, and its relation to the Holy Spirit's work. Consequently, the task of these theologians will be to justify believers' pursuit of spiritual renewal while upholding divine freedom and sovereignty. In the late eighteenth century, Andrew Fuller would chart a revival course under a similar theological rubric, and therefore, it is not surprising to find parallels and patterns in the writings of Owen, Howe, and Cheare.

John Owen

John Owen's influence on Andrew Fuller has been noted in several recent scholarly works.[5] Fuller read broadly and deeply from Owen, liberally citing the Puritan divine, particularly in earlier writings. When an opponent of Fuller, after reading the manuscript to the *Gospel Worthy* decried its, "disrespect to Drs Gill and Owen," Fuller replied that: "I know of no writer for whom I have so great an esteem; it would be a faint expression for me to say I approve his principles–I admire [Owen's]."[6] Andrew Fuller's theology, broadly considered, stood in the orthodox Reformed tradition of Puritans such as Owen.[7] What has not been written is the connection between Owen's theology and Fuller's understanding of revival. It is worth noting that

---

5. See Trueman, "John Owen and Andrew Fuller," 53–70. Morden, *Life and Thought*, 53–55; Box, "Atonement," 46–60. Chun, *Legacy*, 126–31. For Fuller's quotation of Owen in the 1st ed. of *The Gospel Worthy*, 86–88, and 127.

6. Fuller, *Memoir*, in *WAF*, 1:39.

7. Trueman critiques the theological relationship, arguing that Fuller appropriated Owen in a way, "that the latter might well not have recognized." See "John Owen and Andrew Fuller," 67. He continues, 67–68: "Fuller may well have been a great church leader, but his grasp of seventeenth-century theological issues is certainly not as great as that of John Gill; and he is almost certainly not as close to Owen in his view of the atonement as his frequent citations from the Puritan would seem to indicate he believed himself to be."

several motifs in Owen's writings are echoed in Fuller's treatments of revival, including the respective concepts of "means," and "duty,"[8] which were appropriated within a robust biblical theological framework.[9] This chapter will focus on *Pneumatalogia,* an exemplary work by Owen which attempts to reconcile the biblical teaching that the Holy Spirit is sovereignly "poured-out," coupled with Scripture's witness that believers are responsible to act.

John Owen was born in Stadhampton, near Oxford in 1616. After education at a local grammar school, he matriculated at Queen's College, Oxford, in 1631, graduating with a B.A. in 1632.[10] Owen's first published work, *A Display of Arminianism*, published in 1642, brought him instant fame. A high point in his academic career was appointment as Dean of Christ Church and Vice-Chancellor of the University of Oxford in 1651, a position he held for six years.[11] Upon Richard Cromwell's abdication and the restoration of Charles II to the throne in 1660, Owen subsequently wrote and ministered under moderately hostile political conditions.[12]

---

8. Among numerous places within his works, Fuller quotes Owen in *On Spiritual Declension and Means of Revival.* See *WAF*, 3:624. Crawford highlights several of Owen's sermons that touch on importance of the outpouring of the Spirit, and two principal signs of its coming: prayer for the millennial kingdom, and revival of powerful evangelical preaching. See *Seasons of Grace*, 26–28. From my research, I did not find any explicit citations of Owen by Fuller in discussions on revival, the Spirit's outpouring, and the millennial kingdom. I have focused, therefore, on Owen's pneumatology as a theological *leitmotif* for Fuller's understanding of revival. Coffey finds John Owen's willingness to forge a doctrinal consensus to satisfy staunch Calvinists and godly Arminians while excluding Socinians as indicative of a modest "activism," that David Bebbington lists as the fourth component of his quadrilateral, thereby suggesting some continuity with evangelicalism. See Coffey, *John Goodwin*, 233–35.

9. Hindmarsh, discusses the significance of duty in early evangelicalism, noting the popularity of Cicero's *De Officiis*, and John's Locke's *Essay Concerning Human Understanding* during the period. See *Spirit of Early Evangelicalism*, 214–17. Influential works such as *The Whole Duty of Man* (1658), led to Howell Harris's conversion. William Law's *A Serious Call to a Devout and Holy Life* fell in a similar strain. Henry Venn's *The Complete Duty of Man* (1763) presented a distinctly evangelical version of deontological ethics, by incorporating a revelatory element lacking in Cicero and Locke.

10. On Owen's life see Toon, *God's Statesman*; Trueman, *John Owen.* Ferguson, *John Owen.* Cooper, "Owen's Personality," 215–26. For early biographies see Asty, "Memoirs of the Life of Owen."

11. "Owen, John (1616–1683)" in Greaves and Zaller, *Biographical Dictionary.*

12. While Owen did not experience persecution to the level of Baptists like John Bunyan and Abraham Cheare (Owen was never imprisoned), his political influence would never attain the level of Cromwell's Protectorate. Nevertheless, it is surprising Owen was treated as favorably as he was under Charles II considering his participation in the death of the monarch's father. For persecution of Dissenters after the restoration, see Brown, *Spirituality in Adversity.*

Owen's greatest legacy lies in his reputation as theologian and polemicist.[13] He stands among the most prolific contributors to orthodox Reformed theology in the seventeenth century with notable works on the Holy Spirit, The Trinity,[14] Justification,[15] and Christ's atonement.[16] Owen composed what remains the most comprehensive commentary on the book of Hebrews, and several devotional works including the popular *Mortification of Sin*.[17]

Pneumatalogia

From the years 1674 till his death in 1683, Owen composed *Pneumatalogia*, alternately termed *Discourse on the Holy Spirit*, a compendium of six books exceeding 650 pages, and intended as a response to the distinctive rationalism embodied in Socinianism, and additionally, the mysticism of the Quakers.[18] The Quaker notion of direct revelation via the "inner light," is the object of his criticism.[19] Owen covers a broad spectrum of subject matter

---

13. Owen was commissioned to write a treatise against Socinianism, *vindicicae-evangelicae* in 1655.

14. See *WJO*, vol. 10; Owen, *Communion with the Triune God*.

15. "The Doctrine of Justification by Faith" in *WJO*, vol. 5.

16. *The Death of Death in the Death of Christ* in *WJO*, vol. 6.

17. The original title is *Of the mortification of sinne in believers: the necessity, nature, and meanes of it. With a resolution of sundry cases of conscience, thereunto belonging* (1656). Owen's rejected practices of Anglo-Catholic piety, including vows, orders, fasting, and penances due to their being "popish religion" and "mistaken ways and means of mortification." For it was "such outside endeavors, such bodily exercises, such self-performances, such merely legal duties, without the least mention of Christ or his Spirit," that motivated him to write *On the Mortification of Sin in Believers*. See Owen, *WJO*, 6:16. Kapic and Gleason see Owen's emphasis on the Holy Spirit and critique of Sacramentarian practices as demonstrative of his being a Puritan *par excellence*. See Kapic and Gleason, *Devoted Life*, 30.

18. *Pneumatalogia, or a discourse concerning the Holy Spirit wherein an account is given of his name, nature, personality, dispensation, operations, and effects: his whole work in the old and new creation is explained, the doctrine concerning it vindicated from oppositions and reproaches: the nature also and necessity of Gospel-holiness the difference between grace and morality, or a spiritual life unto God in evangelical obedience and a course of moral vertues, are stated and declared.* (London: J. Darby, 1674). In the Banner of Truth edition of *WJO*, *Pneumatalogia* is placed in vols. 3 and 4. See Haykin, "John Owen and the Challenge of the Quakers."

19. In his preface Owen distinguishes between "objective" and "subjective" revelation, the latter being, properly speaking, illumination of which, "nothing is intended but that work of spiritual illumination whereby we are enabled to discern and understand the mind of God in the Scripture; which the apostle prays for in the behalf of all believers, Eph. i. 16–19, and whose nature, God assisting, shall be fully explained

that includes the Holy Spirit's existence and activity prior to Christ's birth, the relationship between the Spirit and the Incarnation, and the nature of sanctification. Though Owen did not compose *Pneumatalogia* with revival in its purview per se, the work provides a theological basis for believers to pursue what Scripture teaches about the Spirit's activity while maintaining a traditionally Reformed understanding of divine sovereignty and freedom.[20]

In chapter four of book I, "Peculiar works of the Holy Spirit in the first or old creation," Owen affirms that by faith in Christ alone is a person converted, and consequently, receives the Holy Spirit. Paradoxically, such faith in Christ is itself, "an effect and fruit of that same Spirit."[21] Hence, the question respecting volition arises: can, or should an individual do anything to appropriate what is offered? Owen presents a scripturally-grounded response, noting that "we are bound to pray for him [the Spirit] before we receive him, and therefore the bestowing of him depends on a condition to be by us fulfilled; for the promise is that 'our heavenly Father will give the Holy Spirit to them that ask him.'"[22] In a subsequent chapter, Owen revisits the subject, noting that,

> the promise of bestowing the Spirit is accompanied with a prescription of duty unto us, that we should ask him or pray for him; which is included in every promise where his sending, giving, or bestowing is mentioned. He, therefore, is the great subject-matter of all our prayers. And that signal promise of our blessed

---

hereafter," 18. Owen contends that the Quakers' heterodox, even arguably heretical theology stemmed from their denigration of classic Trinitarian formulations. See *WJO*, 3:69.

20. It should be noted that William Grimshaw (1708–1763), an Anglican parson from Yorkshire was converted through a vivid experience in which he felt a palpable flash of heat upon opening Owen's treatise on justification. For this account and other examples see Walsh, "Origins of the Evangelical Revival," in Bennett and Walsh, *Essays in Modern Church History*, 77. Williams cites *Pneumatalogia*'s usage in Jonathan Edwards's *Religious Affections*, see Williams, "Enlightenment Epistemology," 359.

21. Owen, *Pneumatalogia*, in *WJO*, 3:109.

22. Owen, *Pneumatalogia*, in *WJO*, 3:109. The passage is Luke 11:13, of which Owen, in a later chapter, "General Dispensation of the Holy Spirit with respect unto the New Covenant," cites as providing confidence that believers, "shall succeed in [their] requests." See *WJO* 3:155. In *Death of Death* bk. 4, ch. 7, Owen answers the objection that a person would be hindered from believing if they were not guaranteed Christ purchased their ransom with the following remark: ". . .believing is understood as *a saving application of Christ to the soul, as held out in the promise*, for to believe that Christ died for me in particular, as is asserted to be the duty of every one, can be nothing else but such a saving application." See *WJO*, 10:292.

Saviour, to send him as a comforter, to abide with us forever, is a directory for the prayers of the church in all generations.[23]

Such a petition does, however, not nullify the freedom of God, rendering him a debtor to the supplicant, but rather it "directs us into the way whereby we may be made partakers of them, unto his glory and our own advantage."[24] Owen buttresses his argument with New Testament citations such as 1 Cor 12:3, in which the Apostle Paul asserts that no person can say, 'Jesus is Lord,' except by the Holy Spirit. The following criteria, asserts Owen, constitute the Father's giving of the Holy Spirit: "The greatness of a gift, the free mind of the giver, and want of desert or merit in the receiver, are that which declare bounty to be the spring and fountain of it."[25]

Further in the same section, Owen acknowledges historical examples where the faithful request the Spirit and receive what they seek. For such, "where God intendeth unto any the benefit of his Spirit, he will actually and effectually collate him upon them."[26] Yet, this is not his exclusive order of operations. For, "[s]ometimes he doth it, as it were, by a surprisal, when those who receive him are neither aware of it nor do desire it."[27] Owen concedes that where God intends to act, he prompts people to pursue him, though his absolute freedom remains.[28] On occasion, he will pour out his Spirit

23. Owen, *WJO*, 3:109. For discussion on the concept of duty and distinctions between human and divine agents, see Morris, "On Duty and Divine Goodness." Morris notes that humans, "exist in a state of being *bound* by moral duty, whereas God, "does not share our ontological status," and thus, "share our relation to moral principles—that of being bound by some of these principle duties," he nevertheless, "acts *in accordance with* those principles which would express duties for a moral agent in his relevant circumstances." Morris concedes that although God does not have literal duties, we can anticipate divine conduct in accordance with moral principles on the basis on analogy to the behavior of a completely good moral agent." See Morris, *Anselmian Explorations*, 36–37. Interestingly, Morris cites Jonathan Edwards's *Freedom of the Will* as a classic defense of the relation between God's being bound to his promises and his absolute freedom: "God's absolute promise of any things makes the thing promised necessary, and their failing to take place impossible" (*WJE*, 1:283).

24. Owen, *Pneumatalogia* in *WJO*, 3:109. In his book *The Grace and Duty of Being Spiritually Minded* (1681), Owen explains that the "The Spirit and his Graces," come to dwell in believers' hearts, and this Spirit freely, "doth of itself and from itself, without any external influence on it, inclined and dispose the whole soul until spiritual actings." See *WJO*, 7:279. Cited in Kapic and Jones, *Ashgate Research Companion*, 123.

25. Owen, *Pneumatalogia*, in *WJO*, 3:109–10.

26. Owen, *Pneumatalogia*, in *WJO*, 3:112–13.

27. Owen, *Pneumatalogia*, in *WJO*, 3:113.

28. In *Death of Death*, bk. 3 ch. 2, Owen concedes that, "First, commands do not signify what is God's intention should be done, but what is our duty to do; which may be made known to us whether we be able to perform it or not: it signifieth no intention or purpose to God." See *WJO*, 10:131.

at unexpected times and in unexpected places.²⁹ Owen's comments on the Holy Spirit's work are particularly insightful. Doctrinal consistency leads him to affirm a causal relationship from scriptural examples that the Spirit effects particular outcomes under certain conditions. Nevertheless, the wind still "blows wherever it wishes."³⁰ Owen is content to live in this tension.

In a series of extended essays on revival, Andrew Fuller would emphasize the confidence believers have wherein God has explicitly promised to answer particular prayers, though he is inherently free not to grant others. Thus, we read in instances of "spiritual and eternal blessings," God has in fact, "bound himself to grant the desire of the righteous, and to perfect that which concerns his praying people."³¹

Returning to *Pneumatalogia*, the recurrent question of human response as relates to God, whose will is immutable, the third person of the Trinity is no less subject than the Father and Son. Whoever queries therefore, whether action on their part is actuallynecessary, Owen gives a striking, if not terse, response:

> It is brutish ignorance in any to argue in the things of God, from the effectual operations of the Spirit, unto a sloth and negligence of our own duty. He that doth not know that God hath promised to "work in us" in a way of grace what he requires from us in a way of duty, hath either never read the Bible or doth not believe it, either never prayed or never took notice of what he prayed for. He is a heathen. . .who doth not pray that God would work in him what he requires of him.³²

With an appeal to Scripture and experience of the Christian life, Owen anticipates that his readers will be sufficiently persuaded that human response and divine action harmonize. He explains that believers ought to do whatever God has commanded them to do, a motif recurrent throughout Andrew Fuller's writings.³³ Whatever God prompts believers to do, they should do, "with diligence and earnestness," if they value the eternal

---

29. Owen cites King Saul in 1 Sam 12, the elders Eldad and Meldad in the wilderness (Num 11), prophets Amos (7:14-15) and Jeremiah (1:5-7) as exemplary of an unanticipated calling.

30. John 3:8.

31. Fuller, *Spiritual Declension and Means of Revival*, in *WAF*, 3:621.

32. Owen, *Pneumatalogia*, in *WJO*, 3:203-4.

33. Owen explains, "From our duty to God's purpose is no good conclusion, though from his command to our duty be most certain." See *Death of Death*, in *WJO*, 10:282. Cf. *Gospel Worthy*, in *WAF*, and *Divine Efficiency*, in *WAF*, 2:730 for Fuller's detailed understanding of "duty" and its relation to the Holy Spirit's work.

well-being of their souls.[34] There is certainly an element of mystery in this biblical, though not strictly logical, pattern. Nevertheless, confidence remains, "...that whatever God hath promised he will do himself in us, toward us, and upon us, it is our duty to believe that he will so do."[35] In his series of essays on revival, Andrew Fuller would sound a similar note, exhorting hearers to pray for outcomes God has explicitly revealed will come to fruition.[36]

Anyone who finds inconsistency between these things, "is to charge God foolishly."[37] A succinct and clear summary of Owen's overarching argument is found in the following:

> The Holy Spirit so worketh *in us* as that he worketh *by us*, and what he doth in us is done by us. Out duty is to apply ourselves unto his commands, according to the conviction of our minds; and his work is to enable us to perform them.[38]

The confessor content to resign to inaction is guilty of sloth and negligence, revealing that he or she has no interest or concern for the promised Spirit of grace. For the Spirit,

> ordinarily giveth not out his aids and assistances anywhere but where he prepares the soul with diligence in duty. And whereas he acts us (sic) not otherwise but in and by the faculties of our own minds, it is ridiculous, and implies a contradiction, for a man to say he will do nothing, because the Spirit of God doth all.[39]

Owen's proposals on the relationship between the Spirit's work and the believer's duty are particularly insightful in relation to Andrew Fuller's

---

34. Owen, *Pneumatalogia* in *WJO*, 3:204.

35. Owen, *Pneumatalogia* in *WJO*, 3:204. Owen takes "duty," in diverse contexts with broad application. For example, in a chapter on "deceitfulness," in his *Indwelling Sin* he proposes two "duties of the mind." First, "To keep itself and the whole soul in such a frame and posture as may render it ready unto all duties of obedience, and watchful against enticements unto the conception of sin." Second, "to carefully attend unto all particular actions, that they be performed *as* God requireth, for matter, manner, time and season, agreeably unto his will." See *WJO*, 6:217. In the subsequent chapter he lists prayer and meditation as specific duties incumbent on believers in their battles against sin. See 224–32.

36. Fuller said: "In respect to spiritual and eternal blessings, God has bound himself to grant the desire of the righteous, and to perfect that which concerns his praying people" (*Spiritual Declension and Means of Revival*, in *WAF*, 3:621.)

37. Owen, *Pneumatalogia*, in *WJO*, 3:204.

38. Owen, *Pneumatalogia*, in *WJO*, 3:204.

39. Owen, *Pneumatalogia*, in *WJO*, 3:204.

theology. The thrust of *The Gospel Worthy* and additional writings will stress biblical mandate and dutiful obedience to revealed commands. Fuller, like Owen, shared several presuppositions on divine revelation, verbal inspiration, and the overall trustworthiness of Scripture. For such reasons, obedience to the Bible—"duty"—is assumed. It should be noted Fuller's citation of *On Indwelling Sin* in subsection II of *Gospel Worthy*, is aptly titled: "Every man is bound cordially to receive and approve whatever God reveals."[40] As this proposition remains central to Fuller's thesis in *Gospel Worthy*, attribution to Owen is significant. Fuller draws from Owen the latter's notion that, "indwelling sin" *alone* hinders men from believing, and that,

> Men are made blind by sin, and cannot see his excellencies; obstinate, and will not lay hold of his righteousness; senseless, and take not notice of their own eternal concernments.[41]

A final note on *Pneumatalogia*: Fuller's sermon, *The Promise of the Spirit* will follow a progression of thought similar to Owen's, but with an explicit exhortation to pursue revival. Though *Pneumatalogia's* final section would be completed two generations prior to the evangelical awakenings in Britain and North America, Owen's modest, if not necessary theological contribution to the relation between the Holy Spirit's work and the believer's duty is evident in Fuller's theological trajectory, his understanding of revival included.

John Howe

On several accounts, John Howe is a seminal figure in late Stuart Dissent.[42] Though comparatively few of his written manuscripts are extant, Howe's impact on the spirituality of later figures such as Philipp Doddridge (1702–1751) and Isaac Watts (1674–1748), places him in a lineage that culminated in the revivals of the eighteenth century. Several aspects of his theology, namely his eschatology and pneumatology, impacted the earliest generation of evangelicals.[43] A brief overview of Howe's life reveals that he was born at

---

40. Fuller, *Gospel Worthy*, in *WAF*, 2:349.

41. Fuller, *Gospel Worthy*, in *WAF*, 2:357. Italics are Fuller's, not Owen's. With a few variants (Fuller has "excellency," and omits, "own") the quotation of Owen is close to that found in *On Indwelling Sin*, in *WJO* vol. 6. The usage of this citation and others by Owen, notably in *Death of Death*, will be further addressed in ch. 3.

42. On Howe's life, see Rogers, *John Howe*; Calamy, *Memoirs*. For a contemporary assessment of Howe and his historical context: Sutherland, *Peace, Toleration, and Decay*.

43. For a brief overview of Howe as a philosopher and apologist, notably his arguments in the *Living Temple*—a polemic against deism, see Sell, "Howe's Eclectic

Loughborough, Leicestershire in 1630.[44] His father, a minister at Loughborough, was ejected by Archbishop William Laud (1573–1645). In May 1647 Howe was admitted to Christ's College, Cambridge, but by 1648 he had left for Oxford where he took a B.A. In July of 1652 Howe was awarded an M.A., after which, he was ordained at Winwick in Lancashire. In March of 1654 he married. The same year he took up the perpetual curacy at Great Torrington.[45] Some biographers have argued that John Howe was a Congregationalist on account of his succeeding the Independent, Lewis Stucley (1632?–1687) at Torrington. His ordination, however, came at the hands of Presbyterian Charles Herle in 1652.[46] Like John Owen, Howe served under Oliver Cromwell, appointed in 1657 as a domestic chaplain.[47]

Beyond this, relatively scant knowledge of his personal life remains. On his deathbed in 1705, Howe requested that his son, George, burn his manuscripts.[48] This paucity of information leaves historians with few insights into his personal life. Yet a dearth of biographical data did not deter biographers, especially those in nineteenth century, from composing hagiographic works on Howe.[49] These accounts gloss unedifying accounts from Howe's contemporaries, or revealing statements from the man himself. By the end of the nineteenth century, Howe had become, in the words of Martin Sutherland, "an icon of nonconformist piety."[50] These historiographic considerations noted, the most reliable biography is the earliest: Edmund Calamy's *Memoirs of the Life of the Late Rev. Mr. John Howe*, published in 1724. There are several combinations of Howe's extant works, the only version available is a reprint of Calamy's 1724 collection, *The Works of John Howe, M.A.*[51]

Theism," 187–93. Cf. Field, *Rigide Calvinisme*.

44. Rogers, *John Howe*, 5.

45. Though several biographers portray Howe's ministry at Torrington as peaceful and tranquil, Sutherland cites sufficient evidence to question this thesis. See *Peace, Toleration, and Decay*, 48.

46. Calamy, *Memoirs*, 31.

47. Correspondence with Richard Baxter reveals that Howe was discontent in this role. See Sutherland, *Peace, Toleration, and Decay*, 42–44.

48. Calamy, *Memoirs*, xlviii–xlix.

49. Calamy, *Memoirs*, 30. Martin Sutherland, in his study of the ecclesiology of later Stuart Dissent, calls the uncritical pattern of historical analysis, "the Howe myth."

50. Calamy, *Memoirs*, 33.

51. *Works of the Rev. John Howe, M.A.* Also, Howe, *Whole Works*.

By a Plentiful Effusion of the Holy Spirit

In 1678, Howe preached a series of fifteen sermons from the singular text of Ezek 39:29 under the title, *The Prosperous State of the Christian Interest Before the End of Time, By a Plentiful Effusion of the Holy Spirit.*[52] The messages contained two principle themes. First, "a state of permanent serenity and happiness appointed for the universal church on earth," and second, "that the immediate original and cause of that felicity and happy state, is a large and general effusion or pouring forth of the Spirit."[53] The structure and progression of the sermons oscillates between arguments for the unfolding reality of this effusion on earth, the nature of the period, and the church's appropriate response.

Howe makes the general observation that that the church, from its inception, has not experienced a "considerable season of tranquility and serenity," both universal and simultaneous. A "long retraction" of the Holy Spirit that began gradually after Pentecost has rendered the church a body, "destitute of a soul."[54] Even times of reformation have been brief; supplanted by returns to arid religious formality, wherein prevailing concern is the church's external prosperity rather than the, "effusion and communication of the Spirit."[55] On the textual basis of Ezek 39:29, a time is coming when the institutional church and outpouring of the Spirit will coincide—a state he argues has no historical precedent. Howe understands this to be the millennial kingdom spoken of in Revelation 20.[56] Foreseeing possible exegetical objections, Howe weights the interpretive options and judges all literal fulfillments inadequate.[57] Though he concedes that Scripture does not

---

52. The AV reads, "Neither will I hide my face any more from them: for I have poured out my Spirit upon the House of Israel, saith the Lord God." The sermons were not published until 1725. Howe mentions several "operations," by which the Holy Spirit works in individual persons through regeneration, of, "implanting principles of divine life," and lastly, for the, "prosperous state of the church in general." It is of the latter category that Howe judges this text to pertain. Howe's first sermon was preached May 8, 1678; the last on October 16, 1678.

53. Howe, Sermon 1:3, *Prosperous State of the Christian Interest...in Works of John Howe*, 564. The entire collection of sermons can be found in 562–607.

54. Howe, Sermon 1:5.

55. Sermon 1:7. In Sermon 9, Howe claims that a withholding of the Spirit in his day proves that, "this age hath highly displeased the Lord...," 6.

56. Sermon 1:9. In Sermon 2:7 Howe claims that a such a time, "God shall be visibly owned in the world, and when it shall cease to be a reproachful thing to be a religious man, a fearer of the Lord." For Howe's understanding of the millennium see Sermon 2:4–6.

57. Howe gives three considerations: 1. The destruction of their external enemies; 2. A very peaceful, composed, united state of things among themselves; and, 3. A very

give chronological certainty as to the inception of the Spirit's outpouring, Howe encourages his hearers to embrace a, "dutiful love unto the blessed God himself," that sincerely rejoices over spiritual abundance bestowed to a later generation. He asks his hearers to envision, the magnitude of God's glory displayed in the same place where he had long been "so insolently affronted and provoked."[58] With these considerations in mind, believers should aspire to attain contentment, what Howe calls, "complacency." Such is the appropriate and necessary disposition towards what will likely unfold in the distant future. Notwithstanding, this extended period may function to sanctify Christ's church. In the meantime, believers are called to, "a serious diligence in the present duty."[59]

In his fourth sermon, Howe considers the nature and evidence of the Spirit's outpouring, which includes the *charismata*—gifts of the Holy Spirit—being distributed in a plenteous degree.[60] Whereas the present age exudes a general distrust of the Holy Spirit's efficacy to bring about "universal tranquility and peace," the future period will witness the removal of such hindrances.[61] Commitment by preachers to practice "affective" preaching, oriented toward "awakening" those with false security, and persuading the obdurate, though advisable, will be manifestly more operative after the Spirit's effusion. At such a time, ministers, "shall know how to speak to better purpose, with more compassion and sense, with more seriousness, with more authority and allurement," then at present.[62]

Howe anticipates the twin possibilities of a discouraged, struggling church that has not experienced this outpouring, and concurrently, an externally-prosperous institution that is neither guided, nor enlivened by the

---

lively, vigorous state of religion. See Sermon 2:4.

58. Sermon 3:3. Andrew Fuller would pose a similar question with an answer corresponding to Howe's when he said in *A Few Persuasives for the Revival of Religion* that, "Suppose we should never live to see those days, still our labour shall not be in vain in the Lord. God would be glorified; and is this of no moment?" (*WAF*, 3:670).

59. Sermon 3:7. In his fourth sermon given on May 29, 1678, Howe explicitly states his belief that his generation has "little prospect" of living through the blessed period of the Spirit's outpouring. Moreover, he warns against the respective errors of interpreting prophecies as having a far-too distant, or too-near fulfillment. There were of course, notable instances of such among radical millenarian Puritan off-shoots such as the Fifth Monarchists.

60. On the manifestation of the miraculous gifts of the Holy Spirit Howe is open to such a possibility, yet he concludes that, "Whether ever any extraordinary gifts shall be renewed, that because I know nothing of it, I shall affirm nothing in." Sermon 4:7. Cf. his comments on tongues in Sermon 6:2.

61. Sermon 4:5. Howe laments a proclivity to trust in "other means," for accomplishing what only the Spirit can do.

62. Sermon 4:6.

Holy Spirit. Each respective set needs the Spirit's power and anointing despite their apparent incongruence. Howe's counsel touches on the theme of hope, advising an optimistic disposition, allowing the promise of the Spirit to, "habitually possess [their] souls." In his fifth sermon, practical counsel is offered, namely, that families tend towards the cultivation of piety, attributing prevailing immorality and irreligiosity to the, "disuse and deficiency of this means."[63] Andrew Fuller would offer similar counsel in several writings on revival.[64] It should be noted that Howe's usage of "means," though having some parallels to Fuller in *Causes of Declension and Means of Revival* and *On Spiritual Declension and Means of Revival*, is orientated less towards practical appropriations.[65]

In seeking to persuade his hearers from Scripture the reality of Spirit's outpouring, Howe exposits several Old Testaments texts, drawing heavily from Isaiah to prove a case for the aforementioned earthly millennium kingdom, a time in which there will be not only an abundance of converts, but the, "high improvement" (e.g. spiritual quality) of such converts.[66] In the following century, Jonathan Edwards and Andrew Fuller would make similar arguments for a period of "spiritual outpourings," employing exegetical arguments, and language similar to Howe's.[67] For hearers receptive to Howe's opinion that this outpouring will not likely occur in their lifetime, the question may arise as to why. With a return to the theme of hope, and humbly acknowledging God's inscrutable wisdom, Howe proposes that an extended period of spiritual barrenness may function to lead the church in seeking the omnipotent God, thereby removing all doubt as to the source of her renewal.[68]

Regarding recognition and evidence of the Spirit's outpouring, there will be unmistakable marks such the dramatic conversion of previously

---

63. Sermon 5:1.

64. See the importance of "cultivating Christianity in the home," as a means for revival in Fuller, *Causes of Declension and Means of Revival*, in WAF, 3:318–24. Cf. *On Spiritual Declension and Means of Revival*, in WAF, 3:615–34. These will be examined in detail in ch. 4.

65. In many instances, "means" denotes the Holy Spirit itself.

66. Sermon 5:2; 6:1. Howe cites Isa 2:2; 32:14, 15; 35:1, 2; 54:1–3; 60:5, 8; 66:6–9; Mic 4:1–2; Joel 2:28; Dan 2:24–35; Ps 110:3; Mal 4:1, 2. In the case of Peter's Pentecost sermon and its stated fulfillment of Joel 2:28–32, Howe argues that the "completion," of the prophecy was not confined to that point of time.

67. See Fuller, *Promise of the Spirit the Grand Encouragement in Promoting the Gospel*, in WAF, 3:359–63 and, *A Few Persuasives to a 'General Union in Prayer' For the Revival of Religion*, in WAF, 3:666–70 and Edwards's *Humble Attempt* each of which will be the focus of ch. 5 of this monograph.

68. Howe, Sermon 5:7.

dissolute and irreligious people, coupled with a newfound boldness among converts.[69] Interestingly, Howe notes that when believers unite on account of the effusion of the Holy Spirit, they will increase in knowledge, and yet, "shall be more patient of dissent from one another in things less necessary to be known," as such knowledge will tend toward holiness.[70] An entrenched self-love, the source of all idolatry and evil in the world, and division within the church, will be removed by the Holy Spirit's outpouring, replaced by a deep and abiding divine love that renders the church on earth, "the very image of the church of God in heaven."[71] This state of affairs will serve to improve the very physical health of those influenced by the Spirit's effects.[72] The love of God communicated to believers will obviate pride, jealousy, and even proneness to take offense at others, and intimate trust between individual Christians will prevail.[73]

Howe's eleventh sermon forms a thematic transition in which he explains the nature of an external "union," between churches. As an indisputable mark of the Holy Spirit, pursuing unity is a duty incumbent on every individual believer.[74] Nevertheless, the nature of such a union is not one of strict uniformity in every respect, and Howe lists four areas of acceptable divergence.[75] Notwithstanding a spiritual union shared through participation in the Holy Spirit, there can exist outward cooperation between churches of like doctrine. And while Howe acknowledges incommensurability between churches of the Reformed tradition, and those of Rome, and does not advocate dilution of theological distinctives, he proposes a set of core doctrines—similar to what later figures such as Philip Doddridge and especially Andrew Fuller—cited as requisite to cooperation.[76] Though the

---

69. Sermon 6:5.

70. Sermon 13:2, 5. Howe claims then men and women will demonstrate a great degree of contentment in their respective vocations and rank in society.

71. Howe, Sermon 8:4–6; Sermon 9:2. "But when persons shall become one, consenting and agreeing, by the influence of that great principle of divine love, in the main design and business of religion, this must produce a happy harmony," 9:3.

72. Sermon 9:4.

73. Sermon 10:4–5.

74. See Sermon 11.

75. These include: measure of knowledge, degrees of holiness, intensity of joy, and rank and station. See Sermon 12:1, 2.

76. Howe proposes the following: "God considered as God, the end, and Christ the mediator, the way to that end." Citing Acts 20:21 (a favorite of Andrew Fuller) "repentance towards God and faith in Jesus Christ." The twofold love for God and neighbor from Matt 22:37 and the baptismal formula with its attendant discipleship mandate in 28:19–20. He concludes, saying, "Now there are none, that are sincere and living Christians, but do and must unite in such things as these, these great essentials and

divisions across churches are doleful, Christians ought to place themselves in a posture of sorrow that is simultaneously expectant. The effusion of the Spirit will one day heal divisions.

Though acknowledging ignorance concerning the precise time of outpouring, Howe's concluding sermon posits that believers should expect "a dismal state of things," prior to the Spirit's effusion, as a series of aforementioned prophetic texts with some newer citations, serve to support.[77] Within the church there ought be an insatiable passion for the Spirit's work, though Howe fears that many would be satisfied with "peace and tranquility, free trade, and [civil] liberty. . ." to achieve happiness.[78] Granted, this is so, the church without the Spirit's effusion is a body without a soul, likened to a carcass that though it retains a human form gradually dissolves into a substance beyond recognition. Likewise, ". . .great external prosperity to the church without the Spirit accompanying it, commonly issues in irreligion."[79]

In comparison to later writings examined in this monograph, Howe's Ezekiel sermons are markedly less "practical" in nature, particularly in comparison to Andrew Fuller. Thematically, hope seems to be the characteristic message, which Howe describes as, ". . .a kind of anticipated enjoyment." Hope provides a kind vicarious participation in what may commence far in the future, consequently, bestowing present joy.[80] Belief in the blessed period of the Spirit's effusion ought to elicit, "an expecting, a waiting posture," on account of the certainty that,

> . . .. this dark and gloomy night will be succeeded by a morning.
> It will not be a perpetual, eternal night. There will be a time, when the hid face will again appear, and the cloud removed.[81]

Howe's impact on the subsequent generation Dissenters including Isaac Watts and Philipp Doddridge is evident in explicit references to Howe, a comparison of their writings, and an overarching pattern of revival emphases.[82] William Cooper (1694-743), in his preface to Jonathan Edwards's

---

substantial of the Christian religion." Howe's doctrinal distinctives are minimal compared to Doddridge, and especially, Fuller.

77. Howe, Sermon 15:2. Passages listed include: Isa 32:13, 14; 34:5; Jer 17:17; Ezek 37:1–14; 39:29; Deut 31:17; 32:40, 41; Pss 106:35, 39, 40.

78. Sermon 15:5.

79. Sermon 15:6. Howe acknowledges that gospel proclamation, and even the working of miracles will not accomplish a good end with the outpouring of God's Spirit.

80. Sermon 5:7.

81. Sermon 12:7.

82. Literary critic Hoxie Neal Fairchild, could claim that, "He who listened to the

Distinguishing Marks, quoted extended passages from the Ezekiel 39 sermons.[83] Particular Baptist pastor Robert Hall Sr. (1728-91) wrote that as a minister, he had, "derived more benefits from John Howe than all other divines put together."[84] Several themes in Howe's writings are shared by Andrew Fuller, notably his broad understanding of millennial kingdom, the nature of its inauguration, and vital need for an outpouring of the Holy Spirit.

Abraham Cheare

Among English Baptists from the Stuart period, Abraham Cheare (1628-1668) is among several lesser-known figures. With a brief life that spanned only 41 years, eight of which were spent in prison, he appears an unlikely candidate to exhort a fledgling denomination toward renewal and revival. Until recently, little had been published on Cheare. *Waiting on the Spirit of Promise: The Life and Theology of Suffering of Abraham Cheare*, a recent monograph draws scholarly attention to Cheare's life and writings.[85] The authors note, that with exception of John Bunyan (1628-1688), Puritan studies over the past fifty years have focused exclusively on Presbyterians and Congregationalists.[86] This Puritan renaissance has overlooked Particular Baptist figureheads such as Hanserd Knollys (1599-1691),[87] William Kiffin (1616-1701),[88] and Benjamin Keach (1640-1704),[89] each of whom guided their own churches through a century fraught with political persecution,

---

sermons of John Howe lived long enough to clasp the hands of Zinzendorf and Whitefield," and that, "this connection is not merely an accident of chronology: it implies a tenuous but unbroken continuity of doctrine and temperament" (*Religious Trends in English Poetry* [New York: Columbia University Press, 1939], 123).

83. Crawford, *Seasons of Grace*, 264n16.

84. Crawford, *Seasons of Grace*, 15. John Ryland Jr., in his biography on Fuller, cites another work of Howe, *The Bessedness of the Righteous*, quoting an extended passage in *Fuller*, 27.

85. Hanson and Haykin, *Waiting on the Spirit*.

86. Hanson and Haykin, *Waiting on the Spirit*, ix.

87. See Duncan, *Hanserd Knollys*; White, *Hanserd Knollys and Radical Dissent*; "Knollys, Hanserd (c. 1599-1691)" in Greaves and Zaller, *Biographical Dictionary*, 2:160-62. Cf. Knollys's works at https://www.mupress.org/The-Collected-Works-of-Hanserd-Knollys-Pamphlets-On-Religion-P934.aspx.

88. On Kiffin, see Ivimey, *Life of William Kiffin*. This work is an annotated and edited version of Kiffin's autobiography. White, "William Kiffin," 91-103; Kreitzer, *William Kiffin and his World*.

89. For a recent monograph on Keach see Riker, *Catholic Reformed Theologian*; Arnold, *Reformed Theology of Benjamin Keach*. Cf. Walker, *Excellent Benjamin Keach*.

and doctrinal compromise, and whose theological and devotional writings served to invigorate the denomination.[90]

Abraham Cheare was born in Plymouth, and baptized as an infant on May 28, 1626.[91] Little is known of his upbringing, except that he had four older siblings, and that his father was a fuller. According to Nathan Brookes, publisher of one of Cheare's books, Cheare's parents were believers who carefully nurtured their son in God's ways.[92] Cheare did not receive a university education, nor did he ever marry. He was baptized as a believer in 1648, and, "joined himself in an holy covenant, to walk in all the ordinances of the Lord blameless to best of his light and power, in fellowship with a poor a despised people."[93] Cheare joined the Calvinistic Baptist church in Plymouth, and the same year was ordained as their minister.[94]

Cheare was imprisoned shortly after the ascent of Charles II to the English throne in 1661. During the reign of Oliver Cromwell (1599–1658), Presbyterians, Congregationalists, and Baptists were granted religious freedom under the Commonwealth.[95] After the restoration of Charles II, the Act of Uniformity, passed in May of 1662, was executed on August 24, after which two-thousand ministers were ejected from their churches for refusal to give, "unfeigned assent and consent to all and everything contained in the Book of Common Prayer."[96] Though an independent, Cheare had been imprisoned for three months in Exeter prior the Act's passage after being convicted of, "encouraging religious assemblies."[97] After his release, Cheare refused to subscribe to several provisions of the Act including the Oath of Allegiance, and was imprisoned in 1662 for holding, "unlawful assemblies" and refusing, "to conform to the laws of the Established Church."[98]

Cheare would spend three grueling years in an Exeter jail, and though the horrid prison conditions tested his fortitude, the church at Plymouth was of greatest concern for the young pastor.[99] Several congregants would

---

90. On these figures, see Ivimey, *History of the English Baptists*; Haykin, *Rediscovering our English Baptist Heritage*.

91. Nicholson, *Authentic Records*, 6.

92. Cheare, "Post Script" to *Words in Season*, 293.

93. Cheare, "Post Script" to *Words in Season*, 293.

94. Nicholson, *Authentic Records*, 5. Cf. Briggs, "Influence of Calvinism on Seventeenth-Century English Baptists," 8–24.

95. Whitley, *History of British Baptists*, 61–62.

96. Whitley, *History of British Baptists*, 113.

97. Ivimey, *History of English Baptists*, 2:104. Cheare's imprisonment was partly a result of a violent rebellion led by Fifth Monarchist Thomas Venner (d. 1661).

98. Nicholson, *Authentic Records*, 19.

99. Thomas Crosby writes, "This worthy good man, after full three years suffering

be imprisoned alongside Cheare, and the Plymouth church would suffer greatly during the 1660s.[100] Remarkably, his personal afflictions did not eclipse heartfelt concern for his congregation. On his deathbed, Cheare admitted that, "he had oft, since sickness, on his bed, begg'd of God, that the Lord the God of the spirits of all flesh would send a man over that church."[101]

While two published writings, *A Looking Glass for Children* and *Words in Season* were composed while Cheare was in prison, the Plymouth pastor had an active ministry prior to confinement that included several published works.[102] Under Cromwell's Commonwealth, Baptist denominational life flourished.[103] The Western Association, of which Cheare's church was an early member, was founded in 1653 for the expressed purpose that,

> The Gospel may have a free course and be glorified everywhere, to the gathering in all the elect to the faith and obedience of Christ and to that end that much of the Spirit may be given to churches to the preparing and thrusting forth fit labourers not only among the gentiles, but also, if it be His pleasure to us, among the house of Abraham His friend.[104]

Cheare engaged fellow pastors, encouraging them to pursue regional missionary activity, and was instrumental in planting a Particular Baptist church in Cornwall around 1655.[105] A circular letter, composed after 1656 even suggested the possibility of Baptist mission work beyond British shores, "as the Lord may open a way."[106] The Western Association's flourishing under the leadership of Cheare and his contemporaries reveals a spiritually-robust Particular Baptist denomination. In spite of High Calvinism's enervating effects on Particular Baptist churches early in the succeeding century, the

---

under very hard circumstance, enduring many inhumanities from merciless gaolers, was continued a prisoner under military guards, in the Isle of Plymouth" (*History of the English Baptists*, 13). Cheare's extant writings are distinctive for their remarkable transparency and anguish at his sufferings. See Hanson and Haykin, *Waiting on the Spirit of Promise*, 7.

100. The Plymouth church was without a pastor until November of 1687 when they called Robert Browne (d. 1688). See Nicholson, *Authentic Records*, 53–55.

101. Cheare, *Words in Season*, 176.

102. Thomas Crosby described Cheare as, "a very pious and laborious minister, took great pains, and wrote many seasonable lessons to youth, which he was in bonds for the truth of Christ; calling them early to remember their creator" (*History of the English Baptists*, 12).

103. See Conner, "Early English Baptist Associations," 163–85.

104. Nicholson, *Authentic Records*, 25.

105. Hanson and Haykin, *Waiting on the Spirit of Promise*, 12.

106. Nicholson, *Authentic Records*, 6–7.

missional ethos of the Western Association, exemplified in the Bristol Baptist Academy would serve to brighten otherwise bleak conditions.

Sighs for Sion

Sighs for Sion, though chiefly Cheare's work, was co-signed with four other Particular Baptist leaders Henry Forty (1625–1692), John Pendarves (1622–1656), Thomas Glasse (d. 1666), and Robert Steed (d. 1703?). The composition's stated purpose was for, "awakening them that are at ease, and pressing and encouraging all the upright in heart," for the welfare of "Sion," Christ's church.[107] A recurring Old Testament motif, particularly in the Psalter, "sion," is a rich and typologically-nuanced reference to God's dwelling generally, and a distinct locale in Israel, particularly. Cheare has a spiritual sense in mind when he describes sion as the, "whole election of God, whose names are written in heaven, that whole body for which Christ gave himself, and whereof Christ is given to be Head; not only those who have believed, but those also who shall believe. . ."[108] Sion, in this broad sense, includes all the elect, chosen before the foundation of the world, of whom regenerate believers should presently labor to convert. In the second sense, Cheare understands Sion as, "God's called and faithful people, Jews and Gentiles, fellow-citizens in Christ, even the whole Israel of God, as considered or concerned in a controversy with Babylon. . ."[109] Sion refers, therefore, to the universal church—militant and triumphant—the redeemed of God in

---

107. Cheare, *Sighs for Sion*, title page. Nicholson, *Authentic Records*, 6–7.

108. Cheare, *Sighs for Sion*, title page. John Howe, in *The Prosperous State of the Christian Interest* finds "house of Israel," as appropriately descriptive of the New Testament church when he writes, ". . .it is an obvious observation. . . .that the universal church, even of the Gospel constitution, is frequently in the prophetical scriptures of the Old Testament represented by this, and by the equivalent names of Jerusalem and Zion, and the like. And the reason was as obvious as the thing itself. For they were the church of God, that people, and they who were proselyted to them. And the prophecies of the Old Testament we know were first and most immediately directed to them; and were more likely to be regarded by them, by how much the more the church, whom these prophecies did concern, was more constantly designed, or set forth by their own name" (Sermon 1:2–3, in Howe, *Works of John Howe*, 563–64).

109. Cheare, *Sighs for Sion*, 7.

heaven, and those present on earth.[110] It should be noted that several Particular Baptist works on Sion were composed in the seventeenth century.[111]

Employing an array of scriptural allusions, Cheare describes Sion as, "God's glorious building and workmanship in Christ, the true seed of Abraham, and heirs of promise."[112] Yet of this same body, God has chosen to hide its glory in apparent weakness to, "let the manifestations of it in the world, and his dispensations about it, be very various, and seemingly to carnal eyes, unsuitable to such intendments, through the many deaths, distresses, and unlikelihoods with which he cloatheth it in their sight. . ."[113] Cheare further explains that Sion's tenuous existence amid persecution, though including the future reign of the antichrist, should not discourage her as Christ himself will, "plead the cause of his own," repaying the generation who shed the blood of the saints by pouring out his wrath.[114] Yet, *Sighs to Sion* was not intended to instill fear, but rather to encourage, for, "The day of Sion's full deliverance, the destruction of her enemies, and the setting up of Christ's glorious kingdom, is very much upon his heart (Isa 63:4) as

---

110. Augustine connects zion with the "City of God," in a sermon on Ps 142: "The origin of this city goes back to Abel, as that of the evil one to Cain. It is, therefore, an ancient city, this City of God: always enduring its existence on earth, always *sighing* (emphasis mine) for heaven—whose name is Jerusalem and Sion." See Brown, *Augustine of Hippo*, 314. cf. John Calvin's comments on Ps 24 fall along similar lines, "Mount Sion, it is true, is not at this day the place appointed for the sanctuary, and the ark of the covenant is no longer the image or representation of God dwelling between the cherubim; but as we have this privilege in common with the fathers, that, by the preaching of the word and sacraments, we may be united to God. . ." (*Commentary on Psalms*, 1:413). Calvin will freely substitute "church," for zion. Commenting on Ps 87, he writes, "Although Zion was not the place of their natural birth, but they were to be grafted into the body of the holy people by adoption; yet as the way by which we enter into the Church is a second birth. . .The condition upon which Christ espouses the faithful to himself is, that they should forget their own people and their father's house, and that, being formed into new creatures, and born again of incorruptible seed, they should begin to be the children of God as well as that of the Church. And the ministry of the Church, and it alone, is the means by which we are born again to a heavenly life" (*Commentary on Psalms*, 2:402). Like Calvin, Benjamin Keach draws ecclesiological conclusions from Ps 87. He unequivocally declares on the basis of verse two that, "the publick worship of God ought to be preferred before private" (*Glory of a True Church*).

111. See William Kiffen's preface to Thomas Goodwin's *Glimpses of Sion's Glory*. On the disputed authorship of this work see Toon, *Puritans, the Millennium and the Future of Israel*. See also, a compilation of poems by Keach, *Sion in Distress*.

112. Cheare, *Sighs for Sion*, 8.

113. Cheare, *Sighs for Sion*, 8.

114. Cheare, *Sighs for Sion*, 8. On the Antichrist in Puritan literature see Hill, *Antichrist in Seventeenth-Century England*; Gribben, *Puritan Millennium*.

a fruit of the sore travail of his soul (Isa 53:11, 12) and recompense of that unworthy usage that himself, his cause, and people had upon earth."[115]

As noted, Cheare's robust ministry prior to imprisonment included, among pastoral and denominational duties, church planting. Cheare was acquainted with the spiritual condition of Particular Baptist churches in the Western Association, and *Sighs for Sion* discloses the contextual distinctives of the congregations there. His writings disclose an awareness that spiritual lethargy was a dire threat to seventeenth-century Baptist churches. Disputes over eschatology, notably the millenarianism of the Fifth Monarchists, divided members in several congregations.[116] Sundry temptations plagued the churches, among which Cheare mentions, "a self-seeking and self-pleasing spirit" centered on comfort rather than the glory of God.[117]

Though incarcerated, and under duress, Cheare expressed concern for the flourishing of Particular Baptists in Plymouth. Cheare claimed the churches greatest need was "a mighty spirit of faith and prayer," and that through this,

> The zeal of the Lord's house would eat us up, and love of it would crucify us more unto, and wean us from those interests of earth, and men, whereupon we have apt to lean, and whereunto we have been deeply and dangerously engaged: causing us also to wait to be with Jesus, which is best of all; and in the mean time to pant, and thirst incessantly, for that Holy Spirit of promise, that alone can present us with the ravishing glory of that expected day, and raise up our spirits to a sweet and suitable disposition, according to the will of God, and act aright toward it.[118]

Cheare's insistence that believers "pant and thirst," for the Holy Spirit is a critical component to his spirituality. Confident that a zeal for Christ's church leads believers away from worldly interests, it furthermore serves

---

115. Cheare, *Sighs for Sion*, 9.

116. Hanserd Knollys, controversial among contemporaries, and no less so centuries after his death, espoused an eschatology that has prompted some historians to place him in the Fifth Monarchist camp. Knolls's eschatology drew from the medieval threefold hermeneutic of the literal sense, Israel, and the Messiah as paradigmatic for a "threefold coming of Christ." Knolls took the 1,260 days of Rev 11:3 and 12:6 as literal years, taking 407–28 as the beginning of Papal Rome, making AD 1667–1688 the beginning of the great tribulation and Christ's "spiritual reign." See *The World that is Now, and the World that is to Come* (1681). For the wider discussion see Garret, *Baptist Theology*), 62–65. On Fifth Monarchism see Capp, "Extreme Millenarianism," 66–90.

117. Cheare, *Sighs for Sion*, 5.

118. Cheare, *Sighs for Sion*, 19. Ps. 69:9 is referenced on the margin of the page. Andrew Fuller would frequently echo the need for a "might spirit of prayer," in many writings, including those pertaining to revival.

to instill vibrant prayerfulness. Cheare's evocative imagery, reminiscent of Psalm 42, gives insight into the responsibility incumbent on human agents to seek spiritual renewal. It should be noted that Cheare juxtaposes "waiting to be with Jesus," with "incessant," panting and thirsting for the Holy Spirit of Promise, disclosing compatibility between divine activity and human agency. Cheare acknowledges that the Holy Spirit alone can, "present us with the ravishing glory of that expected day." Yet, as John Owen himself argued in *Pneumatalogia*, this reality does not inhibit the church's pursuit of that same Spirit.

Cheare carefully weaves the inviolability of God's decrees with the obligation that believers respond in fitting obedience. In *Sighs for Sion*, he writes, "Notwithstanding that salvation he works for them, and his pleading their cause, lays them under no small engagement to him. . ."[119] Spiritual aridness, discouraging as it may be, should not dampen the church's zeal. Drawing from Isa 59:16, Cheare concludes that widespread apostasy does not preclude momentous divine intervention. He explains, "great defection of saints themselves, from following the lamb in this special service, together with the fixation of the work upon the heart of Christ, notwithstanding this, serveth highly now more than ever, the day drawing near. . ."[120] If a reader accepts Cheare's premises, little room remains for despair.

A passion for prayer ought to increase the zeal of local congregations. A small remnant of faithful intercessors typifies the biblical pattern, often preceding dramatic and supernatural intervention. Even adverse conditions, such as Cheare himself experienced ought, ". . .commend, and greatly to encourage and excite the faithfulness of any, though the weakest and most despised of the Lord's holy ones, who are in a right spirit engag'd for, and together with Christ, making prayers also for him continually, and preferring him and his interest before their chief joy, through the spirit of faith and love. . ."[121]

Sighs for Sion carries a distinctly optimistic view of the Protestant church's future, though he is not advocating a naïve, superficial triumphalism. Though Cheare witnessed a brief period of denominational growth under favorable political circumstances, the latter half of his life would be marked by imprisonment, isolation, and illness—all of which led to a premature death. Cheare believed that for an undisclosed period, the church militant would exist alongside, and be oppressed by, the antichrist. Cheare also acknowledged the reality of apostasy among scores of confessing

---

119. Cheare, *Sighs for Sion*, 10.
120. Cheare, *Sighs for Sion*, 10.
121. Cheare, *Sighs for Sion*, 10–11.

believers. Yet, none of these trials dampened the prospect of kingdom of advancement.

In *Sighs for Sion*, Cheare perceives a passion for intercession among congregations in the Western Association as plausible evidence of an impending awakening. Thus, he asks:

> For the quickening of our hearts to this work, and the heightening of our expectations therein, hath not the Lord given us, among many other, this remarkable sign of the times, even a mighty spirit of faith and prayer, through some choice discoveries of grace raised up in his people?[122]

The divine will underscores Cheare's interpretation of the church's present condition as well as its future prospect. The church should perceive God's foreordained plan as enjoining her in his mission. Prayer is the fitting response. Even bleak conditions, where spiritual attrition is high, fits a scriptural pattern. Dramatic intervention in supernatural form should engender an increased zeal for prayer.

Conclusion

Several patterns of spiritual renewal can be detected in the Puritans cited above that will later serve to ground and inspire evangelical revival in the eighteenth century. This chapter has focused on three representatives from the Stuart period: John Owen, John Howe and Abraham Cheare. In each of their works, we find emphasis on the Holy Spirit as sovereign and free—who does the unexpected at divinely-appointed times. Nonetheless, Scripture reveals means by which believers should pursue the Holy Spirit and anticipate his activity. Preeminently, the Spirit is a promised gift, sent by the Father and Son to the church.

In *Pneumatalogia*, John Owen considers the broad scope of biblical data, concluding that duty in matters of revealed doctrine is the proper response to the Holy Spirit. The Spirit accomplishes its mission by means of human agency, even if the relationship is not contingent. Owen summarizes the believer's proper disposition to the Spirit as follows: "Our duty is to apply ourselves unto his commands, according to the conviction of our minds; and his work is to enable us to perform them."[123] Dutiful obedience to revelation in scripture would be a centerpiece of Andrew Fuller's theology. It

---

122. Cheare, *Sighs for Sion*, 15.

123. Owen, *Pneumatalogia* in *WJO*, 3:204.

was this very notion that freed Particular Baptists from logical quandaries that bound high Calvinists to a no-offers-of-grace theology.

In *The Prosperous State of the Christian Interest* John Howe expresses hope that an outpouring of the Holy Spirit would inaugurate the millennial kingdom on earth. Though he concedes that this period, deduced from sundry Old Testament passages, is likely to commence beyond his own lifetime, the proper disposition is one of hope. The simultaneous flourishing of visible congregations, and the individual spiritual lives of believers across the globe is certain to occur. Yet, this feat will only be done through divine fiat. All human attempts, even those within the church to bring universal tranquility, mass conversions, even denominational unity, will fail dismally without effusion of the Spirit. Andrew Fuller would later stress the Spirit's crucial role for bringing revival, sharing with John Howe, belief in a spiritualized millennial reign of Christ on earth. Unlike Howe, who advocated a disposition of passive receptivity, Fuller would place more emphasis on means of a practical nature in preparation for, and participation in, revival.

The seventeenth century marked the genesis of prayer calls, and Calvinistic Baptists were no exception to this movement. Efforts to unite churches in corporate intercession were inspired by theological and contextual distinctives. Like many of his Puritan contemporaries, Abraham Cheare typologically interpreted prophetic passages such as refer to Zion, as promises given to the New Testament church. These texts disclose God's love for his people, and zeal for their spiritual vitality. Furthermore, Zion's prosperity, spoken of in magnificent terms, and whose crowning glory lay in the future, provided a major impetus to pray for its arrival. Cheare's acknowledgement of spiritually-famished times should not discourage churches since the biblical paradigm is of God's drawing a remnant to initiate change.

The theological foundation for Andrew Fuller and his contemporaries and their approach to spiritual renewal had its roots in seventeenth-century Puritanism. Dissenting congregations who maintained Reformed orthodoxy would define and evaluate revival from a distinctly Calvinistic perspective, striving to balance the divine decrees, biblical prophecy, duty, and means, for proposing a coherent, honest, and persuasive case for pursuing it. The work of Owen, Howe, and Cheare, provided critical theological insight with methodological implications for successive generations who looked to the recent past for sympathetic voices to the nascent revival they were experiencing in the present, and longed for in the future.

Chapter Two

"The Spirit has Departed"
Dissents' Declension and its Relationship to the Evangelical Revivals

THOUGH DISSENTING CHURCHES EXPERIENCED reprieve from state-sponsored persecution after the assumption of William and Mary and consequent passage of the Edict of Toleration in 1689, the first third of the eighteenth century was marked by widespread decline. Trends in contemporary philosophy and science had begun to undermine the theological consensus among the Puritans, leading to the increasing popularity of Arianism, Socinianism, and Deism.[1] But while liberal views adversely affected Anglicans first, then Presbyterians, Congregationalists, and General Baptists, Antinomian controversies were the primary concern among Calvinistic Dissenters in early to mid-century.[2] Concurrently, Particular Baptist churches came to embrace an expression of high Calvinism that rejected offering Christ to sinners, and consequently stymied growth among their churches. Several notable figures, however, perceived a need for revival, writing and preaching in accordance with this conviction. This chapter will seek to trace developments that led to decline among early eighteenth-century Particular Baptists with

---

1. On Baptist persecution from 1660–88 see White, *English Baptists*, 95–133. Popular unorthodox works indicative of Enlightenment rationalism includes: John Toland's (1670–1722), *Christianity not Mysterious* (1696), and the deist Matthew Tindall's (1657–1733) *Christianity as Old as the Creation* (1730). On deism during the period see Sell, *Enlightenment*, 112–31. Webb, "Emergence of Rational Dissent," 12–41.

2. This includes Calvinistic Presbyterians, Independents, and Particular Baptists. See Toon, *Emergence of Hyper-Calvinism*, 36, 40. Peter Naylor notes some positive aspects of high Calvinism within the Particular Baptist denomination. See *Calvinism, Communion and the Baptists*, 165–67. For full discussion see 164–82. On the broader theological boundaries of Puritanism, see Coffey, "Puritanism," 263.

focus on several exceptions to the pattern within the denomination, and in Dissent as a whole.³

To understand the malaise of Particular Baptists in the first thirty to fifty years of the eighteenth century, several theological and historical considerations warrant attention. In the latter half of the seventeenth century, their churches experience substantial growth through robust evangelism and evangelical preaching, yet by 1720, high Calvinism was the denomination's theological hallmark. Peter Toon and others have judged high Calvinism a theological overreaction to Neonomianism.⁴ Antinomianism, prominent in the seventeenth century, preoccupied the careers of later Puritans such as Richard Baxter (1615–1691).⁵ Baxter had witnessed its effects firsthand as a chaplain in Cromwell's army, an experience that led him to publish *Aphorismes of Justification* (1649), a novel and doctrinally-controversial work.⁶

---

3. To conclude that churches of this time were oblivious or unconcerned with spiritual enervation prior to the evangelical awakenings would be a major oversight. A survey of literature, particularly from the 1720s and 30s reveals a deep pastoral concern for an outpouring among the Holy Spirit in Britain and North America. See Kidd, "'Vital Breath of Christianity,'" 27–30; Nuttall, "Methodism and the Older Dissent," 259. Roger Hayden has argued against the pervasiveness of high Calvinism in British Baptist churches, asserting that, "From the very beginning Particular Baptists had been evangelical in their Calvinism." Hayden's thesis posits that many churches, especially those of the provinces maintained evangelical Calvinism over and against the theology of London Baptists. See *Continuity and Change*, xi. Hayden's thesis, though provocative, struggles to account for why numerical decline among Particular Baptist churches was widespread throughout Britain.

4. Toon distinguishes between "high," and "hyper" Calvinism, the latter being, "a system of theology, or a system of the doctrines of God, man and grace, which was framed to exalt the honour and glory of God and did so at the expense of minimising the moral and spiritual responsibility of sinners to God. It placed excessive emphasis on the immanent acts of God—eternal justification, eternal adoption, and the eternal covenant of grace." Others, however, object to the qualifier "hyper." Geoffrey Nuttall for instance, judges it as question-begging. That Fuller used the terms interchangeably adds to the ambiguity. For the purpose of avoiding equivocation, I will use "high" throughout this monograph. For full discussion see Toon, *Emergence of Hyper-Calvinism*, 143–52. See also Sell, *Great Debate*; Daniel, "Hyper-Calvinism and John Gill," Shaw, *High Calvinists in Action*, 11–25. For a recent appraisal of eternal justification and its acceptance in the Reformed tradition see Crisp, *Deviant Calvinism*, 41–69. For the roots of Antinomianism in seventeenth-century England, see Watts, *Dissenters*, 180–86.

5. Popular amongst Puritans between 1640 and 1660, antinomianism was condemned at the Westminster Assembly. For history of the Assembly see Paul, *Assembly of the Lord*. For Baxter and antinomianism see Cooper, *Fear and Polemic*. On Baxter's life see Powicke, *Life of Richard Baxter*; Nuttall, *Richard Baxter*.

6. This work aroused more criticism than any of Baxter's publications. The author's comment to a neighbor that it was "hissed at" by "most divines" is indicative. See Nuttall, *Richard Baxter*, 119. For a recent account of the justification debate, see Boersma, *A Hot Pepper Corn*. For Baxter ecclesiology see Lim, *In Pursuit of Purity, Unity, and*

When Antinomian tendencies cropped-up forty years later, notably in the ministry of Welshman Richard Davis, Baxter commenced a full-throttle attack.[7] Only a year before his death, Baxter composed *Scripture Gospel Defended... Against the Libertines*. Baxter's concern that antinomianism would prevail, making England "believe that elect wicked infidels are as righteous as Christ," and that "it is impossible that any sin should hurt them," led to a lament that, "I should have more hope for the Turks and heathens, than of the land that receiveth and practiseth these principles."[8] Baxter's unique, though, controversial understanding of justification incited fears among Calvinists who saw in Baxter's views a mere rehashing of Arminius and Rome. Particular Baptists were especially wary of Baxter and his successor, Daniel Williams (1643–1716), whose "middle way" Calvinism broke with traditional Reformed orthodoxy's understanding of the law.[9]

In addition to the law, Middle-way Calvinism diverged from historic Reformed theology's understanding of the doctrine of election at several levels. First, Reformed divines had held that Christ' death made satisfaction for the elect only.[10] Second, it was stressed that Christ died to make satisfac-

Liberty; Packer, "Redemption and Restoration."

7. In 1690, the thirty-one-year old Davis was ordained in the Congregational church at Rothwell in Northamptonshire. Davis incited controversy among Dissenters and Anglicans who felt his novel evangelistic campaigns encroached on their territory. Furthermore, Davis appointed untrained laymen as evangelists whose meetings frequently incited hysterical fits, notably among female hearers. Yet, the most worrisome aspect of Davis's ministry were his theological views. His various opponents leveled the accusation of antinomianism. See Toon, *Emergence of Hyper-Calvinism*, 28. Coincidentally, 1690 is the same year the works of Tobias Crisp (1600–1643), the early seventeenth-century Antinomian, were republished. John Gill would himself write a glowing preface to the fourth edition of Crisp's works.

8. Baxter, *Scripture Gospel Defended*, cited in Toon, *Emergence of Hyper Calvinism*, 56–57.

9. Throughout his life, Andrew Fuller repeatedly denied any accusation of being a Baxterian and expressed no sympathy toward Baxter's theology. See Letter I 'Narrative,' in *WAF*, 2:702 and "Letter VI 'Baxterianism,'" in *WAF*, 2:714–16—the latter written to John Ryland Jr. in 1803. Under the middle Calvinist scheme, the law of God was understood as extrinsic, rather than intrinsic to his character. Baxter taught that Christ, in his priestly office, offered his death to God, as Rector, as the basis for the relaxation of the original penal law of the covenant of works. Consequently, Christ's death rendered only a certain satisfaction to divine justice. This allowed Baxter to introduce the gospel as a new law. Middle-way Calvinism denied both the imputation of Christ's righteousness to the sinner, and additionally the sinner's unrighteousness to Christ. Daniel Williams could therefore assert, "I deny that Christ by his obedience made atonement as a proper Pecuniary Surety in the Law of Works" (Toon, *Emergence of Hyper-Calvinism*, 56–57).

10. I am using the Canons of the Synod of Dort and the Westminster Assembly as representative of Reformed orthodoxy. A further conclusion drawn from middle-way Calvinist theology was universal redemption, that is, hypothetical, not actual

tion to the holy, just, righteous God, whose law arises from his very nature. Thus, double imputation was a logical conclusion.[11] The crux of the debate centers of the reality and nature of imputation. Tobias Crisp, for instance, wrote fourteen sermons on Isa 53:6 alone, and was maligned by critics who claimed Crisp made Christ an *actual* sinner as he bore the sins of the elect. Although some of his language suggests this, Crisp denied teaching such.[12]

Crisp's position stems from several considerations drawn from a covenantal theological framework. If the *pactum salutis* (covenant of redemption) precedes the creation of the world, and hence, is unconditional; if the active and passive righteousness of Christ is effected only to the elect, what role then, do good works have in the Christian life? For Baxter and Williams, such conditions made antinomianism inevitable. For the Middle-way Calvinists, the covenant of grace came through the preaching of the gospel, the proclamation that Christ had died and gained forgiveness for the whole world. This gospel-covenant, coined "the law of grace," commanded obedience by means of repentance and faith in Christ. It is from the so-called "law of grace," that the term Neonomianism arose.

In addition to Crisp, several popular teachers preached doctrinal antinomianism, notably by framing grace in such a way as to lead hearers away from the disciplines of confession and prayer. Lay antinomians failed to demonstrate steadfast trust in God, and love for others, an observation Andrew Fuller would make in several writings on the subject.[13] Theologically, a preoccupation with justification, understood as an eternal decree given to elect sinners prior to birth, served as a pretext to neglect holiness.[14]

---

universalism.

11. Toon, *Emergence of Hyper-Calvinism*, 57.

12. The text reads "The Lord hath laid on him the iniquity of us all." In his own words, Crisp explains, "It is iniquity itself, as well as the punishment of it, that the Lord laid upon Christ: he bare the sins of many, as well as he was wounded for them: this is a real transaction; Christ stands as very sinner in God's eye, as the reprobate, though not as the actor of sin; yet as he was the surety, the debt became as really his, as it was the principal's before it become the surety's. . . ." in *Christ Alone Exalted*, 1:562 cf. 447–583.

13. These include John Saltmarsh (d. 1647), John Eaton (b. 1575), and Robert Lancaster. Cited in Toon, *Emergence of Hyper-Calvinism*, 28. See Fuller, *Picture of an Antinomian*, in WAF, 3:829–31; *Antinomianism*, in WAF, 2:660–62 and *Antinomianism contrasted with the Religion of the Holy Scriptures*, in WAF, 2:737–62. Fuller writes that antinomianism's "distinguishing feature. . .is selfishness" (738) an echo of Jonathan Edwards's statement in *The Nature of True Virtue* that "All sin has its source from selfishness, or from self-love not subordinate to a regard for being in general" (*Ethical Writings* in WJE, 8: 614). Online: http://edwards.yale.edu/archive?path=aH-RocDovL2Vkd2FyZHMueWFsZS5lZHUvY2dpLWJpbi9uZXdwaGlsby9nZXRvYmplY-3QucGw/Yy43OjYud2plbw.

14. As a modern Reformed theologian, Oliver Crisp questions this thesis, noting

Whereas previous generations of Puritans, most of whom affirmed unconditional election, wrestled deeply over how a confessing Christian could attain assurance of salvation, antinomians advocated a subjective experience, the inner voice of the Spirit saying: "You are elect."[15] Crisp, and others sympathetic to his views, did not believe good works were grounds for, or indicative of, assurance.

The preservation and promulgation of Tobias Crisp's theology would come through the Presbyterian Joseph Hussey (1660–1726) whose notable treatise, *God's Operations of Grace, but no Offers of Grace* (1706) was a quintessential work of eighteenth-century high Calvinism. Hussey argued against free offers of the gospel, and proposed that although the grace of God should not be offered to all, the doctrines of the gospel should be preached indiscriminately.[16] In defense of his dichotomous scheme, Hussey gave a detailed reply of 20 propositions defending gospel-offers despite inherent limitations as to who was invited, or could be offered, grace.[17] Hussey's influence would extend beyond his lifetime, notably through the high Calvinist John Skepp (d. 1721), pastor of the Particular Baptist church in Cripplegate, London, who was initially converted under Hussey's ministry.

To give a summary of high Calvinism, five central tenets should be noted.[18] First, election is unconditional on the basis of a supralapsarian

---

that motivation to act morally prior to conversion is a duty incumbent on all on the basis of general revelation. As for those who acquire epistemic knowledge that they've been justified *in* eternity (they are elect), these, "have more reason to act morally, not less reason." See *Deviant Calvinism*, 64. For full discussion, see 55–65.

15. The Westminster Catechism gives three means by which a believer can attain assurance, first, the objective work of Christ given in the gospel, two, evidence of the virtues faith, hope and love; third, the witness of the Holy Spirit. For an expanded exposition on assurance see Watson, *Body of Divinity*, 250–60. Representative of those Puritans who understood good works as instrumental in providing assurance of election, and therefore, salvation, was Perkins, particularly in *A Case of Conscience* in which he writes, "This is one of the chiefest uses of good works that by them, not as by cause, as by effects of predestination and faith, both we and also our neighbors are certified of our election and salvation too" (*Works of William Perkins*, 1:437–38).

16. Hussey gives three reasons why he disapproved of offers of grace. First, the Bible presents preachers, and describes preaching, not "offering" the gospel. Second, irresistible grace alone makes Christians. Third, because the elect have been purchased from eternity, invitations are intended for them alone. See Hussey, *God's Operations of Grace*.

17. Hussey's rigid conclusions stemmed from an extreme supralapsarianism, with its novel God-man Christology that rendered the covenant of redemption as an "everlasting," though not eternal, relationship between Father and Son. Hussey compared this subservient hypostatization to personified wisdom of Proverbs eight. See *God's Operations of Grace*, 103–10. On the distinction between preaching and "offering" see 111–25.

18. For a useful chart comparing evangelical Arminianism, hypothetical

understanding of Adam's fall. Second, atonement is particular in scope. Third, Christ's righteousness is imputed to the elect from eternity, before the actual exercise of faith (eternal justification). Fourth, final perseverance is a corollary of election. Lastly, free offers of the gospel are constrained or repudiated. Controversy arose from points three and four, where doctrinal antinomianism was implied, and point five, with its denial of duty faith, served to impede evangelism and evangelistic preaching.

High Calvinism and Declension among Particular Baptists

Divine Energy, John Skepp's only published book, a posthumous work, can be summarized under three headings: The true nature of conversion, the inability of human power to convert sinners, and the Spirit's energy in conversion.[19] In presenting rigorous criteria as prerequisites for a true confession, Skepp believed that admitting a person to church membership on account of their belief that Jesus is the Messiah was simply inadequate.[20] Various unorthodox views which plagued English religion in the 1720s precipitated his doctrinal fastidiousness. Skepp criticized "Pelgian preachers" who relied on rhetorical persuasion and rational arguments to persuade unbelievers.[21] He averred that though the scriptures present cases where gospel exhortations are indiscriminately given, God "always superads the efficacious power of His Spirit. . .to quicken and renew those souls of men whom he has an eternal purpose of love and grace."[22]

Unlike Middle-Way Calvinists, Skepp did not see any obligation or "law" incumbent on hearers of the gospel. Rather, the gospel was itself, "nothing but the blessed news and glad tidings of a salvation that is all grace," and that the promises, encouragements and reproofs connected with it were but, "a sort of adjuncts or necessary concomitants attending the ministry of the Word."[23]Skepp typified much of Hussey's tendencies, placing

universalism, strict Calvinism and High Calvinism, see Hindmarsh, *John Newton*, 124–25. James Leo Garret lists five of his own tenets of hyper-Calvinism that share with those listed above but add the covenant of redemption while omitting final perseverance as a corollary of election. (*Baptist History*, 89).

19. Skepp, *Divine Energy*.

20. This is apparent in John Howe's minimalist doctrinal standards drawn from a few texts with corresponding nebulous propositions. See ch. 1.

21. See Skepp, *Divine Energy*, chapter 3, "Showing the Insufficiency of Moral Suasion to effect true conversion to God, and Faith in Christ," 50–116.

22. Skepp, *Divine Energy*, 50–51.

23. Skepp, *Divine Energy*, 53.

heavy emphasis on opposing Arminianism to such a degree as to neglect scriptural examples that juxtaposed divine sovereignty and human responsibility. Skepp is a critical figure among Particular Baptists as he formed a connecting link between Hussey's theology and the high Calvinism that beleaguered the denomination until the latter half of the eighteen-century.[24] It was through John Brine (1703–1765), and especially John Gill (1697–1771) that Hussey's no offers-of-grace scheme prevailed. John Skepp participated in Gill's ordination ceremony on March 22, 1720 and Gill's respect for Skepp is evinced in his preface to the second edition of *Divine Energy*, in which he wrote: "The worthy author. . .was personally, and intimately known by me and his memory precious to me."[25] Gill even purchased most of Skepp's Hebrew and Rabbinical books upon the latter's death in 1721.[26] Like Skepp, Gill perceived his role as an apologist and polemicist for Reformed orthodoxy in an age of infidelity.

A contemporary of Gill, and converted under his ministry, John Brine established himself as a leader among Particular Baptists. He expressed his conviction that pastoral ministry has a twofold purpose: First, "the defence of the principle of our religion, and that of revelation" and second, the necessity of convincing churchgoers of their "lukewarmness, indifferency, and sad declension."[27] Brine's words reveal a disposition centered on preservation. Andrew Fuller would later attribute these factors to enervation among Particular Baptist churches, and additionally his long, torturous conversion.[28] Those theological authorities whom Brine quotes, find approval in John Gill, and although Brine did not uncritically accept all John Hussey's doctrines, he shared Hussey's belief that grace should not offered indiscriminately.[29]

Though Skepp's adoption of Hussey's non-invitation scheme hindered the growth of Particular Baptist churches, ecclesiological considerations should not be neglected. Within the young tradition, denominational

---

24. Toon, *Emergence of Hyper-Calvinism*, 88–89.

25. See Gill, "A Recommendary Preface," in *Divine Energy*, 1.

26. Gill, "A Recommendary Preface," in *Divine Energy*, 1.

27. Brine, *Preface to Treatise on Various Subjects*, iii.

28. On Fuller's conversion see *Memoir* in *WAF*, 1:1–8. Fuller's detailed systematic rejection of high Calvinist tenets is found in *Gospel Worthy* part II, in *WAF*, 2:343–67.

29. In *God's Operations of Grace*, Hussey wrote that "An offer always keeps aloof from the Man, never closes with him nor changes him, but clucks here 'I offer you grace,' 'I offer you Christ,' 'I propose him to you Acceptance,' which never effects any Thing, never comes home upon him. Offers are not through the Gospel, and so can never be effectual, as Operations are." Cited in Naylor, *Calvinism, Communion and the Baptists*, 175.

paragon Benjamin Keach (1640–1704)[30] could speak in terms that Brine, Gill, and others could easily appropriate to a high Calvinist framework. Commenting on the parables of Jesus and Ezek 34:14, Keach wrote that the church,

> Shall wander no more on the mountains of error and heresy; Christ leads them out of all idolatry and superstition, out of Babylon and all false worship; they shall no more be defiled with women, that is, by pollution of false churches, or with harlot worship; the church of Rome is called the mother of harlots. . .Were the gospel churches national, or did they receive into those churches profane persons? No, no, they were a separate people, and a congregational and a holy community, being not conformable to this world; and into such a church Jesus Christ brings his sheep. And from hence it followeth that he carries his lost sheep when he hath found them into his own fold, or into some true gospel church.[31]

As an original drafter of the 1677/89 *Second London Confession of Faith*, Keach wrote in *Gospel Mysteries Unveiled* (1701) what was to become the quintessential ecclesial metaphor for Particular Baptists, "a garden enclosed," an allegorical rendering of Song 4:12.[32] This is, however, far from a complete picture. Keach and other signers of the Confession anticipated high Calvinism, and thoroughly addressed churches with such theological leanings. Andrew Gifford Sr. (1642–1721), pastor of Pithay Calvinistic Baptist Church in Bristol wrote that he knew of ministers who preached that "none could pray acceptably without the influence of the Holy Spirit, and unconverted men being destitute of those influences, that therefore it was not their duty to pray, nor the duty of ministers to exhort them to prayer." In a reply, written two years prior to the Confession's 1677 composition,

---

30. Keach was also known for introducing hymn-singing into congregational settings. See Givens Jr., "'And They Sung a New Song,'" 406–20.

31. Keach, *Gospel Mysteries Unveil'd*, 65–66. Perhaps unsurprisingly, the pastoral metaphor is found in an earlier Baptist document, section 34 of the 1644 London Confession of Faith, where all people are invited acknowledge Christ as "prophet, priest, and King, to be inrolled amongst his household servants, to be under his heavenly conduct and government, to lead their lives in his *walled sheep-fold, and watered garden*, to have communion here with the Saints, that they may be made to be partakers of their inheritance in the Kingdome of God." Cited in Lumpkin, *Baptist Confessions*, 166.

32. This view was first propounded by Augustine in the fifth century. See *Song of Songs*, 4, 12–13, cited in Brown, *Augustine*, 207–8. It is a fascinating paradox that Augustine seeks to navigate the tension between the moral purity of the church—even to employ the garden metaphor—and its broad, universal scope in the context of the Donatist controversy, where separation from the world was a central issue.

prayer is described as "a duty belonging to natural, and not only instituted religion."[33] Close examination of the Confession reveals a firm evangelical Calvinism. Article 7.2, for example states,

> Man having brought himself under the curse of the law by his fall, it pleased the Lord to make a covenant of grace wherein he freely offereth unto Sinners, Life and Salvation by Jesus Christ.[34]

As a significant number of Calvinistic Baptist preachers would reject evangelical aspects in the London Confession, no new editions of the document would appear from 1720 to 1791. By contrast, five editions were published between 1689 and 1720. Robert Oliver draws from this gap a suspicion that many eighteenth-century Calvinistic Baptists did not fully accept the Confession, as its content and the writings of its framers were incompatible with high Calvinist views.[35]

John Gill

As the leading theologian among eighteenth-century Particular Baptists, the influence of John Gill (1697–1771) is extensive.[36] His complete commentary on the Old and New Testaments ensures placement among a select group of biblical exegetes in church history. Gill's *Body of Practical Divinity*, the first Baptist systematic theology, was a standard text for Particular

---

33. See Ivimey, *History of English Baptists*, 1:416. In response to the objection that those without the Spirit have are not required to pray, the Confession states: "This object is not cogent, forasmuch as neither the want of the Spirit's immediate motions to, or its assistance in the duty, doth not take off the obligation to the duty. If it would, then also, from every other duty; and consequently, all religion would be cashiered. If the obligation to this and other duties were suspended merely for want of such motions or assistance, then converted persons are so far from sinning in the omission of such duties, that it is their duty to omit them. Tis certain no man can, without the assistance of the Holy Spirit, either repent or believe; yet it will not follow, that impenitency and unbelief are no sins, then the contrary must be their duty," 417–18.

34. See *Second London Baptist Confession* in Lumpkin, *Baptist Confessions*, 295. Additionally, Hanserd Knollys could speak of the gospel being "preached to every creature in all parts of [the] world. None are exempted or prohibited from hearing the Gospel preached, but everyone that hath an eare is required to heare, Rev. 2:7." See *Christ Exalted*, 12. Keach maintained that the Holy Spirit is "a River of Life that lieth open to all poor Sinners; whoever may come to these waters; none are forbidden, no restraint is laid upon any soul that desires to have them." See *Tropologia*, bk. 2, 512.

35. Oliver, "Emergence of a Strict and Particular Baptist Community," 16.

36. On Gill see Haykin, *Life and Thought of John Gill*; George and Dockery, *Theologians of the Baptist Tradition*, 11–33; Nettles, *By His Grace*; Oliver, "John Gill 1697–1771," in Haykin, *British Particular Baptists 1638–1910*, 144–65.

Baptist pastors during his lifetime and well into the nineteenth century. While Gill's exegetical and theological contributions served to preserve Reformed dogma against strains of Arianism and Socinianism prevalent among Dissenters of the era, most Baptist historians in the last two centuries have made distinctly negative assessments of Gill.[37] On account of his adopting Hussey and Skepp's no-offers-of-grace" theology, Gill's name has long been synonymous with high Calvinism. As a resolute defender of eternal justification, Gill has been associated with antinomianism, though that charge has recently been refuted.[38]

Several historians in the recent past have contested the thesis that Gill was a high Calvinist or that he was unconcerned with evangelism.[39] Thomas J. Nettles, citing Gill's own words, demonstrates that the London pastor did not hesitate to affirm that the gospel should be preached to all people. In describing the preacher's evangelistic role, Gill claimed, "The ministers of the gospel are sent to preach the gospel to every creature."[40] Moreover, the very commission of gospel ministers. . .[is] to go into all the world, and preach the gospel to every creature."[41] In assessing Gill's relationship to the evangelical Awakenings, Nettles concludes that Gill had no qualms with the gospel being preached to wide audiences, rather "He took exception to the *manner* in which this was done, and sometimes to the *matter* of what

---

37. George and Dockery, "John Gill," in *Theologians of the Baptist Tradition*, 30. In "Ecclesiology of John Gill," George cites McBeth in *The Baptist Heritage* whose claim that Gill's theology "brought a kiss of death to Particular Baptists," is indicative of an unbalanced assessment of Gill.

38. George and Dockery, *Theologians of the Baptist Tradition*, 92–94, 78. Henry Vedder whose criticism was widely-adopted by historians in the nineteenth and early twentieth century accused Gill of Supralapsarianism and high Calvinism that was hardly distinguishable from "fatalism and antinomianism," and that his non-invitation to sinners was "practically to nullify the Great Commission." See *History of the Baptists*, 239–41. Gill summarizes the close relationship between the divine decrees of election and justification: "Justification may well be considered a branch of election; it is no other, as one expresses it, than setting apart the elect alone to be partakers of Christ's righteousness; and a setting apart Christ's righteousness for the elect only; it is mentioned along with election [Eph. 1:6]. What is this acceptance of Christ but justification in him? And this is expressed as a past act, in the same language as other eternal things be in the context, he 'hath' blessed us, and he 'hath' chosen us, and 'having' predestined us, so he hath made us accepted; and, indeed, as Christ was always the beloved of God, and well pleasing to him; so all given to him, and in him, were beloved of God, well pleasing to him, and accepted with him, or justified in him from eternity." See Gill, *Body of Practical Divinity*, bk. 2, ch. 5, sec. 2b2.

39. Nettles, *By His Grace*; Ella, "John Gill and the Charge of Hyper-Calvinism," 160–70. White, "Theological and Historical Examination of John Gill's Soteriology."

40. Gill, *Answer to the Birmingham Dialogue-Writers Second Part*, 21.

41. Gill, *Answer to the Birmingham Dialogue-Writers Second Part*, 21.

was preached, but not *that* it was done."⁴² Though this assessment does not minimize Gill's theological disagreements with evangelicalism's leaders, it does mitigate the common notion that John Gill was at worst, hostile to evangelism. Among Baptist scholars, debate over Gill's theology and legacy is ongoing.⁴³

If Gill believed universal gospel proclamation was the duty of pastors, what brought controversy during, and after Gill's lifetime? First, Gill opposed a form of rationalism, prevalent in eighteenth-century Britain, that reduced conversion itself to the rational discovery that they were elected and saved.⁴⁴ Conversion was a distinctly spiritual, not merely intellectual act.⁴⁵ Consequently, a person must come to Christ spiritually. He or she must experience godly affections, be overcome by the beauty and holiness of Christ, and sense their own corruption.⁴⁶ By scriptural and logical argument, Gill concludes that proclamation of the gospel should extend to all people, but invitation should be offered to those who possessed spiritual affections. Gill called the latter, "sensible sinners," that is, those who became "sensible of their lost and perishing condition."⁴⁷ Christ did not invite "all the individuals of mankind to come to him for salvation, but limited it to "such who groan, being burdened with the guilt of sin upon their consciences."⁴⁸

---

42. Nettles, "John Gill and the Evangelical Awakening," 147. Gill's assertion that a minister is "not to offer, but to preach Christ. . . ..to proclaim the peace [offered by Christ] but not to offer it." See *Answer to Birmingham Dialogue Second Part*, 21. Of course, this could be argued for Skepp and Brine as well, since they made a hard distinction between "offers of the gospel," which have supposed scriptural warrant, and "offers of grace," which do not.

43. In a recent article, David Mark Rathel argues that Gill's very soteriological project minimized human responsibility, leading to practical rejection of gospel offers and duty faith. Rathel's criticism is levelled primarily at Nettles whom he believes (wrongly) defends Gill as a "theoretical hyper-Calvinist." See "Was John Gill a Hyper-Calvinist?" 47–59.

44. Wills, "Spirituality of John Gill," 209.

45. This echoes Skepp's own beliefs as expressed in *Divine Energy* though there would prove to be some theological irony in high Calvinism's rationalistic trajectory.

46. Wills, "Spirituality of John Gill," 209. Commenting on Isa 6:5–6 and ascribing Isaiah's vision to Christ via John 12:41, Gill writes, "It may seem strange that a sight of Christ should fill the prophet with dread. . .his sight of Christ is given as a reason of his view of his impurity, and his impurity as the reason of his being undone in his apprehension of things." Gill, *Exposition of the Old Testament*, 5:36, commenting on Isa 6:5. On John 12:41 *Exposition of the New Testament*, 42.

47. Wills, "Spirituality of John Gill," 209. David Rathel notes that Gill uses the term "sensible sinners" 49 times in his New Testament commentaries and 80 times in his Old Testament commentaries. See "Was John Gill a Hyper-Calvinist," 55.

48. "Glory of God's Grace Displayed," in Gill, *Collection of Sermons and Tracts*, 1:197.

Gill summarizes his unique resolution to tension between universal gospel proclamation and unconditional election in an exhortation to pastors in *Cause of God and Truth*,

> Ministers, in exhorting men to believe in Christ, do not, and cannot consider them as elect or non-elect, but as sinners, standing in need of Christ and salvation by him. . .not as insensible of it; for I do not find that any such are exhorted to believe in Christ for salvation; but as sensible of it.[49]

While John Gill disagreed with other high Calvinists on several points, he did maintain that the non-elect had no obligation to evangelical obedience, his view being grounded on the supposition that the necessity of such did not exist in unfallen humanity deposited in Adam.[50] Lewis Wayman (d. 1764) was the first known high Calvinist to distinguish between "legal" and "evangelical" repentance. The former required only turning from sin with an attempt to live by the moral law, and intellectual assent to God's revelation, while the latter was a saving gift of God, and therefore not required of the non-elect.[51] Thus, Gill, along with Brine and Wayman, rejected the supposition posed in Matthias Maurice's *Modern Question*.[52] While several Particular Baptist leaders agreed with Maurice and wrote against Gill and company on precisely this point, the influence of the denomination's premier theologian and exegete was extensive. A generation after the Modern Question was proposed, Andrew Fuller would lay the blame at the feet of Gill and Brine for the failure of his own pastor, John Eve, to offer Christ to a young man in Soham.

Exceptions to the Pattern

Though theological-frigidity characterized many Particular Baptist churches, there were exceptions to the pattern. The Western Association, with the city of Bristol, and the Baptist academy founded there, typified spiritual vitality of a robust evangelical Calvinism.[53] Bristol Baptist

---

49. Gill, *Cause of God and Truth*, 38. Cf. 294, 317.

50. Nettles, "John Gill and the Evangelical Awakening," 153.

51. See Wayman, *Further Enquiry After Truth*. Interestingly, Jonathan Edwards, discussing humility in *Religious Affections* distinguishes between what he considered "legal" and "evangelical" humiliation (*Works of Jonathan Edwards*, 294–302).

52. The full title is *A Modern Question Modestly Answered*. For full discussion see Nuttall, "Northamptonshire and the Modern Question," 101–23.

53. Haykin, "Habitation of God," 73. For several of these figures, see Haykin, "'For God's Glory [and] for Good of Precious Souls,'" 279–83.

Academy, founded at bequest of the will of Edward Terrill (1635–1686), elder of Broadmead Church, would produce an impressive roll of graduates through the eighteenth century.[54] Two pastors trained at Bristol, Andrew Gifford (1700–1784), and Benjamin Francis (1734–1799) had successful ministries under which hundreds were converted. Several years before his death, Gifford, an enthusiastic supporter of George Whitfield, and who edited Whitefield's sermons for publication, was responsible for six-hundred individuals coming to faith.[55] A 1745 sermon preached by Gifford on John 4:14, the only extant which survives, captures his evangelistic ethos:

> If there are any here who have not yet received this living water, let it be improved, by way of advice, earnestly to seek it. Oh, that you did but see your need of it; believe the report, and admit the conviction that without it you are parched wilderness, barren and dry, nigh unto cursing, whose end is to be burned! . . .[But] if. . .you are now thro' grace longing to taste of it. . .quench not the Spirit, but labor to feel and lay heart, both the want and worth of it. . .Above all, go to the spring head the Lord Jesus Christ, whose gift it is. . .Tell him you come at his invitation and command, therefore beg he will remember his word, upon which he has encouraged you to hope (Rev. xxii, 17).[56]

After leaving the Bristol Academy in 1756, Francis was called to serve at Horsley, Gloucestershire. Upon arrival, there were sixty-six members, forty-two years later, close to 450 had been converted, baptized, and joined into membership.[57] The meetinghouse at Horsley had to be enlarge three

---

54. Among these are John Collett Ryland (1723–92), John Rippon (1751–1836), successor to John Gill at Carter Lane, London, Samuel Pearce (1766–99), John Sutcliff of Olney (1752–1814), two of Andrew Fuller's closest friends. See Hayden, *Continuity and Change*, 63–103.

55. Haykin, "Habitation of God," 74. On Francis's life see Flint, "Brief Narrative," 42–43; "Benjamin Francis," in Haykin, *British Particular Baptists*, 17–30. For a listing of most of Francis's works see Starr, *Baptist Bibliography*, 8:71–73. Ian Randall attributes Moravian influence to Francis and Gifford, notably, hymnody, personal conversion, and international missions. Included are several other Baptists from the period including Benjamin Beddome, John Rippon, John Fawcett, Anne Steele, and Samuel Pearce. Randall, "Christ Comes to the Heart," 14–15. On Whitefield's sermon published by Gifford see *Eighteen Sermons*.

56. Gifford, *Living Water*, 17–18.

57. Haykin, "Habitation of God," 74. On Francis's life, see Flint, "A Brief Narrative," 33–76.

times to accommodate growth.[58] Francis was himself a vigorous evangelist, traveling weekly to preach in adjacent villages and towns.[59]

Andrew Gifford was not the only Particular Baptist sympathetic to Whitfield and the evangelical revivals. Future pastors Robert Robinson (1735–1790) and John Fawcett (1740–1817) were both converted under Whitefield's ministry.[60] Robinson, later baptized as a believer, ministered at Stone Yard Baptist Church, Cambridge in 1761. Fawcett, like Robinson, embraced believer's baptism and pastored in Yorkshire.[61] While the above representatives would be instrumental in shaping the Particular Baptist denomination in the latter half of the century, they were still the exception in the 1750s and 60s. Regrettably, their impact would not reach churches such as those in Soham where Andrew Fuller was reared.

Notwithstanding the ministries of Gifford and Francis, Particular Baptist churches as a whole languished. The "Evans Manuscript," a compilation named after Dr. John Evans, the minister of the Hand Alley Presbyterian meeting in London, purported to list every church among Dissenting congregations throughout England and Wales in the years 1715–1718 yielded bleak results. On Evans's numbers, as little as four-percent of Londoners embraced the residual Puritan culture.[62] Recorded in the manuscript were 220 Particular Baptist Churches.[63] After a census was taken in 1750, around 150 Particular Baptist churches were listed, a one-third decrease. Writing in 1743, Benjamin Dutton could lament that "The Holy Spirit. . .is despis'd and contemned."[64] This downward trend would eventually reverse, but only through a paradigm shift due in large part to the resolutions of the Northamptonshire Association in the 1780s to seek revival and of which Andrew Fuller made critical contributions by pen and pulpit.

---

58. Haykin, "Habitation of God," 74.
59. Haykin, "Habitation of God," 75.
60. Morden, *Life and Thought*, 28.
61. Morden, *Life and Thought*, 28.
62. Hindmarsh, *John Newton*, 51.

63. Watts, *Dissenters*, 268–69. See 489–550 for discussion on assessing the Evans Manuscript. See also Evans et. al., "Baptist Interest under George I," 95–109; Langley, "Baptist Ministers in England about 1750 A.D.," Gilbert, *Religion and Society in Industrial England*, 35, 37.

64. Dutton, *Superaboundings*, iv.

Dissenting Voices for Revival: Philip Doddridge and Isaac Watts

Though declension marked Particular Baptist churches in the first half of eighteenth century, and concurrently, as revival arose from within the Anglican church, two Dissenting clergymen perceived distinct theological and methodological problems within their own churches. Isaac Watts (1684–1748) and Philip Doddridge (1702–1751) were crucial in the formation of eighteenth-century Nonconformity.[65] Though ordained Congregationalists who addressed problems unique to their respective denomination, Watts and Doddridge made accurate assessments of Dissent as a whole, underscoring the need for passionate, evangelical preaching, and crucial preservation of minimal, yet orthodox confessions of faith among its pastors.[66] As complex characters, their lives and writings defy neat categorization.[67] Watts, for instance, though led by rationalism to entertain heterodox views of the Trinity and the person of Christ, could yet praise John Howe for his openness to mystical encounters.[68] Both figures were sympathetic to continental pietism, and familiar with its German progenitors, providing a notable parallel to Whitefield, and especially Wesley.[69] On such the bases,

---

65. Sutherland, *Peace, Toleration, and Decay*, 179. Watts wrote the preface to the British edition of Jonathan Edwards's *Faithful Narrative*.

66. See Muller, "Philip Doddridge and the Formulation of Calvinistic Theology," 65–84. Crawford cites the example John Jennings (d. 1723), whose *Two Discourses: The First Preaching Christ; The Second Experimental Preaching*, emphasized conversion and were published in 1723 with a preface by Isaac Watts. See Crawford, *Seasons of Grace*, 54–55.

67. Scholars attribute primary influence to diverse figures as Richard Baxter and John Locke. See Nuttall, *Richard Baxter and Philip Doddridge*. Others consider John Howe the exemplar of faith and practice Watts and Doddridge sought to emulate. See Sutherland, *Peace, Toleration, and Decay*, 179. Isaac Watts fell into the Middle-Way Calvinist camp. His belief in universal redemption as justification for free gospel offers was refuted by John Brine in *Certain Efficacy of the Death of Christ*.

68. Nuttall, *Philip Doddridge*, 154–63, 159–62. See Sutherland, *Peace, Toleration, and Decay*, 180. The encounter, which Howe called, "extraordinary witness," is described as a kind of ecstasy that 'far surpass'd the most expressive words my thoughts can suggest. . ." A posthumous discovery by Howe's wife, the account was written in his study Bible in Latin. See Calamy, *Memoirs*, 229–31, and Rogers's *Life and Character of John Howe*, 519–23. Howe's experience was not atypical and Watts's praise for it reveals clear Puritan sympathies. Charles Hambrick-Stowe's survey of devotional works from seventeenth-century New England led to his contention that, "Puritan theology and much of the preaching was rational in nature. But the devotional exercises, when pursued by the contemplative, led to experiences quite beyond the realm of reason." *Practice of Piety*, 286. For a helpful overview of Watts's conflicting views on the Trinity, see Aniol, "Was Isaac Watts Unitarian?" 91–103.

69. Doddridge began correspondence with Zinzendorf in 1737 and maintained

Doddridge and Watts can rightly be considered "evangelicals before the revivals"[70]

Isaac Watts

Isaac Watts stands among the eighteenth century's most influential and iconic Nonconformist figures with noted written contributions to logic, rationality, and apologetics, though his greatest theological legacy is found in his hymnody.[71] Considered a leading figure within English Dissent, Watts preached in the pulpit once occupied by John Owen.[72] During his ministry, Watts served as a model figure in Dissenting churches, being frequently asked to preach at significant events.[73] Though not generally associated with revival, spiritual renewal was a central theme in his thought. His immensely practical *Guide to Prayer* went through eight editions by 1739.[74] Furthermore, several elements in Watts's preaching made him unique to the early eighteenth century.[75] For such reasons, Watts has been understood as

a high view of the Moravians, but later—along with Watts—changed his views. See Harris, "Philip Doddridge," 252–56, and Payne, "Eighteenth Century English Congregationalism," 296. For the influence of Pietism on English Puritans, see Stoeffler, *Rise of Evangelical Pietism*.

70. Nuttall, "Methodism and the Older Dissent," 261. Hindmarsh citing the example of Matthew Henry, gives the following definition of an "evangelical before the revival": "a moderate who could not be identified with late-seventeenth and early-eighteenth-century controversies over Baxterian Neonomianism or Crispian high Calvinism, and who though. . .believed in the Nonconformist conscience, rejected the drift toward heterodoxy evident among some Dissenters." *Spirit of Evangelicalism*, 30.

71. Watts's extant compositions number close to 750. On Watts's life, see Fountain, *Isaac Watts Remembered*; Davis, *Isaac Watts*; Beynon, *Isaac Watts*. Cf. Rupp, *Six Makers of English Religion 1500–1700*, 102–24. On Watt's hymnody, see Manning, *Hymns of Wesley and Watts*, 78–106.

72. Fountain, *Isaac Watts Remembered*, 11, 46.

73. Beynon, *Isaac Watts*, 7. Watt's connection to Fuller is modest, but not insignificant. For instance, in a 1798 compilation of books from his personal library, six belonged to Watts, the same number as John Owen. See *Complete Works of Andrew Fuller Volume*, 215. Fuller would quote a hymn by Watts from *Songs and Spiritual Songs* (1707) in a diary entry on October 31, 1784. "O for this love let rocks and hills their lasting silence break; And all harmonious human tongues, His lasting Praises speak. Angels assist our mighty joys! &c." Cf. Ryland, *Fuller*, 101–2.

74. Watts, *Guide to Prayer*, also in Burder, *Works of Isaac Watts*, 3:107, 188. O'Brien notes that alongside William Law's *A Serious Call to a Devout and Holy Life* (1728), *A Guide to Prayer* was cited among the most common devotional guides prior to the 1740s. "Eighteenth-Century Publishing Networks in the First Years of Transatlantic Evangelicalism," 54n32, cited in Kidd, "'Very Vital Breath of Christianity,'" 21.

75. Graham Beynon observes that these include usage of neoclassical language,

a figurehead of continuity between Puritanism and the evangelical revivals, and an anomaly among English clergy of the time, though there were some exceptions to this pattern.[76]

Watts first read of the awakenings in New England, only to witness revival fervor in his own context soon after. He maintained correspondence with evangelical leaders John and Charles Wesley, George Whitefield, and Jonathan Edwards until his death in 1748.[77] A preface to the English publication of *A Faithful Narrative* was composed by Watts.[78] Watts's relationship to George Whitefield, markedly nuanced, is aptly summarized in a recorded conversation among ministers in April 1742, in which Watts said,

> Tho' I do not fall in with him in all his conduct, yet I cannot but think him a man raised up by Providence in something of an uncommon way to waken a stupid and ungodly world to a sense of the important affairs of religion and Eternity. You may show these letters of mine to what persons you please, and let my opinion of Mr. Whitefield even notwithstanding all his imprudences, be known where you think fit.[79]

Like Jonathan Edwards, Watts was concerned to balance reason with the passions and affections in the religious realm. Whereas Edwards proposed rational analyses to evaluate these faculties in a revival context, Watts's concern was to emphasize the inadequacy of reason alone, devoid of the affections, for knowing and loving God.[80] Watts's target was John Locke,

Puritan focus on the passions, the new religious psychology of the faculties, each underpinned by his theological understanding of sin and regeneration. See *Isaac Watts*, 140. Hence, Beynon's thesis that reason and passion uniquely embody Watts's thought.

76. Beynon, *Isaac Watts*, 11.

77. Watts's familiarity and high regard for Charles Wesley's hymns is evident in a generous comment that "Wrestling Jacob" was worth all that he himself had ever written. Cited in Bernard Manning, *Hymns of Wesley and Watts*, 78.

78. Fountain, *Isaac Watts Remembered*, 90. Fountain notes that Watts kept close contact with New England leadership, acting as a literary agent, purchasing books for prominent men as well as the libraries of Harvard and Yale. He also personally funded Indian missionary work in the colonies. Edwards and Watts wrote on similar subjects including the passions, affections, and human volition, though they ministered in divergent religious climates.

79. Fountain, *Isac Watts Remembered*, 93. Throughout his life Watts, in contrast to Doddridge, disapproved of Methodism as a whole. Cited in Rack, *Reasonable Enthusiast*, 325.

80. *Doctrine of Passions Explained and Improved*, in Watts, *Works of the Late Reverend and Learned Isaac Watts*, 580–633, 636–716. Jonathan Edwards draws a quantitative difference between passions and affections, with passions being more powerful affections. Cf. Smith, *Jonathan Edwards*, 33. For further discussion on Edwards and the passions see Davidson, "Not From Ourselves," 577–81. Watts uses the terms

of whom he chided in a poem for the "wav'ring and cold assent" Locke gave to divine truths, embodied in his appropriate, though tepidly titled, *Reasonableness of Christianity* (1695).[81]

Cold assent remained the greatest enemy of genuine piety, for, "[I]t is not enough for the eye to be lifted up to him. . .for the tongue to speak of him. . .or the hand to act for his interest in the world," wrote Watts. Rather, "the heart with all the inward powers and passions must be devoted to him in the first place: This is religion indeed."[82] Andrew Fuller would make similar arguments against the extreme rationalism of the Sandemanians who defined faith as "bare belief of the bare truth."[83] In an excerpt from a sermon titled, "The World to Come" Watts aptly expresses concern for engaging the passions.

> Our hearts are cold as well as dark: How seldom do we see the fervency of spirit in religious duties which God requires? How cool is our love to the greatest and best of beings? How languid and indifferent are our affections to the Son of God, the chiefest of ten thousand and altogether lovely? And how much doth the devotion of our souls want it's proper ardour vivacity?[84]

In 1712 the Presbyterian Daniel Defoe would observe that English Dissent was in a "declining and decaying posture"[85] from a lack of spiritual

synonymously. Cf. Beynon, "Helpfulness of the Lesser-Known Work," 482. He defines the passions as "[T]hose sensible commotions of our whole nature, both soul and body, which are occasioned by the perception of an object, according to some special properties that belong to it." See Watts, *Works of the Late Reverend and Learned Isaac Watts*, 584.

81. Watts, "Love of God," 2:642, *Horae Lyricae*, 4:397, cited in Beynon, *Isaac Watts*, 96. It should be noted that Watts highly regarded Locke, calling him "the ingenious director of modern Philosophy." Watts attributed his use of clear and distinct language and ideas, a motif repeated throughout his writings, to John Locke. See Watts, *Philosophical Essays* (1733) Essay 6 introductory paragraph, and Preface, cited in Bebbington, *Evangelicalism in Modern Britain*, 54. In *Reasonableness of Christianity*, Locke reduced the faith to a few essentials, including Jesus as Messiah, evidence of fulfilled prophecy and his working of miracles. Faith he defines as "a firm assent of the mind." Salvation comes by those "who make a sincere endeavor after righteousness by obeying God's law." The faith in Christ is counted in place of perfect obedience, and the work of Christ makes up what is lacking in our own efforts." See Rack, *Reasonable Enthusiast*, 25.

82. Watts, *Works*, 2:640.

83. Andrew Fuller, "Strictures on Sandemanianism" in *WAF*, 2:561–646. This phrase was used frequently by Scotsman and eponymous founder Robert Sandeman (1718–71). See Smith, *The Perfect Rule of the Christian Religion*.

84. Watts, *World to Come* in *Works*, 1:626.

85. Defoe, *Present State of the Parties in Great Britain*, 285. For Defoe's relation to Dissent and his own checkered life, see Mursell, *English Spirituality*, 38–48.

vigor, a trend of which Watts was fully aware, and whose lament was expressed in another sermon.

> As for the savour of piety, and inward religion...spiritual mindedness, and zeal for God and for the good of souls; as to the spirit and power of evangelical ministrations, we may all complain, the glory of God is much departed from our Israel.[86]

Watts's comment on the "departing glory" is another recurring theme echoed in predecessors, John Howe among them.[87] Watts's heartfelt desire for a "returning glory"—that is, revival of religion, becomes evident throughout several published works, notably *Humble Attempt at the Revival of Practical Religion* whose focus was on reforming Dissenting churches.[88] Watts understood preaching as the vital means by which churches could be awakened from the spiritual lethargy prevalent in the era. As noted in the prior comment by Daniel Defoe, the early decades of the century disclose a spiritual malaise whose distinctive aspects could be attributed to Latitudinarianism.[89] Moralizing and rationalistic sermons were the result of latitudinarian theology. Under this scheme, the role of the preacher was relegated to persuading the public to "choose moral reform and the Christian life, to teach private and social virtues, and to educate people on their duties."[90] For Isaac Watts, such preaching was inherently flawed. As in the case of John Locke, Watts insisted that rational assent to doctrinal propositions coupled with ethical living as essential Christianity was inadequate.[91] While

---

86. Watts, "Sermons on Various Subjects Divine and Moral," in *Works*, 2:xxiii.

87. John Howe, Preface to *Redeemer's Tears Wept over Lost Souls* in *Works of John Howe*, 2:316–89 and *The Prosperous state*, Sermon 1:5, in *Works of John Howe*, 566.

88. Beynon, *Isaac Watts*, 10. Like Abraham Cheare and most Puritans of the previous century, Watts makes the typological connection between Israel and the church.

89. Latitudinarianism, a term of abuse leveled by High Church opponents against the Cambridge Platonists in the 1660s, whose preaching emphases were commonsense piety and practical morality stemmed from the publication *A New Sect of Latitude Men* by 'S.P.' (probably Symon Patrick). See *Oxford Dictionary of the Christian Church*. See Rack, *Reasonable Enthusiast*, 24.

90. See Ihalainen, "Enlightenment Sermon," 29. Charles Stanford, in his 1881 biography on Philip Doddridge cites an Episcopal prelate, Shenstone, who encouraged preachers to imitate Roman orators and poets: "I should think the clergy should distinguish themselves by preaching on the ordinary virtues extolled by the classics, introducing the ornamental flourishes etc" (*Philip Doddridge, D.D.*, 84).

91. For instance, Locke believed that raising the passions misled people. Cited in Beynon, *Isaac Watts*, 135 Nevertheless, Watts could say in agreement with Locke that "God has given us rational faculties and requires the exercise of them in religious concerns, and he has laid down such grounds for faith in all ages as must approve itself unto reason." Cited in *Blessedness of Faith without Sight*, in Watts, *Wattiana*, 209.

Latitudinarianism and similar expressions of moralism did not characterize Particular Baptist preaching, high Calvinism as a theological system was uniquely formed, and sustained by an implicit rationalism. Consequently, Watts's counsel on preaching would be no less salutary for these churches.

Watts wrote to preachers, giving detailed advice on the content, style, and goal of preaching. He advocated a holistic approach that addressed the mind, will, and passions of hearers.[92] In a sermon titled *Improvement of the Mind*, Watts explains how three elements constitute his rhetorical method:

> 1. Conveying the sense of the speaker to the understanding of the hearers in the clearest and most intelligent manner by the plainest expression of the most lively and striking representation of it, so that the mind may be thoroughly convinced of the thing proposed. 2. Persuading the will effectually to choose or refuse the thing suggested and represented. 3. Raising the passions in the most vivid and forcible manner, as to set all the soul and every power of nature at work, to pursue or avoid the thing in debate.[93]

For Watts, ineffective preaching lay with forms of reductionism that failed to account for the multiplicity of faculties active in the human subject. Passion without content, and reason without passion, would both fail to persuade audiences in a meaningful and substantive way.[94] Andrew Fuller in an essay on revival would make explicit his intent to persuade both head and heart.[95] In the instance of the Puritans, Watts finds an overemphasis on logic and plain language; in John Locke and the Latitudinarians, bare rationalism dominates. Each respective group inadequately addressed the passions and thus fails to persuade. Though commonly interpreted as a preacher in the Puritan mold, Watts puts greater emphasis on reason than his forbearers.[96] He had a higher view of philosophy than most Puritans,

---

92. In *Of the Composure of Sermons*, Watts writes, "Remember that you have to do with understanding, Reason and Memory of Man, with the heart and conscience of man, with the will and affections; and therefore you must use every method of speech which may be most proper to engage and employ each of these faculties or powers of Human Nature on the side of religion and the interests of God and the gospel." See *Humble Attempt Toward the Revival of Practical Religion*, 67–68.

93. Watts, *Improvement of the Mind*, in *Works*, 5:311.

94. Beynon, "Helpfulness of the Lesser-Known Work," 482.

95. In *On Spiritual Declension* he writes, "If this, or any of the foregoing papers, should be the means of reclaiming any from the error of their ways, either mental or practical—if they should tend to excite either myself or others to a closer walk with God, I shall enjoy of the satisfaction of not having written in vain" (*WAF*, 3:634).

96. Beynon, *Isaac Watts*, 139.

and believed philosophical arguments were appropriate for persuading hearers.[97]

Notwithstanding his concern that rationality undergird the form and content of a sermon, Watts did not minimize the role of the Holy Spirit for persuasion and transformation of hearers's hearts and minds. Rather, he boldly asserts that,

> If we should have reason to fear that the Spirit of God is much departed from others, let us cry with great greatness, that the Spirit may never leave our assemblies, and abandon us to labour in vain without his influences.[98]

Resolute in his belief that the Holy Spirit's essential activity is free, Watts nevertheless implored his hearers to "Seek earnestly the influences of the quickening Spirit" for the very reason that "nothing can be done without him."[99] Watts instructed believers to excite love of God in their own hearts by cultivating their passions, acknowledging that though they do not lie under the command of our will, being a response to something, he suggests believers can "raise or suppress the passions" by "applying [their] minds to the perception of those objects, or those truths, which are suited for these purposes."[100] This involves a focus on God as object of devotion and cultivating a love for him. Specific application includes reflecting on his word, works, and character, private meditation and public worship.[101] Like the Puritans before him and evangelical Calvinists after, Watts affirms God's sovereign action stands in accord with, and not in opposition to, human response. Watts's immensely practical counsel to revival mirrors Andrew Fuller's own writings, notably Fuller's rejection of exclusively intellectual-focused

---

97. Watts writes, "It is good to impress the conscience as well as instruct the understanding by the two great lights God has given us (viz.) reason and revelation. Two such pillars will support the structure of religion better than one." See *Humble Attempt Toward the Revival of Practical Religion*, 28. By contrast, William Perkins, in *The Art of Prophesying* writes, "Humane wisdom must be concealed;" private use of philosophy was allowed but it was not to be displayed in the pulpit (132–33), cited in Beynon, *Isaac Watts*, 142–43.

98. Watts, *Rational Foundation of a Christian Church*, in *Works*, 6:109.

99. Watts, *Discourses of the Love of God*, 212. In *Guide to Prayer*, Watts noted a tendency among believers to "run away with extremes. They either attribute too much or too little to the Holy Spirit" (124, 172).

100. *Doctrine of the Passions Explained and Improved*, in Watts, *Works of the Late Reverend and Learned Isaac Watts*, 89.

101. Beynon, "Helpfulness of the Lesser-Known Work," 488. Watts's hymns ostensibly functioned to arouse and direct the passions towards this precise end.

preaching.[102] And yet, though such steps can and should be taken, the Holy Spirit's power remained essential for revival, without which human effort would never avail.

Philip Doddridge

If Isaac Watts enjoined the zeal of the Puritan tradition with the rationalism of the eighteenth century, fellow Nonconformist, Philip Doddridge (1702–1751) was a like-minded co-laborer.[103] Like Watts, Doddridge was influenced by John Locke, composed hymns, wrote on the importance of education—particularly for children, and passionately sought revival among Dissenting churches.[104] Born in London on June 26, 1702, Doddridge came from a Nonconformist heritage of ministers that included paternal and maternal grandfathers.[105] Though he remained a theological moderate by standards of eighteenth-century English Congregationalism, Doddridge claimed Calvinistic orthodoxy throughout his life.[106] Widely-respected among Particular Baptists, Arminian Methodists, even evangelical High Churchmen, denominational unity remained a fitting priority in his ministry.[107] Upon hearing of a regular association founded in Norfolk and Suffolk in 1751, the fruit of an earlier visit, Doddridge reminisced,

102. This is a focus points throughout Fuller's *Strictures on Sandemanianism*.

103. Biographies on Doddridge include Stanford, *Philip Doddridge*; Nuttall, *Philip Doddridge*; Greenall, *Philip Doddridge*; Deacon, *Philip Doddridge*; Striven, *Philip Doddridge*.

104. See Secrett, "Philip Doddridge and the Eighteenth-century Revivals," 242–59. Doddridge wrote to Watts in 1741, telling him the success of Watts's *Catechism*. For Doddridge on education see Murray, "Doddridge and Education," 102–21. On hymnody, see Routley, "Hymns of Doddridge," 46–78; Idle, *Philip Doddridge*.

105. Nuttall, *Philip Doddridge*, 14.

106. Doddridge defended adherents of minimalist confessions of faith, including those that fell along Arian or semi-Arian lines. In the case of a Northampton church who excommunicated a member who would not affirm the deity of Christ beyond a minimalist Scriptural sense, Doddridge demurred, declaring that he would "sacrifice his place, and even his life, rather than fix any such mark of discouragement upon one, who, whatever his doctrinal sentiments were, appeared to be a real Christian." See Nuttall, *Philip Doddridge*, 16. Manning, *Essays in Orthodox Dissent* and others doubted the orthodoxy of Doddridge and Watts, though this is disputed. For a recent examination of Doddridge's theology see Muller, "Philip Doddridge and the Formulation of Calvinistic Theology," 65–84. Clifford describes Doddridge as a theological eclectic in the strain of Richard Baxter combined with the rational curiosity of the Enlightenment and scriptural piety of the Puritan tradition. "Christian Mind of Philip Doddridge," 227–42.

107. See Harris, "Philip Doddridge: Eighteenth-Century Ecumenicist," 251–70. Doddridge maintained correspondence with John Wesley throughout his life.

calling it "one of the most delightful days of my whole life." Of the incident, he adds, "We held a kind of council afterwards concerning the methods to be taken for the revival of religion; and I hope set them on work to some good purpose."[108]

Like Watts, Doddridge's greatest contributions came through writing. This did not, however, preclude an active ministry that included preaching several times a week, even devoting half his holiday to evangelical excursions.[109] Doddridge also appointed members of his congregation to read sermons in cottages licensed for that purpose throughout Northampton.[110] Though initially hesitant to publicly endorse Methodist preachers—Calvinistic or Arminian—he later expressed wholehearted support for the evangelical revival ministers, even asking Whitefield to preach at his church in October 1743.[111] Through various connections, Doddridge turned scores of orthodox Dissenters into friends of revival with Calvinistic Methodists converted under Whitefield now joining their congregations.[112] In concord with Watts, Doddridge was a confirmed admirer of John Howe, noting that Howe's mystical encounter made a deep impression on him.[113] He also praised Howe for his sermons in which Howe insisted that Christians depend upon the "immediate influence" of the Spirit, a lack of which "is the great worm at the root of religion this day."[114] Against high Calvinists, Doddridge was convinced that the gospel should be preached to all; but in

---

108. Nuttall, *Philip Doddridge*, 24. Cf. Jewson, *Baptists in Norfolk*.

109. Though Watts has been given more scholarly attention, some have argued that Doddridge was more typical and influential than his older fellow Congregationalist. See Payne, "Eighteenth Century English Congregationalism," 286–301.

110. Stanford, *Philip Doddridge*, 86. In 1737, Doddridge noted that these appointed representatives, kept up, "four or five 'repetitions' in the neighboring towns, and crowds of people constantly attend at each."

111. Stanford, *Philip Doddridge*, 98–100. In 1748 Whitefield asked Doddridge to revise pages of his journal for a new edition, to which the later acquiesced. Charles Stanford observes such an act as demonstrative of a sincere friendship.

112. Bebbington, *Evangelicalism in Modern Britain*, 32. Upon inviting Whitefield to preach, Doddridge was reproached by fellow Dissenters. As Secrett notes, Doddridge "was the first of the influential leaders of the dissenters to be convinced that the Methodists had been chosen and called by God to rouse the churches and the nation from the sleep of death" ("Philip Doddridge and the Evangelical Revival," 253).

113. In 1726 he wrote to Samuel Clark of St. Albans: "I have lately read Howe on the Spirit. . .I think one may see more of the man. . .by this, than any other of his works which I have yet perused." Nuttall, *Philip Doddridge*, 160. In a letter to John Wesley twenty years later, Doddridge encouraged the Methodist leader to read Howe's works, saying, "I cannot but say that he seems to me to have understood the gospel as well as any uninspired writer I have ever read, and to have imbibed as much of its spirit."

114. See Howe, *Whole Works*, 5:155–56.

agreement with them, that failure to believe should be attributed solely to sin, while "success" owes all to "the sovereignty of Divine grace."[115]

Free Thoughts on the Most Probable Means of Reviving the Dissenting Interest

Doddridge's contribution to the subject of revival is best exemplified in a polemical document written to combat the liberalizing tendencies in Dissenting academies. While Congregationalists, like Particular Baptists, experienced numeric decline early in the eighteenth century, the former faced challenges from heterodoxy within the denomination. Some Congregationalists even ventured to attribute stymied growth to theological strictness of their congregations.[116] One such man was Strickland Gough (d. 1752).

In 1730, Gough, who had just emerged from one of the Dissenting academies composed *An Enquiry into the Causes of the Decay of the Dissenting Interest*.[117] The anonymous pamphlet attributed Dissent's decline to churches that imposed creedal formulations on their pastors. Gough's superficial, and historically-dubious assessment led to a claim that the spirit of their Puritan forbearers was "nothing else but a spirit of liberty," and that, "the fundamental principle of the Dissenters. . .is a liberty for every man to form his own sentiments."[118] Gough's solution to the present problem was that ministers pay less attention to members of their congregations,

---

115. Muller, "Philip Doddridge and the Formulation of Calvinistic Theology," 69. Muller notes that Doddridge's understanding of freedom breaks with a determinism formulated in Jonathan Edwards, 78–81.

116. It should be noted that throughout his writings, Doddridge himself is theologically-generous to a degree uncharacteristic of Particular Baptists at the same period. Though he himself maintained orthodoxy, he could write to Gough that by preaching in a "truly experimental and spiritual strain," the congregation, ". . .instead of studying to find us heretics, will rather put the most favourable sense on ambiguous expressions, and labour to believe us as orthodox as they can: Or, if they suspect us to be in the dark as to some particulars, yet they will charitably hope, that age and experience will perfect what is wanting; and that *God will reveal it to us* in his own time." See *Enquiry*, 28–29. For further discussion on Doddridge's theological inclusion, see Nuttall, *Philip Doddridge*, 122–53.

117. Gough, *Enquiry*.

118. Gough, *Enquiry*, 5, 7. Cf., Philosopher and fellow Dissenter John Locke's claim that toleration is "the chief characteristic mark of the true church," and "The care, therefore, of every man's soul belongs unto himself, and is to be left unto himself" (Locke, *Letter Concerning Toleration*, 115, 128). Nevertheless, Locke does acknowledge an individual congregation's right to excommunication, though not financial deprivation or physical harm.

and more to people of wit and politeness.[119] Though the treatise caused a stir, Gough's enduring legacy among Dissent was nullified—among other reasons—his eventual decision to become a clergyman in the Established Church.

In response to Gough's pamphlet, Doddridge wrote *Free Thoughts on the Most Probable Means of Reviving the Dissenting Interest* that same year. The rejoinder refutes Gough's contention that "a spirit of liberty" was the core principle of Dissent. The actual Puritan concern, claimed Doddridge, "was not merely a generous sense of liberty (which may warm the breast of a deist or an atheist)," but rather, "a religious reverence for the divine authority." It was this which, "animated our pious forefathers, to so resolute and so expensive an opposition. . ."[120] Early Dissenters, claimed Doddridge, fought to preserve freedom of conscience, of which, "the throne of God" was its "only sovereign."[121] He presciently counsels that if such "religious reverence" is not the undergirding principle for freedom of conscience, defense of liberty "will hardly be worth. . .maintaining at all."[122]

From Dissent's history Doddridge draws a lesson on the indispensability of personal piety and the Holy Spirit's anointing. Put simply, religious vitality was a direct result of zealous preaching through holy vessels. Doddridge writes that any "languor and insensibility" on the part of the congregation is a direct reflection of the preacher himself. By contrast, if the minister's heart, "be filled with vital religion, it will have a happy influence on all our ministrations. Our prayers and sermons will be tinctured with it."[123] If Dissenting churches lack fervency, look no further than who occupies the pulpit.[124] Doddridge concedes that though rhetorical eloquence did not characterize Puritan sermons, the effects of such preaching surpassed what most eighteenth-century pastors in England could claim. The source of power in Puritan preachers derived not from their "elegant phrases" or

---

119. Gough, *Enquiry*, 33–34.

120. Doddridge, *Free Thoughts*, 6.

121. Doddridge, *Free Thoughts*, 6. Cf. Andrew Fuller's comments in *Spiritual Declension and the Means of Revival* that religious liberty is "of no further use to us than as it is applied to the discovery of truth, and the practice of righteousness. . .[.]" and a warning that the "spirit of the present age is to boast of the liberty of thinking for ourselves, till we lose all attachment to religious principles." See *WAF*, 3:631.

122. Doddridge, *Free Thoughts*, 6.

123. Doddridge, *Free Thoughts*, 9.

124. In *Enquiry*, 34, Gough shows notable contempt for the congregation, writing that "the being pleas'd, which they so much insist upon, seldom arises from any thing but some oddness that hits their peculiar humour, and is not from any view to edification at all, and therefore too mean to be worthy of any one's study." Doddridge is quick to expose and impugn Gough's haughty disposition throughout *Free Thoughts*.

"ornaments of language," but rather, "great attainments in vital and inward religion."[125]

Doddridge makes several proposals for the substance of preaching in *Free Enquiry*. The preacher's first objective must be to impress on sinners' minds. . ."a deep and an abiding sense of the pollution and misery of that estate into which they are fallen by sin," for, "Here true conversion begins."[126] Only after a sinner recognizes their depravity, will they "rejoice to hear of a saviour."[127] At this juncture, Doddridge addresses Christology, a doctrine he believes stands among, "the distinguishing articles of the Christian religion," and which was denigrated by many contemporaries in the Age of Reason."[128] Doddridge provides what he believes constitutes core Christological content. This includes, "the dignity of [Christ's] person as the Son of God. . .his mysterious incarnation, his holy life, his divine doctrine, his wonderful miracles, his painful and accursed death, his resurrection and ascension into heaven, his exaltation to the right-hand of GOD, and his glorious appearance to the universal judgment," and avers that if such articles are not of high importance, ". . .revelation was given to us in vain."[129] In a treatise on revival, Andrew Fuller would himself list several doctrines he judged essential.[130]

Further proposals include instructing hearers to discern how redemption is applied through the Holy Spirit as to facilitate discussion on "the nature of faith, repentance, and effectual calling."[131] Furthermore, covering these subjects, "may be useful to all sorts of hearers," by which Doddridge understands the unregenerate, who may be convinced of their lack of faith, and repentance, and thereby, be led to seek salvation. Conversely, genuine believers will be comforted by discovering they possess these qualities.[132]

---

125. Doddridge, *Free Thoughts*, 10.

126. Doddridge, *Free Thoughts*, 13.

127. Doddridge, *Free Thoughts*, 13.

128. Doddridge, *Free Thoughts*, 13. Early in his ministry Doddridge was viewed as having some Sabellian accents. See Harris, "Philip Doddridge and Charges of Arianism," 267–72. On Arianism, see Macleod, "God or god?" 121–38.

129. Doddridge, *Free Thoughts*, 13–14.

130. Citing the "generality of the Reformers" as a paradigm, Fuller lists goes as follows: a trinity of persons in the Godhead; the Deity and atonement of Christ; justification by faith; predestination; efficacious grace; the certain perseverance of the saints, & c." He concludes, noting, "These doctrines they preached, and looked upon as consistent with a free and unreserved address to unconverted sinners. How far the body of the reformed churches are gone off from them, I need not say" (*On Spiritual Declension and Means of Revival* in *WAF*, 3:630).

131. Doddridge, *Free Thoughts*, 14.

132. Doddridge, *Free Thoughts*, 14.

Doddridge taught that pastors have a twofold calling: to encourage the weak while simultaneously exhorting confessors to do good works. They should diligently study the scriptures and read them to their families.[133] Their character "must be free from the taint of vice, or of folly, in any remarkable degree." If a man be "a slave to secular interest, or to the little trifles of food, dress, or domestick accommodation," he is not fit for the ministry.[134] The preacher must be accessible to his congregants, approachable, not disposed to favor the rich over the poor.[135] Over half a century later, Andrew Fuller would stress several of these points in a circular letter.[136]

In addition to practical, even predictable counsel for revival, Doddridge critiques the central argument of Gough's treatise: that Dissenting congregations are an uncultured, unlearned, and theologically-rigid bunch. Doddridge asserts that for a pastor to neglect such a humble people "out of complaisance to the taste of a few," most of whom are but "occasional visitants" to Dissenting churches, and whom "we judge by their habits...to be a part of the polite world," is to break with the very pattern of Christ, who ministered primarily to the poor.[137] Dissenters, he writes, "appear to be persons of serious piety," who have a deep regard for the gospel and firsthand experience of such doctrines to, "awaken, and revive, and enlarge the soul."[138] Though not the simpletons of Gough's caricature, Dissenting congregants prefer a plain preaching style from a minister who handles "experimental subjects" with "seriousness and tenderness," and who speaks in a "lively and pathetick, as well as a clear and intelligible manner."[139] The result of such preaching is to increase the congregation's veneration for their minister.[140] To summarize, Dissenters, claims Doddridge, desire an evangelical, experimental, plain, and affectionate preacher.[141]

133. Doddridge, *Free Thoughts*, 16.

134. Doddridge, *Free Thoughts*, 23. This description of the leisure life of a country parson has been well-documented among historians, e.g., Abbey and Overton, *English Church in the Eighteenth Century*.

135. Doddridge, *Free Thoughts*, 16.

136. See *Causes of Declension in Religion* in *WAF*, 3:318–24. This work will be discussed in detail in ch. 4.

137. Doddridge, *Free Thoughts*, 17–18. In undated treatise, Fuller would attribute openness to hear Dissenting preachers on account of the "generality of (established) clergy" having "lost ground in the estimation of the common people" (*Decline of the Dissenting Interest* in *WAF*, 3:484).

138. Doddridge, *Free Thoughts*, 20.

139. Doddridge, *Free Thoughts*, 20.

140. Doddridge, *Free Thoughts*, 20.

141. Doddridge, *Free Thoughts*, 21. Doddridge concedes that though Dissenters certainly appreciate an eloquent and rhetorically-pleasing discourse, their reception of

In response to Gough's criticism of Dissenting academies, Doddridge reiterates the institutional purpose for education. Tutors are to train pastors for ministry, imbibing them with, ". . .a deep and early sense of the importance of the gospel-scheme, for the recovery of man from the ruins of the apostacy, and his restoration to God, and happiness by a mediator."[142] Moreover, as Christ's very mission and ministry exude humility and selfless service, it would befit a tutor to let such theological realities inform their content and method.[143] As Doddridge has labored to show, theological content and a pastor's humble disposition are equally critical for Dissent to flourish. While freedom of thought and rhetorical flourish typify the age, they must not supplant the simple gospel spoken in plain language. For the common Dissenter, the preacher's simple, passionate addresses,

> must have an apparent tendency to fill the mind with sublime and elevated views, and to make a man feel and own too (though it may appear something unpolite) that the salvation of one soul, is of infinitely greater importance, than charming a thousand splendid assemblies, with the most elegant discourses that were ever delivered.[144]

The overarching assessment drawn from *Free Enquiry* is first, that Dissent maintain core doctrines, of which Doddridge deems indispensable to the gospel, and second, that pastors remain pious, passionate, and plain-speaking preachers. Revival cannot be wrought through theological nor methodological compromise. Despite cultural pressure to denigrate orthodoxy and dismiss humble discourse, the allurement of intellectual

---

a sermon is not hindered by a poor oration. Cf. Augustine's comments in *On Christian Doctrine* that "those to be read or heard should be those truly recommended not only for their eloquence but also for the fact that they have written or spoken wisely. For he who speaks eloquently is heard with pleasure; he who speaks wisely is heard with profit" (122). Moreover, his observation that, "People may be taught and pleased and still not consent" (137).

142. Doddridge, *Free Thoughts*, 34.

143. Doddridge frames Christ's humility as the theological foundation and pedagogical model for the tutor who should, ". . .point out the Son of God descending from heaven in favour of this design, pursuing it by humble condescensions for the lowest of the people, and unwearied labours amongst them; and at last, establishing it by agonies and death:—To shew them the Apostles taking up their master's cause, prosecuting it with unwearied vigour and resolution, and sacrificing to it their ease, their reputation, their liberty, and their lives:—To trace out those generous emotions of soul, which still live and breathe in their immortal writings" (*Free Thoughts*, 34).

144. Doddridge, *Free Thoughts*, 35. Like Watts, Doddridge emphasized exciting the passions, calling them the "sails of the soul."

autonomy; "liberty for every man to form his own sentiments,"¹⁴⁵ Dissenting churches must resist the tide if they are to survive, much less flourish in their present context. English Congregational churches who did adopt Doddridge's—and additionally, Watts'—proposals by mid-century, did reap the spiritual fruit of their labors.¹⁴⁶

Evangelical Revivals and Particular Baptist Reception

A surprise from the historical origins of eighteenth-century evangelicalism is the fact that its prominent leaders, whose ministries became synonymous with revival, were priests in the Anglican Church.¹⁴⁷ For Dissenters such as Calvinistic Baptists who strove for decades to preserve the Reformed orthodoxy of their Puritan forbearers, the established church was hopelessly corrupt. Despite state-sponsored systematic persecution, sporadic mob violence, and political, educational, and social disadvantages spanning several generations, Dissenters had survived as distinct congregations.¹⁴⁸ As consequence, when Anglican ministers experienced conversion and began to preach Christ, there was an understandable degree of suspicion, even incredulity.

The lives and ministries of high Calvinists John Gill and John Brine, contemporaneous with Anglican Methodists Wesley, Whitefield, Daniel Rowland, and Howell Harris, form a striking juxtaposition. As noted, Gill, like Brine and others saw themselves as polemicists waging a crusader's war for the preservation of doctrinal purity. Their primary pastoral obligation was as ministers to their existing flock, not pursuers of outsiders. Unsurprisingly, high Calvinists disagreed with evangelical Anglicans that the gospel be offered indiscriminately to sinners. Though Whitefield, Harris

---

145. Gough, *Enquiry*, 7. Cf. 28.

146. Watts, *Dissenters*, 384. Doddridge's most popular and enduring devotional work, *The Rise and Progress of Religion in the Soul* (1745) was instrumental in the conversion of William Wilberforce (1759–1833), nineteenth-century abolitionist and social reformer. In a brief 1814 essay, *State of the Baptist Churches in Northamptonshire*, Andrew Fuller presents an overall optimistic picture of the Baptist churches in the region, noting that half the existing congregations were founded after 1764, and that only four were known high Calvinist (*WAF*, 3:481).

147. See ch. 1, n75.

148. As late as 1710, mobs attacked Dissenting meeting houses in London in what is known as the Sacheverell Riots. See Holmes, "Sacheverell Riots," 55–85. Persecution of Dissenters continued into the nineteenth century. For example, Caleb Evans Birt (1795–1854) studied law at Cambridge but could not graduate because he did not subscribe to the 39 Articles (*Baptist Autographs in John Ryland's University Library of Manchester*, 356).

and Rowland were fellow Calvinists, Gill and others took issue with their methods. In the case of Wesley, there was a greater antithesis, to the level of incommensurability.[149] John Gill not only engaged Wesley personally in the press but insisted till his death that the Church of England was apostate.[150] Andrew Fuller was himself no Wesley sympathizer and expressed doubts about Wesley's salvation for reasons similar to Gill's.[151]

While polemics characterized the Wesley-Gill relationship, a curious exception to an otherwise adversarial relationship is noteworthy. A nineteenth-century biography of Selina Hastings (1707–1791), countess of Huntingdon—an evangelical Calvinist herself—recounts a 1751 breakfast meeting and worship service attended by Wesley, Whitefield, Andrew Gifford, Methodist preachers William Cudworth (1717–1763) and John Cennick (1714–1795) in which Gill is said to have "addressed a short exhortation to his brethren in the ministry."[152] This display of ecumenical fellowship excepted, doctrinal disparity alone, without account of personality, formed a chasm between Gill and Wesley that simply could not be spanned. A closer affinity exists between Gill and Whitefield, primarily on the basis of theological content. Whitefield, for instance, consistently preached on reprobation, unconditional election, imputed righteousness, perseverance of the saints, all hallmarks of Gill's theology.[153] Nettles offers the most sym-

---

149. Wesley's arch-foe was the fellow Anglican and staunch Calvinist Augustus Tolpady (1740–1778). Whitefield's relationship to Wesley was comparatively irenic, though Wesley's famous predestination sermon formed an irreparable breach between the two.

150. Morden, *Life and Thought*, 28. In 1751, Wesley published *Serious Thoughts upon the Perseverance of the Saints*, in which he argued that true believers in Jesus can "fall from God and perish everlastingly." Gill responded publicly with *The Doctrine of the Saints Final Perseverance Asserted and Vindicated*, in which he countered each of Wesley's eight propositions in *Serious Thoughts*. Wesley's rejoinder, *Predestination Calmly Considered*, served to confront the tendency in Methodist circles toward election (Nettles, "John Gill and the Evangelical Awakening," 158).

151. In his divergence from several denominational colleagues on the subject of open communion, Fuller responded to William Ward's listing of Wesley among paedobaptist "worthies" to take the Lord's Supper, by remonstrating that even if "Mr W had been a Baptist I could not have joined him at the L[ord's] S[upper] . . .how a person who opposed the doctrine of salvation by grace as he did, and who held with sinless perfection in this life, could know either himself or the Savior I do not understand." Fuller to Ward, personal letter, July 16, 1809. On this episode see Potts, "I Throw Away the Guns," 115–17.

152. Seymour, *Life and Times of Selina Countess of Huntingdon*, 162. Cf. Orchard, "Selina, Countess of Huntingdon," 77–90.

153. See Nettles, "John Gill and the Evangelical Awakening," 163–70. On election Whitefield expresses his unapologetic support of the doctrine: "For my own part, I cannot see how true humbleness of mind can be attained without a knowledge of it; and

pathetic treatment of Gill in his relationship to the evangelical revivals, notably, Gill's assent to the gospel being preached to sinners. If John Gill made any contribution to Dissent's benefiting from revival, however oblique, it was his defense of Calvinistic orthodoxy. It is significant that churches within Dissent who succumbed to heretical trends eventually died out, thereby placing them beyond the pale of revival's influence.[154]

At his worst, John Gill's unqualified public criticism of Whitefield, the Wesleys, and other evangelicals kept Particular Baptists from experiencing benefits of the awakenings[155] For example, in his *Body of Divinity*, Gill stated that joy, "is not to be expressed by those who experience it; it is better experienced, than expressed."[156] Gill's relentless hostility to the Church of England created unnecessary divisions between Particular Baptists and Calvinistic Anglicans who shared theological ground. As Methodism expanded through the eighteenth century, and with it, increased denominational interaction, Particular Baptists and Methodists would excommunicate respective members who attended meetings or embraced disputed theological positions of their rivals.[157]

The no-offers-of-grace scheme bears primary responsibility for Particular Baptists' resistance to the evangelical revivals. A dogged desire to maintain the Reformed orthodoxy of the Puritans in the context of encroaching heterodoxy, made the high Calvinism of Ames and Owen, the

though I will not say, that every one who denies election is a bad man, yet I will say. . .it is a very bad sign." Cited in *Memoirs of the Rev. George Whitefield*, 366, 641.

154. This would be true of the General Baptists and Presbyterians (Copson, "General Baptists in the Eighteenth-century," 29–56). Exceptions within this trend would come from the leadership of Dan Taylor in forming the revival-birthed and orthodox New Connexion of General Baptists (Rinaldi, *Tribe of Dan*).

155. Morden is unsympathetic to Gill's theology, maintaining that it "greatly contributed to the malaise in [Particular Baptist] life" (*Offering Christ to the World*, 22).

156. Gill, *Complete Body of Doctrinal and Practical Divinity*, 781. Morden detects here an implicit criticism of the emotionalism that marked the evangelical revivals (*Life and Thought of Andrew Fuller*, 27). At other points, Gill is more ambiguous, "It is [believers'] duty to communicate in spiritual things, to mutual comfort and edification; to speak often one to another about divine things; to impart spiritual experiences, and to declare to each other what God has done for their souls," and earlier he stated, "as we are to love our God with all our heart, and with all our strength; we are to give thanks to him in like manner, in the most intense way we are capable of. . ." (*Complete Body*, 255, 161).

157. In 1741–1742, members at Wapping agreed that participation in "religious societies or bands" or in a Methodist "love feast" was to be regarded as 'disorderly' conduct, and in 1753, the Norwich congregation declared it "unlawful for any so to attend upon the meetings of the Methodists" (Brown, *English Baptists of the Eighteenth Century*, 78). Conversely, John Wesley would personally remove any preachers who embraced the doctrine of election (Watts, *Dissenters*, 428–34).

hyper Calvinism of Skepp, Gill, and Brine.¹⁵⁸ Failure to distinguish between the secret and revealed will of God, and a tendency to make logical deductions from biblical texts as if they were premises, minimized plain scriptural teaching, namely, that offers of grace should be given to all people. Assurance of salvation, sought by introspection and internal feelings would lead to antinomianism in some, or, in the case of Andrew Fuller, needless anguish and procrastination instead of bold response. Charles Spurgeon (1834–1892), writing a century after high Calvinism's peak, made the following comment with Gill in mind: "The system of theology with which many identify his name has chilled many Churches to their very soul, for it has led them to omit the free invitations of the Gospel."¹⁵⁹

Political and Sociological Considerations

In considering the evangelical revivals in Britain, Michael Watts poses the intriguing question of whether revival could have arisen from Dissenting denominations. While acknowledging the prevailing impulse of separation forged through years of restricted toleration, Watts perceives that several other factors precluded spiritual renewal at Dissent's hands. By withdrawing from the parish system, Dissenters gained the independence necessary to maintain stringent standards of doctrine and piety among their pastors and laypersons. At the same time, the responsibility to individuals outside their local congregations was lost. By contrast, Anglican Methodists Whitefield and Wesley would both confidently say, "The world is my parish."¹⁶⁰

---

158. Toon, *Emergence of Hyper-Calvinism*, 40–41. As noted the distinction, between "hyper" and high Calvinism given by Toon is not always clear. It seems that "hyper-Calvinism" as Toon understands it, is connected to theological emphases, not a theological system. As Carl Trueman notes, John Owen had more in common with John Gill *as a theologian*—particularly in regard to a soteriology that was covenantal in nature—than Andrew Fuller, though on a practical level, Owen, like Fuller, and unlike Gill, offered Christ to sinners in his preaching (Trueman, "John Owen and Andrew Fuller," 61–66).

159. Quoted in Whitley, *Calvinism and Evangelism in England*, 28. It should be noted that while high Calvinism adversely affected Baptist churches, it did preserve Christian orthodoxy and could therefore be "revived." The same could not be said of churches that embraced Socinianism and Deism.

160. For the discussion see Watts, *Dissenters*, 435–45. Quoted in *WJW* (BE), 19:67. Cf. George Whitefield in March 1739, "The whole world is now my parish," and again in a later sermon, "All the world is my parish" (Thomas, "George Whitefield and Friends," 91) and Whitefield, *Spiritual Baptism* in *Eighteen Sermons*, 310. See also, Hindmarsh, *Spirit of Early Evangelicalism*, 291n31. Watts notes that no eighteenth-century Dissenter would have made such a statement.

In addition to the inherent limitations due to Dissent's ecclesiology, Anglican Methodists had a substantially broader audience. Remaining in the established church, these men could preach at any parish if the minister permitted. Though John Wesley would be censured by the Church of England for ordaining Thomas Coke in 1784, he consistently defended remaining in it, arguing that leaving "would hinder multitudes of those who neither love nor fear God from hearing us at all."[161] A further advantage to conformity was freedom from the social stigma associated with Dissent. An Anglican preaching to large crowds was less likely to incite violence.[162] Thus, attributing Dissent's lack of participation in the revivals to high Calvinism alone does not account for contextual complexities. The ministry of Congregationalist Vavasor Powell (1617–1670) suggests otherwise. During the interregnum Powell engaged in vigorous evangelistic tours, yet the extent and longevity of impact paled that of fellow Welshman Howell Harris. Though sharing Calvinistic theology, Harris's impact far exceeded Powell's on account of the parish system alone.[163]

Conclusion

This chapter has focused on the causes of declension among English Dissenting congregations during the early to mid-eighteenth century. Attention has been given to the Particular Baptist denomination as the ecclesial context of Andrew Fuller's upbringing, where high Calvinism, preached and applied, led to a neglect of evangelism and hindrance to growth. Among Particular Baptists, there were several exceptions associated with the Bristol Baptist Academy, who offered Christ and called for hearers to respond, notably, Andrew Gifford and Benjamin Francis. The majority, however, followed the

---

161. Jones, *Congregationalism in England 1662–1962*, 151. In 1753, upon hearing that several Methodists had embraced Congregationalism, Wesley made the following comment: "Did God design that this light should be hidden under a bushel? In a little obscure, Dissenting meeting-house" (*WJW*, 13:93).

162. Baptists, for instance could not legally do mass evangelism outside their meetinghouses. See Langford, *Polite and Commerical People*, 257. Watts notes that although violent mobs periodically attacked the Methodists, Dissenting preachers in a similar situation would have incurred the wrath of hostile crowds at an exponentially worse level (*Dissenters*, 437).

163. As a Congregationalist, Powell served in a denomination whose members comprised a mere 3 percent of Wales' total population (Watts, *Dissenters*, 437–38). Interestingly, Powell preached in nearly every Welsh parish before being imprisoned on account of his Fifth Monarchist connections (Milton, "Pastoral Predicament of Vavasor Powell," 520). On Powell's life and ministry, see Nicholson, *Vavasor Powell 1617–1670*; Nuttall, *Welsh Saints: 1640–1660*.

theological trajectory set by John Gill and John Brine. It is no small irony that in their zeal for combatting Enlightenment rationalism, overtly rationalistic elements characterized their theological method. Preoccupation with the immanent acts of God, a systematization of God's decrees entailed high Calvinism's carrying the seeds of its own destruction.

As "evangelicals before the revivals," Isaac Watts and Philip Doddridge functioned as transitional figures who bridged the gap between orthodox Dissent and nascent evangelicalism. Both men accurately assessed the decline of its churches, proposing solutions through preaching, networking, and publication. Zeal and passion, central components of a powerful pulpit ministry cut against the grain of contemporary trends. Watts and Doddridge were likewise aware of rationalism's pull towards theological liberalism and affirmed that certain core doctrines not be compromised if the gospel were to remain.[164] With focus on preaching the gospel indiscriminately, they prefigured Andrew Fuller's own theology and ministry. Incidentally, despite its Anglican origins, Dissent would experience the greatest benefits from the evangelical revivals in the long-term.[165]

When revival began its sweep through England in the 1730s, Particular Baptists—with some noted exceptions—remained resistant to it. This would change, but not until the last quarter of the eighteenth century, when Andrew Fuller's ministry was in its early stages. Several non-theological factors precluded revival beginning, much less flourishing within Dissent. It was Isaac Watts himself who echoed Dissent's ecclesiological self-understanding in *Hymn no. 74*.

> We are a garden wall'd around chosen and made peculiar ground; a little spot enclosed by grace, Out of the world's wide wilderness.[166]

---

164. As noted, this is not to say Watts and Doddridge were unaffected by their intellectual context. Watts wrestled deeply over the doctrine of the Trinity. A posthumous excerpt reveals his anguish, "How shall a poor weak creature be able to adjust and reconcile these clashing ideas to understand this mystery?...I want to have this wonderful doctrine of the all-sufficiency of thy Son and thy Spirit for these divine works made a little plainer...Surely I ought to know the God whom I worship, whether he be one pure and simple being or whether thou are a threefold deity...Help me, heavenly Father, for a I am quite tired and weary of these human explainings, so various and uncertain..." (Watts, *Works*, 9:506–10). See also, Aniol, "Was Isaac Watts Unitarian," 101.

165. Watts, *Dissenters*, 440, Rack, *Reasonable Enthusiast*, 167. Bebbington, *Evangelicalism in Modern Britain*, 32.

166. Fountain, *Iaac Watts Remembered*, 16. Also: *Hymns and Spiritual Songs*, bk. 1 hymn 74 in *The Works of the Reverend and Learned Isaac Watts* (1810), 4:274.

Like Benjamin Keach, who also drew from Song 4:12, the case of Isaac Watts proves that soteriology was not the sole contributor to high Calvinism's resistance to revival. Andrew Fuller's Biblicism, coupled with the philosophical contributions of Jonathan Edwards would break high Calvinism's siege, and reorient Particular Baptists toward an evangelical Calvinism with a revival trajectory.[167]

---

167. Cf. Oliver Crisp's observation that official ecclesiastical documents such as creeds, confessions, and catechisms are "metaphysically underdetermined" for a variety of reasons including minimizing, "theological and metaphysical hostages to fortune" (*Deviant Calvinism*, 81–83). High Calvinism's tendency to go beyond the Second London Confession's soteriological teaching affirms Crisp's thesis, showing that some aspects of the Enlightenment held Gill, Brine and other high Calvinists, "hostage."

Chapter Three

Andrew Fuller and Revival

THIS CHAPTER SEEKS TO articulate Andrew Fuller's understanding of revival by examining major influences in his life—personal and literary—and additionally, events which uniquely shaped his theology. This includes fellow Baptists John Ryland Jr. (1753-1825), John Sutcliff (1752-1814), and Robert Hall (1764-1831). The works of Jonathan Edwards, notably *Freedom of the Will* and *An Humble Attempt at Extraordinary Prayer* would be instrumental in Andrew Fuller's composition, *The Gospel Worthy of All Acceptation*, formation of the Northamptonshire Baptist Association, and the Prayer Call of 1784. Edwards's distinction between natural ability and moral inability will undergird Andrew Fuller's entire theological project, the nature of revival included. Furthermore, the centrality of the Bible and the practice of Puritans in offering Christ to sinners supported a categorical rejection of high Calvinism. Lastly, the enduring impact of Fuller's revival-oriented ministry will be examined, notably in the formation of the Baptist Missionary Society.

Biographical Background

Andrew Fuller's life has been discussed in detail by several older works and in recent literature.[1] Fuller was born on February 6, 1754 at Wicken, a village near Ely in Fenland Cambridgeshire, the youngest son of Robert Fuller (d. 1781) and Philippa Gunton (d. 1816).[2] Robert and Philippa were both Dissenters, though the latter was more religiously committed

---

1. For these sources see introduction, n14.
2. Morden, *Life and Thought of Andrew Fuller*, 11.

than the former.³ In 1761 the Fuller's moved to Soham, where the whole family attended worship at the Baptist church there.⁴ Andrew Fuller's two older brothers, Robert (1747–1829) and John (b. 1748), themselves committed Christians, would serve as deacons in respective Particular Baptist churches.⁵ Of Fuller's early life, there is a dearth of extant material, and the meager, fragmentary evidence led to the statement by one of Fuller's earliest biographers, John Webster Morris, that "Mr. Andrew Fuller arose out of obscurity."⁶

Fuller's inauspicious, plebeian upbringing belied the profound impact he would have as pastor, theologian, and missionary advocate. Fuller's conversion, which occurred in 1769, is in several respects, a parable on the folly of eighteenth-century high Calvinism. John Eve, pastor of Soham Baptist church had, in Fuller's own words, "little to say to the unconverted."⁷ High Calvinists had rejected the "Modern Question," the soteriological inquiry as to whether non-elect sinners had obligation to exercise faith and repentance.⁸ Only those who possessed the "warrant of faith"—a subjective apprehension that one is elect—should come to Christ. The warrant was typically understood as a singular text of scripture forcibly impressing itself on a hearer.⁹ Fuller believed he had such an experience after Rom 6:14 was

---

3. Soham Baptist Church Book, 1752–1868, 1. Interestingly, Philippa's mother, who bore the same name as her daughter, was one of the six founding members of the Baptist church in Soham. See Ryland, *Fuller*, 8–10.

4. Ryland, *Fuller*, 9. Fuller's parents both came from non-conformist backgrounds, a detail which John Ryland Jr., his earliest official biographer, and close friend, makes much of. Ryland mentions Honour Hart, a "pious woman" who was an Independent that later became convinced of believer's baptism and joined the church at Isleham. Philipp's parents, Friend Stevenson and Mary Malden, are cited as exemplary Dissenters, and additionally, Mary's parents, John and Joan Malden, who, upon the restoration of Charles II to the throne in 1661, became "objects of ridicule and persecution, because of their nonconformity," 10. In evaluating the form and content of Ryland's biography Peter Morden notes the author's intention to present "a lineage of determined, principled Nonconformity before his readers," with heavy emphasis on personal faith and holiness alongside other elements of the Dissenting tradition. Moreover, he notes that the church book at Soham has no record of Honour Hart. See Morden, *Life and Thought*, 12–13.

5. Ryland, *Fuller*, 9.

6. Morris, *Memoirs*, 17.

7. Ryland, *Fuller*, Letter I, 11.

8. See Nuttall, "Northamptonshire and the Modern Question," 101–23.

9. Ryland, *Fuller*, Letter I, 14. It should be noted that scriptural "impressions" were not unique to high Calvinists. Many Methodists attributed their conversions to verses being brought forcibly to their minds, though Methodism in its Arminian expression denied the necessity of a warrant. For several of these accounts see Jackson, *Lives of the Early Methodist Preachers*, 2:4, 27, 60.

brought to his own mind.¹⁰ Despite this, and other "impressions," he felt that "the bias of heart" remained unchanged.¹¹

Perhaps unsurprisingly, Fuller wrestled in his early teens over conviction from books he read, not John Eve's sermons.¹² For two years Fuller vacillated over whether he was "in a state of salvation," and though the weight of sin and guilt led Fuller to bouts of weeping, any spiritual resolve was transient. By 1769 this had changed. Fuller had a deep sense of God's judgment, aptly summarized in a letter to John Ryland Jr.,

> The fire and brimstone of the bottomless pit seemed to burn within my bosom. I do not write in the language of exaggeration…I saw, that there was no truth in me. I saw, that God would be perfectly just in sending me to hell, and that to hell I must go, unless I were saved of mere grace, and as it were in spite of myself…I never before knew what it was to feel myself an odious, lost sinner, standing in need of both pardon and purification. Yet although I needed these blessings, it seemed presumption in hope for them, after what I had done.¹³

Fuller was overwhelmed, as he did not believe he possessed the requisite warrant to trust in God.¹⁴ The solution to this existential dilemma did come, even if from unlikely quarters. Fuller found from two passages in the Old Testament, the courage to place his faith in Christ: Job 13:15, and Esth 4:11.¹⁵ Fuller's son Andrew Gunton narrates his father's conversion experience:

> He…came to this resolve, 'I must, I will—yes, I will—trust my soul, my sinful, lost soul, in his hands: If I perish, I perish.' As

10. "Sin shall not have dominion over you, for ye are not under the law, but under grace." (AV)

11. Ryland, *Fuller*, 14. See Morden, "Andrew Fuller: A Biographical Sketch," 6.

12. Ryland, *Fuller*, Letter I, 11. Prior to his mid-teens, he confessed to have "seldom thought of religion." Gunton Fuller, *Memoir*, in *WAF*, 1:4. These works include two staples of Nonconformity piety, *Grace Abounding to the Chief of Sinners* (1666) and *The Pilgrim's Progress* (1678) by John Bunyan. Fuller mentions a lesser-known work by the Scottish evangelical Ralph Erskine (1685–1752), *Gospel Sonnets: or, Spiritual Songs, in Six Parts*, which upon reading, he "was almost overcome with weeping," for "so interesting did the doctrine of eternal salvation seem." Ryland, *Fuller*, Letter I, 11. See Morden, "John Bunyan: A Seventeenth-Century Evangelical?," 33–52.

13. Ryland, *Fuller*, Letter II, 17.

14. Ryland, *Fuller*, Letter II, 18. Consequently, he spoke of seeking salvation as "presumption."

15. Job 13:15 reads, "Though he slay me, yet I will trust in him." In Esth 5:1–2, the Queen boldly enters King Ahasuerus's presence without being summoned, thereby risking her life yet succeeding in saving her own people.

he looked away from self, and fixed his eyes upon a crucified Saviour, his guilt and fears began to dissolve. . .and he found how true were the words of Christ, 'Come unto me all ye that labor and are heavy laden, and I will give thee rest.'[16]

Fuller's conversion brought immediate relief and a deep sense of joy, it remained a pivotal moment for his life and ministry, and precipitated a commitment, in his own words, "to devote [his] future life to God."[17] Fuller's conversion was seminal in that its very nature served to fundamentally reject high Calvinism. John Eve baptized Fuller in 1770. His journey from convert to pastor came after only five years, and in 1775 the church became embroiled in an antinomian controversy that would deepen Fuller's dissatisfaction with high Calvinism, particularly its tendency to erode human responsibility.[18]

Formative Influences

As noted, the evangelical Calvinism associated with Andrew Fuller, revival-oriented and missionary-conscious, originated from several sources, most of which were interconnected.[19] Fuller's friendships in the Northampton-

---

16. Gunton Fuller, *Memoir*, 28. The last line is from Matt 11:29.

17. Morden, *Life and Thought*, 31. See Ryland, *Fuller*, Letter II, 20. For Morden's analysis of Fuller's conversion narrative see *Life and Thought*, 31–33. Keith Grant's reading of Fuller's conversion narrative in *Fuller and the Evangelical Renewal of Pastoral Theology*, 23–50, is the most detailed analysis to date in its immediate and wider context. For the conversion narrative as a literary genre see Hindmarsh, *Evangelical Conversion Narrative*.

18. Ryland, *Fuller*, Letter III, 23–24. A certain James Levit, who had been guilty of excessive drinking, and defended his actions on grounds that he had no power in himself to refrain from sin. John Eve condemned Levit's drunkenness, yet upon exclusion from membership, a seemingly innocuous comment by Eve that individuals did possess power to obey God "as to outward acts," incited controversy. Some in the church challenged their pastor on this point, asserting that believers possessed no power in themselves to refrain from evil, except what God provides, citing Jer 10:23 (AV), "The way of a man is not in himself: it is not in him that walketh to direct his steps." Fuller initially sided with Eve but was exonerated by Eve's opponents on account of being young in the faith. John Eve would resign in 1771, but the disputed subject—human responsibility—remained salient in Fuller's mind. This event discloses the detrimental effects of high Calvinism on Particular Baptist churches like Soham. See Morden, *Life and Thought*, 35. Commenting on the Modern Question, Fuller opined that, "I perceived that some kind of power was necessary to render us accountable beings." See Ryland, *Fuller*, 40.

19. See Clipsham, "Andrew Fuller and Fullerism," 99–114, 146–54, 214–25, 268–76. Morden, "Andrew Fuller and the Birth of Fullerism," 140–52. Fuller expressed disapproval of a label—penned as early at 1804—that suggested theological innovation.

shire Association led to his reading Jonathan Edwards. Edwards's revival writings, notably *Humble Attempt to Extraordinary Prayer*, initiated a call to prayer in 1784 for "revival of religion," which in turn, led to the formation of the Baptist Missionary society. This selection of figures, their writings, and historical events are crucial to understanding the substance and development of Andrew Fuller's theology of revival.

Northamptonshire Baptist Association

Andrew Fuller was ordained in the spring of 1775; Robert Hall Sr. (1728–1791) preached the service, after which he commended "Edwards on the Will" to settle Fuller's conflict over the Modern Question.[20] Additionally, a compelling scriptural basis for imploring sinners to repent and have faith in Christ came through Abraham Taylor's *The Modern Question Concerning Faith and Repentance*.[21] Fuller proposed that Soham join the Northamptonshire Association of Particular Baptist Churches, to which the congregation unanimously agreed in 1775. The association, formed in 1764, was, in the words of John Briggs, "the archetype of the new associations, born out the Evangelical Revival."[22] Membership served to invigorate an otherwise difficult pastorate that was exacerbated by personal tragedies.[23] Hall, John

Peter Morden cites two pamphlets. One by an opponent: Hupton, *Blow Struck at the Root of Fullerism*, and a sympathizer: Stonehouse, *Fullerism Defended*. See Morden, "Andrew Fuller and the Birth of Fullerism," 140. In a recent work, Mauldin argues that "Fullerism" is a better nomenclature for Baptists than Calvinism on the basis of missiological differences between Fuller and John Calvin (*Fullerism as Opposed to Calvinism*).

20. Ryland, *Fuller*, 38. As has been noted, Fuller mistakenly read *Veritas Redux* by the Cambridge minister John Edwards (1637–1716). Fuller appreciated this solidly-Calvinistic work yet was puzzled as it said nothing regarding "the power of man to do the will of God." It was not until 1777 that Fuller realized he read the wrong book, after which he acquired the correct work: *A Careful and Strict Inquiry into the Modern Prevailing Notions of That Freedom of Will, Which is Supposed to be Essential to Moral Agency, Virtue and Vice, Reward and Punishment, Praise and Blame*.

21. Ryland, *Fuller*, 60. Priest, "Andrew Fuller, Hyper-Calvinism, and the 'Modern Question,'" 47; Sell, *Great Debate*, 54–55. Taylor's work was published in 1742.

22. Briggs, *English Baptists of the Nineteenth Century*, 203. See Elwyn, *Northamptonshire Baptist Association*.

23. Soham Baptist gave Fuller a paltry stipend of 13 pounds a year, making supplementary sources of income necessary. This led to Fuller's failed attempt to run a school which closed in 1780. See Morris, *Memoirs*, 34. Cf. Morden, *Life and Thought*, 42. Fuller, *Memoir* in *WAF*, 1:1, 18–19; Ryland, *Fuller*, 44. Fuller's marriage to Sarah Gardiner—which happened in 1776—though strong in the early years, was marked by the loss of three of the first four children born to the couple (88). Morris, *Memoirs*, 34. See Haste, "Marriage and Family in the Life of Andrew Fuller," 28–34.

Sutcliff (1752–1814), and John Ryland Jr. (1753–1825) formed a deep and lasting friendship with Fuller that expanded his theological horizons.[24]

As the years progressed, Fuller's unease with high Calvinism increased. Though already rejecting its salient theological points, he resolved to proceed with "slow and trembling steps," as he knew a break with the system would affect the "whole tenor" of his preaching.[25] In 1779, after Fuller introduced direct appeals to the unconverted, the reception was characterized by consternation and "bitterness of Spirit."[26] Personal attacks were especially painful, though these seem to have come from a small, albeit, antagonistic and vocal minority.[27]

Though Fuller's emphases in preaching shifted in 1779, it is difficult to demonstrate how, since evidence from this period is minimal, as Fuller's sermons were brief and composed in shorthand.[28] Diary entries from the Soham period reveal a gradual shift, with periodic struggles to overcome a deeply engrained theological framework.[29] Coincidentally, 1779 was the same year the Baptist church at Kettering, a congregation already committed to evangelical Calvinism, invited Fuller to be their pastor. He initially declined on grounds of his commitment to Soham.[30] Over the next three years, Kettering made further proposals. Meanwhile, Fuller's variegated struggles continued at Soham. Among these, cases of immorality with several members, opposition to Fuller's preaching style, and financial strain.[31] On October 2, 1782, nearly three years after the initial proposal, Fuller decided to leave Soham and take the Kettering pastorate.[32] Participation in the

---

24. Morden, *Life and Thought*, 57. See Haykin, *One Heart and One Soul*.

25. Ryland, *Fuller*, Letter IV, 32.

26. Fuller, *Memoir*, 45.

27 Ryland, *Fuller*, 44.

28. Ryland, *Fuller*, 45. Morden analyzes possible shifts through nuanced vocabulary (*Life and Thought*, 43–44).

29. This includes Fuller's deathbed conversation about the spiritual condition of his father, Robert, in which Fuller expresses regret at being insufficiently emphatic about his father's faith, and even posing a question suggestive of a "warrant." See Ryland, *Fuller*, 87–88.

30. Fuller, *Memoir*, 45. See Kirkby, "Andrew Fuller," 197.

31. Robert Robinson of Cambridge counseled Soham to raise Fuller's salary to 26 per annum, though it is unclear if the church ever did. Fuller himself insisted that financial considerations were never his reason for departure. See Narration of. . .the Baptist Church at Soham, 48–49.

32. There is evidence of regret from the Soham church. The Soham Association Letter for 1783 reads, "Surely Mr Fuller's leaving Soham was attended with many tears, some reflecting on themselves as having bin instruments of Wo!" See Letters of the Soham Church, Letter 8, June 10, 1783.

Northamptonshire Association provided the sources sufficient not only to repudiate high Calvinism, but to articulate a theologically-sound evangelical alternative. Foremost among these works came from the pen of the New England theologian Jonathan Edwards.

Influence of Jonathan Edwards

As noted, Fuller's introduction to Edwards at the behest of Robert Hall came at a critical juncture in his theological development.[33] Edwards's writings would have a profound impact on the young English pastor and his close friends.[34] Roger Hayden traces the earliest Baptist teaching on Edwards's distinction between natural and moral inability to Caleb Evans, principal of the Bristol Baptist Academy, who adopted Edwards's dichotomous proposal in 1772.[35] Fuller adopted various aspects of Edwards's theology, though it is the proposals in *Freedom of the Will* that most fully permeate Fuller's thought.[36] Thus, Fuller writes in *Gospel Worthy*,

> It is abundantly, improved for this purpose by President Edwards, in his Inquiry into the Freedom of the Will. A book which has been justly said to go further toward settling the main points

---

33. Works on Edwards are extensive. For an annotated bibliography see Lesser, *Jonathan Edwards*. Early biographies include Hopkins, *Life and Character of Jonathan Edwards*; Dwight, *Life of President Edwards*. Standard contemporary biographies include Miller, *Jonathan Edwards*; Marsden, *Jonathan Edwards*; Murray, *Jonathan Edwards*. Cherry, *Theology of Jonathan Edwards*. Works by contemporary theologians include: Holmes, *God of Grace and God of Glory*; Jenson, *America's Theologian*; Lee, *Philosophical Theology of Jonathan Edwards*; McDermott, *Jonathan Edwards Confronts the Gods*. For an applied theological contribution, Piper, *God's Passion for His Glory*.

34. See Hindmarsh, "Reception of Edwards by Early Evangelicals in England," 201–21; Haykin, "Great Admirers of the Transatlantic Divinity," 197–207.

35. Hayden, "Evangelical Calvinism," 217. John Ryland would read *Freedom of the Will* in 1775 and in 1780 publish the New England divine's sermon "The Excellency of Christ." John Ryland, *Pastoral Memorials*, 1:15, cited in Bebbington, "Remembered Around the World," 183. On Caleb Evan's life, "Evans, Caleb (1737–1791)," in *Oxford Dictionary of National Biography*: http://ww.oxforddnb/view/article/40192.

36. Of authors listed in Fuller's library from 1798, 11 titles belong to Edwards. Second to the New England divine was his son, Jonathan Edwards Jr. with seven. See *The Complete Works of Andrew Fuller Volume 1*, 215. Chun, in *Legacy*, critically and comprehensively examines the relationship between these men at several levels. Chun explicitly identifies natural and moral inability, metaphysics of causality, volitional freedom, and "Use of Means" as concepts drawn from *Freedom of the Will*. See Chun, *Legacy*, 2:32–65. For further discussion on *Freedom of the Will* see Guelzo, *Edwards on the Will*. For a recent appraisal see Fisk, *Jonathan Edwards's Turn from the Classic-Reformed Tradition*.

in controversy between the Calvinists and Arminians, than any thing that has been wrote.[37]

Edwards's argument was that "the freedom human beings possess, when properly understood, is not inconsistent with our actions being predictable or indeed necessitated—not incompatible fundamentally with predestination."[38] The will, claims Edwards, "is simply that by which the mind chooses anything" and these choices are always determined by the strongest motive "in view of the mind."[39] Edwards explains the basic conception:

> For in every act of will whatsoever, the mind chooses one thing rather than another; it chooses something rather than the contrary, or rather the want or nonexistence of that thing.[40]

This definition is distinct from the historically dominant philosophical understanding of the will as *liberum arbitrium*—"absolute power to the contrary," and diverged from John Locke's own view that, "the will is perfectly distinguished from desire."[41] Such cannot be the case, claims Edwards, as "a man never, in any instance, wills anything contrary to his desires, or desires anything contrary to his will."[42] Though a comprehensive and seminal work, *Freedom of the Will*, as its full title suggests, was a polemical document against an encroaching Arminian theology.[43] Edwards fundamentally

---

37. *The Gospel Worthy of All Acceptation*, at Eighteenth Century Collections Online: http://www.galenet.galegroup.com, 192.

38. Holmes, *God of Grace and God of Glory*, 153. Bebbington notes that Fuller's reliance on Edwards's thought was "sufficient to ensure" that the evangelical movement was "built on Enlightenment Foundations" (*Evangelicalism in Modern Britain*, 3).

39. Edwards, *Freedom of the Will*, in *WJE*, 1:137.

40. Edwards, *Freedom of the Will*, in *WJE*, 1:137. See Chun, *Legacy*, 17.

41. Edwards, *Freedom of the Will* in *WJE*, 139. See Chun, *Legacy*, 17. Locke writes, "the greatest and most pressing should determine the will to the next action; and so it does for the most part, but not always. For the mind having in most cases, as is evident in experience, a power to *suspend* the execution and satisfaction of any of its desires, and so all, one after another, is at liberty to consider the objects of them; examine them on all sides, and weigh them with others. . .In this lies the liberty man has; and for the not using it right comes all that variety of mistakes, error, and faults which we run into, in the conduct of our lives, and our endeavors after happiness; whist we precipitate that determination of our *wills*, and engage too soon before due *examination*. To this we have a power to suspend the prosecution of this of that desire, as everyone daily may experiment in himself" (*Essay Concerning Human Understanding*, 105–6).

42. Edwards, *Freedom of the Will*, in *WJE*, 1:139.

43. Chun notes that one of Edwards's antagonists who advocated the "prevailing notions" was the Arminian, Daniel Whitby, a minister of the Church of England who wrote against Calvinism in *Discourse on the Five Points* (1710) (*Legacy*, 15n22). The

disagreed with the notion that the will moves itself. The will, according to Edwards, is determined by the strongest motive at any given moment.⁴⁴ Andrew Fuller heartily embraced Edwards view, referencing it throughout his works. In *The Free Agency of Man* for instance, he writes, "No one can conceive of a power of voluntarily acting against the prevailing inclination, for the thing itself is a contradiction."⁴⁵ Fuller would apply the natural ability, moral inability model to a diversity of theological, and practical dilemmas.⁴⁶ Though it is *The Gospel Worthy of All Acceptation* that Edwards's thought in *Freedom of the Will* is most conspicuous, other works by Edwards made additional contributions to Fuller's understanding of revival.⁴⁷

The Prayer Call of 1784

The convergence of Jonathan Edwards's thought and the community of Northamptonshire Baptist pastors bore spiritual fruit after John Ryland Jr. received *An Humble Attempt for Extraordinary Prayer* from the Scottish

---

others were the deist Thomas Chubb and fellow Congregationalist Isaac Watts. Cf. Ramsey, "Editor's Introduction," in *WJE*, 1:65–118.

44. Chun, *Legacy*, 18.

45. Fuller, *Free Agency of Man*, in *WAF*, 2:657.

46. For example, in *Calvinistic and Socinian Systems Examined*, Fuller contrasts the natural ability of an unbeliever to perform good deeds with the moral inability to act virtuously apart from supernatural grace (*WAF*, 2:174). David Bebbington notes an increasingly negative reception of *Freedom of the Will* by theologians in the nineteenth-century and additionally, intellectuals such as the romantic poet Samuel Coleridge. See "Remembered Around the World," 177–95. Stephen Holmes weighs Edwards's dichotomous proposal in *Freedom of the Will* and concludes that philosophical developments, particularly that of twentieth-century philosophies of language by Ludwig Wittgenstein and Alasdair McIntyre have shown that a multiplicity of language games operate in human discourse. Thus, Edwards's assumption regarding "ordinary language," in Holmes's words, "relies on the assumption that this language game will produce meaningful and non-contradictory results when subjected to rigorous philosophical analysis" (*God of Grace and God of Glory*, 154). For alternative proposals that employ resources contained in *Freedom of the Will* (Holmes, *God of Grace and God of Glory*, 154–59). See Guelzo, *Edwards on the Will*, "Critics and Criticism," 54–86.

47. These include *Humble Attempt to Extraordinary Prayer* and Edwards's apocalyptic writings. Both will be discussed in ch. 5. Additionally, *Religious Affections* was read and highly regarded by Fuller and others in the Northamptonshire Association. In a diary entry from 1781, Fuller wrote, "I think I am by the ministry, as I was by my life as a Christian before I read *Religious Affections*. I had never entered into the spirit of a great many important things. O for some such penetrating, edifying writer on this subject! Or rather, O that the Holy Spirit would open my eyes and let me into the thing things that I have never seen" (Fuller, *WAF*, 1:25). See "Fuller's Theological Indebtedness to *Religious Affections*," in Chun, *Legacy*, 110–41.

Presbyterian pastor John Erskine (1721–1803) in April 1784.[48] While in his twenties, Erskine had entered correspondence with Edwards as part of a letter-writing network of Scottish, English, and American pastors committed to the cause of evangelical revival.[49] Erskine corresponded with Sutcliff and Ryland until Erskine's death in 1803, regularly sending books and tracts he thought worth promoting. After reading *Humble Attempt*, Ryland enthusiastically shared its insights with Fuller and Sutcliff, who upon reading the book themselves, embraced its vision with zeal equal to Ryland's. This was the occasion for the pastors' resolution to "seek revival or real religion, and extension of Christ's kingdom in the world."[50]

At the behest of John Ryland Jr., the Northamptonshire Baptist Association in Nottingham initiated designated times for congregational prayer, one hour every second Tuesday of the month. The uniqueness of these meetings was their outward, missional focus, though not their existence within the Baptist tradition.[51] The 1784 Call to Prayer became a denominational catalyst for meetings of a similar nature by Baptist churches in Northamptonshire and beyond, which in turn invigorated evangelism and prompted church planting.[52] It was, however, overseas missions, particularly in the ministry of William Carey (1761–1834), that solidified the Prayer Call's legacy. Fuller's indefatigable role as secretary of the BMS until his death in 1815 expresses his concrete personal commitment to revival, even to an international level.

---

48. For recent appraisals of John Erskine, see Yeager, *Enlightened Evangelicalism*. For an early biography, see Wellwood, *Life and Writings of John Erskine*.

49. Haykin, *One Heart and One Soul*, 158.

50. Ryland, *Fuller*, 96.

51. Revival was a concern among several pockets of Baptists in colonial Pennsylvania. In 1734, The Philadelphia Association advised their churches to "set a day apart, once a month, to implore the Lord of the harvest to thrust forth faithful labourers into his harvest; by fasting and prayer, continue in a faithful depending, waiting and heartily crying to God, until he be pleased to grant you desirable blessing." The chronological parallels to the Northampton awakening is noteworthy (Gillette, *Minutes of the Philadelphia Baptist Association*, 35).

52. For more details on the call, see Payne, *Prayer Call of 1784*, and Haykin, *One Heart and Soul*, 153–71. For a summary of *Humble Attempt* and its connection to the 1784 Call to Prayer, see Chun, *Legacy*, 66–71. Fuller specifically mentions that "seven or eight new churches have been raised amongst [us] within the last 20 years" (Morden, *Life and Thought*, 111).

The Gospel Worthy of All Acceptation: Fuller's Break with High Calvinism

As has been noted, several theological distinctives constituted eighteenth-century high Calvinism—what Andrew Fuller coined, "false Calvinism," or "Crispism."[53] Joseph Hussey's *God's Operations of Grace: But no offers of His Grace* argued that to offer Christ indiscriminately would imply that natural man had the ability to respond in faith, and that failure to consider the imputation of Christ's righteousness to the elect alone would undermine the Holy Spirit's work.[54] Practically, this meant that the gospel should be preached, but Christ not offered to the non-elect, since doing so would ". . .rob the Spirit of his power, degrade the gospel, and flatter men that they have some ability to receive it."[55] Gill and Brine concurred with Hussey on this point, though dissenters such as Abraham Taylor stressed duty faith.[56]

Aware of theological nuances in the debate, Andrew Fuller had deep personal interest in the outcome. His own creative, enduring theological contribution to the subject is *The Gospel Worthy of All Acceptation*, which Fuller published after ten years of pastoral ministry, denominational interaction, and theological and biblical study.[57] Fuller begins by challenging the prevailing the definition of faith proposed by high Calvinists. He cites Lewis Wayman's *Further Inquiry* as representative of the view that if "there be any act of special faith," it must necessarily have "the nature of appropriation in it."[58] Fuller understands "appropriation" to mean "a persuasion of our

---

53. Fuller, *Calvinism*, in *WAF*, 2:713. Fuller called his own position "Strict Calvinism." See "Confession of Faith" in Fuller, *Last Remains*, 209–17.

54. Hussey writes, "The Spirit will not, and cannot honourably work without the imputation of Christ. . .without a due regard of the imputation of his righteousness, or the work of the Spirit, therefore are not fit means to work this ability" (Priest, "Andrew Fuller's Response to the 'Modern Question,'" 46); Sell, *Great Debate*, 53–54.

55. Sell, *Great Debate*, 54.

56. Priest, "Andrew Fuller's Response to the 'Modern Question,'" 47. Nuttall, "Northamptonshire and the Modern Question," 101–23. For further discussion see ch. 2.

57. Fuller began work on *Gospel Worthy* as early as 1781. Morden lists several factors that contributed to Fuller's theological shift from high, to evangelical Calvinism: Biblicism, Puritan writers, John Calvin (possible influence), Associational life, Jonathan Edwards, notably, *Freedom of the Will*, and the Transatlantic evangelical network (*Life and Thought*, 50–67).

58. Fuller, *Gospel Worthy* in *WAF*, 2:333. The full title of Wayman's work is *A Further Enquiry After Truth, wherein, is shown what faith is required of unregenerate persons*.

interest in spiritual blessings," and it is precisely this notion that he resolves to overturn.[59]

Though high Calvinists distinguished faith from assurance, and acknowledged that reliance on Christ is sufficient for salvation, consistently, "speak as if they did not believe what at those times they say."[60] Exhortations by high Calvinists to "be strong in the faith" meant that professing believers should, "without doubting, believe in the goodness of their state."[61] Such a scheme is impotent, even dangerous for unconverted sinners, who under its terms, possess no duty to believe. As "they are not interested in Christ," and since "it cannot possibly be their duty to believe a lie," unbelief is not a sin.[62] The subjectivity in high Calvinist discussions on faith was detrimental to deluded confessors and outright unbelievers, both of whom overlooked the imperatives in Scripture to repent and believe. Fuller counters by noting the implications of an outward-oriented understanding of faith:

> . . .if it can be proved that the proper object of saving faith is not our being interested in Christ, but the glorious gospel of the ever-blessed God (which is true, whether we believe it or not), a contrary inference must be drawn; for it is admitted, on all hands, that it is the duty of every man to believe what God reveals.[63]

Fuller devotes the remainder of *Gospel Worthy* to biblical, historical, and philosophical arguments to defend the thesis that faith is a duty, obligatory to all who hear the gospel, and that resistance stems from human unbelief, not God's decrees. The course Fuller embarked upon in *Gospel Worthy* can be attributed first, to extensive and thorough examination of biblical passages. Though Fuller does not claim a presupposition-free reading of the Bible, upon critical examination, he found the tenets of high Calvinism and its prevailing understanding of faith deeply problematic.[64]

---

59. Fuller, *Gospel Worthy*, in *WAF*, 2:333.

60. Fuller, *Gospel Worthy*, in *WAF*, 2:333.

61. Fuller, *Gospel Worthy*, in *WAF*, 2:333.

62. Fuller, *Gospel Worthy*, in *WAF*, 2:333.

63. Fuller, *Gospel Worthy*, in *WAF*, 2:333. For a further exposition on faith and its relation to duty see a letter written to Mr. M'Lean of Edinburgh (1797) in Ryland, *Fuller*, 257–67.

64. The most audacious attempt at such a project came from the American Restorationist Alexander Campbell (1788–1866), who co-founded the Disciples of Christ and advocated a "confessional principle" that made the New Testament the sole authority for believers, even rendering the canonical Old Testament to a secondary position. All creeds and confession were rejected as illegitimate. See Thirteen Propositions in Garrison and De Groot, *Disciples of Christ*, 145–61. Cf. Pelikan, *Credo*, 261.

In the Scripture, Fuller finds gospel "offers" abundantly interspersed, particularly in the New Testament. "Calls, warnings, invitations, expostulations, threatenings and exhortations, even to the unregenerate" are common.[65] Several examples are worthy of attention. Fuller observes that in Gospel accounts where individuals are healed, the subjects approach Jesus by an appeal to his power and/or authority. The centurion, seeking healing for his servant, tells Jesus, "speak the word only, and my servant will be healed." A leper, in his plea for healing reasons, "Lord if you are willing, you can make me clean." Fuller concedes that the promise of healing is not offered in the same univocal sense as salvation, yet Christ, "has graciously bound himself not to cast out any who come to him for mercy."[66] Thus, *a fortiori*, "there is a greater ground for faith in the willingness of Christ to save than there was in his willingness to heal."[67] Consequently, there is less unbelief in the leper's plea, "if you will" than the same proposal from a sinner seeking salvation—salvation that is promised.[68] The high Calvinist claim of a requisite "persuasion" that an individual is a child of God, and "interested in the blessings of the gospel," is speculative, subjective, and without precedent in Scripture.[69]

Common in high Calvinist teaching was the notion that a grant, or gift, was necessary to believing in Christ, and that a warrant was evidence of that gift. This Fuller denies. On the contrary, "The gospel is a feast, freely provided, and sinners of mankind are freely invited to partake of it. There is no mention of any gift or grant, distinct from this, but this itself is a ground sufficient."[70] The gospel of Jesus Christ is the warrant. Fuller cites two texts: 1 John 1:9 and Rom 4:24 to demonstrate that salvation is given to whoever receives it without preconditions.[71] Fuller lists a string of consecutive

---

65. Fuller, *Gospel Worthy* in WAF, 2:373. Fuller's usage of "commands, promises, and threatening" echoes John Owen verbatim where he writes, "Neither, indeed, is the intention and purpose of God, concerning which we now inquire, proposed as the object of the faith of any; but only his commands, promises, and threatening" (*Death of Death* in WJO, 10:293).

66. Fuller, *Gospel Worthy*, in WAF, 2:335.

67. Fuller, *Gospel Worthy*, in WAF, 2:335.

68. In *On Spiritual Declension*, Fuller discusses varying degrees of certitude a believer should have in prayer on the basis on biblical revelation. Applying this principle to prophetic texts that Fuller interprets as having future fulfillment in the millennial reign of Christ should instill confidence that God will answer the church's prayer for revival (see WAF, 3:621–22).

69. Fuller, *Gospel Worthy*, in WAF, 2:335.

70. Fuller, *Gospel Worthy*, in WAF, 338.

71. Fuller, *Gospel Worthy*, in WAF, 338. Authorized Version: "If we confess our sins, he is faithful and just to forgive us our sins"; "To us it shall be imputed, if we believe on

New Testament passages to support his claim that saving faith is "belief of the truth which God hath revealed in the Scriptures concerning Christ."[72] Among the most persuasive listed is John 12:36, "While ye have light, believe in the light, that ye may be the children of light," to which Fuller comments, "The *light* they then had was that of the gospel; and had they believed it, they would have been children of *light*, or true Christians."[73]

As Peter Morden argues in his recent biography on Fuller, biblicism was a major factor in Fuller's criticism, and repudiation of high Calvinism.[74] Naturally, scriptural exegesis comprises major portions of *Gospel Worthy*. In separate writings, including those which pertain to revival, engagement with biblical texts is a dominant feature. For Fuller, this entails accepting the tension inherent in disparate Bible passages rather than rigid adherence to a theological system. Moreover, passages understood as having future fulfillment will provide an impetus for believers to seek revival. Biblicism alone, however, did not constitute Fuller's strongest arguments for duty faith in *Gospel Worthy*. The conceptual apparatus for rendering unconditional election and free choice compatible in an Enlightenment philosophical context, and adopted by Fuller, came through Jonathan Edwards's *Freedom of the Will*.

Returning to the content of Gospel Worthy, under a lengthy subheading, "The Want of Faith in Christ is Ascribed in the Scriptures to Men's Depravity, and is itself represented as a heinous sin," Fuller reasons that, "If faith were no more a duty than election or redemption, which are acts peculiar to God, the want of the one would be no more ascribed to the evil dispositions of the heart than that of the other."[75] Scripture speaks of faith, however, as that which the human agent has both the ability and responsibility to perform, something a pre-modern Puritan such as John Owen was well aware.[76] Fuller concedes that if the natural ability of any man to

---

him that raised up Jesus our Lord from the dead." Responding to what scripture reveals is a key tenet throughout *Gospel Worthy*.

72. Fuller, *Gospel Worthy*, in *WAF*, 2:338.

73. Fuller, *Gospel Worthy*, in *WAF*, 2:338.

74. The well-known, and widely-accepted term comes from David Bebbington's *Evangelicalism in Modern Britain*. Bebbington does not give a precise definition of "bliblicism" though he notes that "evangelicals revered the Bible," and were "certain they understood the Bible clearly," and most importantly "agreed that the Bible is the inspired word of God" (13). He cites several historical examples. For full discussion see, 12–14.

75. Fuller, *The Gospel Worthy*, in *WAF*, 2:355.

76. In *Death of Death* Owen defends the notion that all people remain culpable for failure to exercise faith despite particularity of redemption, the Holy Spirit's prompting, and God's sovereign mercy. Owen denies that ". . .any internal assistance is required to

believe was illustrated by example of say, a dead man being commanded to rise, then, "it were absurd to suppose that they would on this account fall under Divine censure," for, "no man is reproved for not doing that which is naturally impossible."[77] Yet sundry biblical texts condemn unbelief without qualification, ascribing such to, "criminal ignorance, pride, dishonesty of heart, and aversion from God."[78]

Further in the same section, Fuller explicitly states that the moral and natural inability dichotomy is necessary for harmonizing duty faith with passages such as Matthew 11:28 where, Jesus says, "Come to me all who labor and are heavy laden."[79] For, writes Fuller, "if there be no other inability than what arises from aversion, this language is not accurate; for it conveys the idea that if all aversion of heart were removed, there would still be a natural and insurmountable bar in the way."[80] Fuller, citing a favorite text from John's Gospel, "Why do ye not understand my speech? *Because ye cannot hear my word*" suggests that unbelief is dispositional in nature.[81] He argues further that if no distinction is drawn between natural and moral inability, and sinners are unable to believe univocally, what logically follows is that "they would be equally unable to disbelieve; for it requires the same powers to reject as to embrace."[82] Under such conditions, a hard determinism absent in the biblical witness is unavoidable.

render a man inexcusable for not believing, if he have the object of faith propounded to him, though of himself he have neither power nor will so to do, having lost both in Adam" (*Death of Death*, in *WJO*, 10:272).

77. Fuller, *Gospel Worthy*, in *WAF*, 2:355.
78. Fuller, *Gospel Worthy*, in *WAF*, 2:355.
79. Fuller, *Gospel Worthy*, in *WAF*, 2:356-57.
80. Fuller, *Gospel Worthy*, in *WAF*, 2:357.
81. Fuller, *Gospel Worthy*, in *WAF*, 2:357. John 8:43 (AV) D. A. Carson's comments on the sovereignty-responsibility tension inherent in the structure of this passage are provocative: "The Jews remain responsible for their own 'cannot', which, far from resulting from divine fiat, is determined by their own desire (*thelousin*) to perform the lusts (*tasephithymias*) of the devil (8:44). This 'cannot', this slavery to sin (8:34) itself stems from personal sin. Sin enslaves." See *Divine Sovereignty and Human Responsibility*, 166. Anthony Thiselton's consideration of "dispositional accounts of belief" leads to the insightful claim that "...*a belief becomes articulated precisely when someone denies it, distorts it, or attacks it in the hearing of Christian believers*" (*Hermeneutics of Doctrine*, 37). For full discussion see 19-42.
82. Fuller, *Gospel Worthy*, in *WAF*, 2:357. In further defense of a moral inability distinct from what is arguably, natural, Fuller draws again from John Owen's work, *On Indwelling Sin*, in which Owen writes that [sin], "disenableth men unto, and hinders them from believing, and that alone. Blindness of mind, stubbornness of the will, sensuality of the affections, all concur to keep poor perishing souls at a distance from Christ. Men are made blind by sin, and cannot see his excellency; obstinate, and will not lay hold of his righteousness; senseless, and take no notice of their eternal concernments" (*On

Use of Means

To continue discussion on Andrew Fuller's indebtedness to Jonathan Edwards, a soteriological insight he judged applicable for preaching is found in part 4 of *Freedom of the Will*.[83] If, as Edwards argued, inability to believe stems from "voluntary ignorance of, and total aversion to, the nature of God and spiritual things," then, reasoned Fuller, "letters, syllables, words, and propositions" can be employed in service to change a disposition. In fact, it would be "a great absurdity to refuse to use them."[84] Chris Chun explains the connection.

> As Edwards articulated the concept of necessary connection, not eliminating the means, but in those connections reside the variables that make the means *effective* in the causal chain of events.[85]

In addition to Edwards, Fuller discovered in Scripture and church history that preaching the gospel is the means God uses to save the elect.[86] John the Baptist proclaimed, "Repent, for the kingdom of heaven is at hand." Jesus pleaded with his hearers, "strive to enter the narrow gate." His Reformed forbearers, by whom God wrought powerful ministries, "all went forth in use of these weapons."[87] Always apt to return to the biblical text, Fuller finds disputes over "metaphysical subtleties" at the expense of preaching the gospel to the unregenerate, as the source of high Calvinism, and consequent declension among Particular Baptist churches.[88] Though he never disavowed traditional tenets of Calvinistic soteriology and insisted that Total Depravity requires the Holy Spirit to grant a holy disposition to a sinner, Fuller believed that the revealed means to a salvific end was preaching and

---

Indwelling Sin, ch. 16, in *WJO*, 6:308).

83. Edwards, *Freedom of the Will*, in *WJE*, 1:337–439. Fuller draws particularly from section 4, "It is agreeable to common sense, and the natural notions of mankind, to suppose moral necessity to be consistent with praise and blame, reward and punishment." Cf. 357–64.

84. Fuller, *Gospel Worthy*, 21.

85. Chun, *Legacy*, 62.

86. Robert Jenson notes that "means" had a very exact sense for Puritans as "natural events ordained by God as the necessary but insufficient conditions of supernatural grace; such as are, on Calvinist interpretation, baptism, preaching, and the Lord's Supper" (*America's Theologian*, 48). Cf. Edwards, *Miscellanies* in *WJE*, 18:532.

87. Fuller, *Gospel Worthy*, 178.

88. Fuller, *Gospel Worthy*, 182. Considering Fuller's reliance on *Freedom of the Will*, there is some irony in this statement.

offering Christ.[89] While Fuller cited respected Puritans such as Owen and Bunyan, his position drew criticism from Reformed pastors and theologians who believed he had gone too far, and evangelical Arminians such as Dan Taylor who believed he had not gone far enough.[90] Fuller's application of means will be the subject of several sermons and circular letters in which he proposed specific communal activities performed for the purpose of revival. Moreover, that William Carey's mission manifesto bore the title: *An Enquiry Into the Obligations of Christians to Use Means for the Conversion of the Heathens* bears the imprint of Edwards and Fuller.[91]

Andrew Fuller's Definition of Revival

In Fuller's entire corpus, three compositions cite the term "revival," in the respective title, a fourth, arguably addresses the subject on basis of content.[92] Furthermore, several letters and diary entries mention revival with brief, but insightful commentary.[93] Though Fuller considers revival a critical component of spiritual vitality in the local church, and cites causes of declension with corresponding remedial measures, he does not give an explicit definition of revival. While technical terminology assists a reader intent on discerning a systematic pattern of a topic, deductions and inferences can be made from the relevant extant data. In the case of Fuller and revival, repeated terms, general argumentation, and biblical exegesis give

---

89. Chris Chun's comments are helpful. He notes that Fuller "never advocated that unregenerate sinners *use their self-determining will* as the basis for the exercise of the will but rather, encouraged using means to persuade sinners to *use their will*." The reason for this is such persons have no natural limitations to exercise the will necessary for coming to Christ (*Legacy*, 63).

90. Noteworthy among them was William Button, pastor at Dean Street, Southwark who composed *Remarks on a Treatise entitled The Gospel Worthy of All Acceptation* in 1785, and John Martin, whose publication was titled, *Thoughts on the Duty of Man Relative to Faith In Jesus Christ*. Taylor, leader of the New Connection of General Baptists argued that "'the universal calls and invitations' of the gospel could only be based on the 'universality of Divine love, and the death of Jesus Christ, as the propitiation for the sins of the whole world,'" in *Observations of the Rev Andrew Fuller's late pamphlet*, title page.

91. Seven years prior, Carey would have heard a message at the Northamptonshire Association meeting in which Fuller exhorted ministers "to preach the gospel to every creature, private Christians, situated in this or that dark town or village, to *use all means* to have it preached" (Haykin, *Armies of the Lamb*, 104, 108).

92. *Causes of Declension in Religion, and Means of Revival* in *WAF*, 3:318–24; *On Spiritual Declension and the Means of Revival*," in *WAF*, 3:615–34; *A General Union of Prayer for the Revival of Religion* in *WAF*, 3:666–70; *The Promise of the Spirit and the Grand Encouragement in Promoting the Gospel* in *WAF*, 3:359–66.

93. Ryland, *Fuller*, 86, 96, 97, 98, 103, 104, 107, 122.

a reasonably clear picture of what the author means by revival. It could be argued that Fuller simply assumed his readers understood his intention and therefore, found it unnecessary to define revival proper.[94]

Several historical considerations provide further insight, notably that spiritual awakenings had been ongoing in Britain and America since the early 1730s, and that the Prayer Call of 1784 came after the zenith of the evangelicalism's first generation.[95] Consequently, fifty years-worth' of preaching, organization, and observation provided time for reflection and analysis.[96] Several Baptist pastors had even been converted earlier in the century through Whitefield and Wesley.[97] As noted, the writings of Edwards and others found their way into the hands of Particular Baptist pastors in Britain. Furthermore, the frequency and fluidity with which Fuller discusses revival suggests a thematic pervasiveness that warranted minimal concrete delineation.[98]

In compositions with exclusive revival emphases, Fuller provides sufficient data for a clear picture of what he understands revival to be. Structurally, these compositions are individual pieces embedded in a larger corpus, and therefore, must be analyzed and interpreted within the scope of Fuller's overarching theology. For example, in Fuller's circular letter *The Promise of the Spirit*, there will be interaction with other writings on pneumatological and eschatological themes. Writings such as *Expository Discourses on the Apocalypse* will be crucial for understanding how revival and a future millennial reign of Christ coincide.[99] Exegetical pieces on various Old Testa-

---

94. Richard Hays's "seven tests," in *Echoes of Scripture in the Letters of Paul*, 29–33, are useful when applied to the termrevival, particularly (2.) volume (3.) recurrence, and (4.) thematic coherence. This framework allows comparison to revival in writings by other historical figures, the meaning of revival within Fuller's own corpus, and the frequency with which he cites it.

95. Edwards had died in 1758; George Whitfield in 1770; Howell Harris followed in 1773, John and Charles Wesley in 1788 and 1791, respectively.

96. As early as 1736, Jonathan Edwards had published *Narrative of Surprising Conversions*; in 1741, *The Distinguishing Marks of the Spirit of God*, followed by *Some Thoughts concerning the Revivals* in 1742. *Religious Affections* was released in 1746. Additionally, Wesley and Whitefield's journals, widely distributed and read in Britain and North America, made first-person accounts of revival popular reading

97. This would include Robert Robinson (1735–90), and the General Baptist Dan Taylor (1738–1816).

98. Michael Crawford notes that during the early 1740s *revival of religion* was used in two ways: as a singular phenomenon, and second, to local awakenings. By 1743 "religion" was dropped altogether. Not until the nineteenth-century that the term revival was used to refer to special services to promote piety (*Seasons of Grace*, 180, 183).

99. See *Discourses on the Apocalypse*, in *WAF*, 3:201–307. Fuller's commentary on Revelation exceeds 100 pages in the 1845 Belcher edition. Like John Howe, prophetic

ment passages will offer additional illumination, in addition to the mature synthesis of Fuller's thought: *The Gospel Worthy of All Acceptation*. Authors whom Fuller cites, whose language and terminology he borrows, and whose theology he explicitly approved, provide additional insight.

With these considerations in mind, sound, working conclusions can be made on Fuller and revival. First, revival is a sovereign work of God. Consistent with historic consensus among Calvinists, the divine will actively directs human affairs to a determinant end. Revival cannot be created, manufactured, or duplicated by mere human agency, a conviction Fuller will repeat throughout his works.[100] Second, commands from scripture function as a warrant. The duty incumbent on human agents to respond in faith at particular existential situations finds coherence via Jonathan Edwards's natural ability-morality inability dichotomy.[101] Third, others within the Reformed tradition preached that to have faith in Christ is obligatory on all humans without exception, for, as Fuller oft repeats, "it is the duty of every man to believe what God reveals."[102] Though the relationship of means to revival when properly understood is not strictly that of cause and effect, as with the Sacraments, believers meet God where he has promised to meet them.[103] In his *Promise of the Spirit* letter, for example, Fuller urges

---

and apocalyptic writings in the Bible will be interpreted by Fuller as having future fulfillment, thereby grounding assurance that spiritual awakenings are imminent in the church and around the world. As with the concepts of duty and means, revelation provides the justification for acting with expectation of success. Various Old and New Testament texts, understood typologically in the context of a post-millennial eschatology will be source of optimism for the advancement of God's kingdom.

100. In *Spiritual Declension* Fuller writes, "That in the use of all means we consider them but as means, place no dependence on them, but entirely on the Spirit of God as the first cause. We can of our own accord find the way out of God's path, but if to ourselves, we shall never find our way in again" (*WAF*, 3:626).

101. Fuller's insistence that appropriated means for accomplishing a biblically-revealed end is fully consistent (i.e., compatible) with pre-ordained divine decrees. Proclamation of the gospel through the preacher's persuasive pleas, even the missionary's winsome tracts, is not to transgress theological boundaries but to humbly obey disclosed instruction. "God's ordinances are the means by which he ordinarily works...[a]t the same time, I think, we should be careful lest we cherish in them an opinion, that when they have done this, they are under no further obligations" (*Reply to Mr. Button's Twelfth Letter* in *WAF*, 2:452).

102. Fuller, *Gospel Worthy*, in *WAF*, 2:333. Fuller argues that neither Augustine, Calvin, the Puritans, nor Nonconformists ever believed or taught that predestination obviated duty faith (see *WAF*, 2:367). Peter Morden cites John Bunyan's later work, *Come and Welcome to Jesus Christ* which reads, "Coming to Christ is by virtue of the gift, promise, and drawing of the Father...Thou art coming, therefore, Christ hath given thee, promised thee, and is drawing thee to Jesus Christ" ("John Bunyan,"86).

103. "Though there is nothing in our doings from which we could look for such

believers to labor faithfully, using the ordained means—preaching and evangelizing—though he concedes that a spiritual harvest may possibly come generations later. Nonetheless, on basis of biblical revelation, certain activities performed by the church will precede spiritual outpourings. If revival comes, means will be present.[104]

To conclude, the above considerations constitute the basis for the thesis that Andrew Fuller's theology of revival was constructed, and methodologically applied, within a framework of compatibility between divine sovereignty and human responsibility. To give an inferential definition from Fuller's thought, revival is a free and gracious act wherein God spiritually enlivens the church instrumentally through revealed means to achieve a predetermined end.

Andrew Fuller's Perspective on Revival in his Historical Context

In *Causes of Declension in Religion, and Means of Revival*, a circular letter composed in 1785, Fuller makes several prefatory comments on the state of Northamptonshire Association congregations.[105] Based on the content of letters from several local churches, their respective spiritual status is mixed. Two congregations "continue destitute of the means of grace," others remain engaged with, "things of an uncomfortable nature," and most "complain of the want of a spirit of fervor and constancy in the ways of God."[106] Fuller thus addresses the most pressing and pervasive need—spiritual renewal.

---

great things," yet, "God is frequently to crown our poor services with infinite reward" (*Causes of Declension* in *WAF*, 3:323). Cf. John Calvin on the Lord's Supper writes, "The rule which the pious ought always to observe is, whenever they see the symbols instituted by the Lord, to think and feel surely persuaded that the truth of the thing signified is also present. For why does the Lord put the symbol of his body into your hands, but just to assure you that you truly partake of him? If this is true let us feel as much assured that the visible sign is given us in seal of an invisible gift as that body itself is given to us" (*Institutes*, Book IV, ch. xvii), 564.

104. An illuminating diary entry from 1791 reads, "Towards the latter end of the summer I heard of some revival of religion taking place in certain individuals about Walgrave and Guilsborough and that the means of it were setting apart days for fasting and prayer. From hence, I thought, we had been long praying for revival of God's cause, the spread of the gospel amongst the heathens &c and perhaps God would begin with us at home" (*Complete Works of Andrew Fuller Volume I: The Diary of Andrew Fuller*, 181).

105. See Fuller, *Causes of Declension*, in *WAF*, 3:318–24. This letter was composed the same year *Gospel Worthy* was published.

106. Fuller, *Causes of Declension*, in *WAF*, 3:318.

His letter has a twofold purpose: first, to identify "causes of declension in religion," and second, propose "means" for revival.[107] Though the task is great, and implementation urgent, signs of hope are evident as,

> Many of our congregations are well attended; a spirit of desire after the word is, we think, upon the increase; nor are our labors, we hope, altogether in vain, as the work of the Lord, in a way of conversion, appears to be going on, though in instances very remarkable.[108]

Fuller finds satisfaction that the monthly prayer meetings, implemented in 1784, have taken root among some congregations. He notes the "manner" in which they have been carried out, claiming that, "God has been evidently present in those meetings," specifically in, "stirring up the hearts of his people to wrestle hard with him for the revival of his blessed cause."[109] Interestingly, Fuller notes that though the prayer meetings had not experienced numerical increase, yet, "a spirit of prayer in some measure being poured out more than balances in our account for this effect."[110] A subsequent comment by Fuller illuminates his theological understanding of revival, particularly its relation to prayer. He says,

> We cannot but hope, wherever we see a spirit of some earnest prayer generally and perseveringly prevail, that God has some good in reserve, which in his own time, he will graciously bestow.[111]

This observation is critical in its disclosure of Fuller's compatibilist understanding of divine and human action. An increased fervency in prayer provides no certainty that revival will commence, nor is God obligated to comply with human wishes. A "spirit of earnest prayer," however, reveals a supernaturally bestowed desire, and suggests revival is imminent. In consistent form, Fuller does not allow his readers to remain passive on account of God's present working. "While we rejoice to see such a spirit of united prayer," he says, "we must not stop here." Rather, "If we would hope for the blessing of God upon us, there must be added to this a spirit of earnest inquiry into the causes of our declensions, and a hearty desire and endeavor for their removal."[112] Human responsibility is not obviated by divine sov-

---

107. Fuller, *Causes of Declension*, in *WAF*, 3:318.
108. Fuller, *Causes of Declension*, in *WAF*, 3:318.
109. Fuller, *Causes of Declension*, in *WAF*, 3:318.
110. Fuller, *Causes of Declension*, in *WAF*, 3:318.
111. Fuller, *Causes of Declension*, in *WAF*, 3:318.
112. Fuller, *Causes of Declension*, in *WAF*, 3:318.

ereignty. The remainder of the letter probes into corporate and individual negligence in spiritual matters, of which believers are accountable.[113]

Diary Entries and Written Correspondence

In addition to sermons and theological treatises pertaining to revival, diary entries and written correspondence disclose Andrew Fuller's disposition, including his psychological state, in transparent form. An inquisitive reader may wonder how writings on revival correspond with Fuller's experience in corporate prayer and personal devotion. Does he believe the prayer meetings are proving effective? Is there confidence that God will grant the request for an "outpouring of the Spirit?" Moreover, Fuller's subjective apprehension toward the prayer meetings and the relationship to their efficacy has important theological implications.

A few preliminary remarks on the nature of diary entries from Fuller's are warranted. Originating with the early Puritans, the employment of diaries and journals served as means of introspection and spiritual examination. Emphasis on sin and spiritual languor are predominant themes, giving the modern reader a strikingly bleak impression of their lives. As Bruce Hindmarsh and others have noted, this was intentional.[114] Diaries were published for purpose of their readers' spiritual edification. To rightly understand these compositions is to interpret them as a unique genre, that, ". . .served chiefly as a means of disciplined self-examination and a way of focusing religious affections."[115] Notwithstanding, Fuller's diary is our sole access to his mind. Thus, the entries should be taken at face value, though not in isolation from the above considerations.[116]

The earliest diary entry compiled by John Ryland Jr. in *Work of Faith and Labour of Love* that mentions revival dates from March 11, 1781 and reads, "I had an effecting day, especially in singing and prayer. The revival of nature, at this season in the year, seemed to kindle an earnest desire for the

---

113. The content of this letter, namely, Fuller's proposed "means" will be discussed in ch. 4.

114. Hindmarsh, *Evangelical Conversion Narrative; John Newton*, 222. Cf. 221–42; "The Antecedents of Evangelical Conversion Narrative: Spiritual Autobiography and the Christian Tradition," 4–13; See William Haller on the Puritan diary in *Rise of Puritanism*, 38.

115. Hindmarsh continues, "Its picture is therefore not only a man at his prayer, but also, more often than not, of a man in confessional" (*John Newton*, 22).

116. Hindmarsh's conclusion that John Newton's diaries, while being the primary source for understanding his spirituality, do not necessarily give a rounded picture of his spiritual life, could be true of Fuller as well.

revival of religion."[117] Written when Fuller was 27 years old and nearing the conclusion of his Soham pastorate, the entry reveals a nascent passion for spiritual renewal. This diary entry, though it provides no setting or further contextual clues, is unique in its predating the Prayer Call of 1784 by three years.[118] The Northamptonshire Baptist Association's decision to institute prayer and fasting on May 11, 1784 was recorded in Fuller's diary as including those "who have agreed thus to spend the second Tuesday in every other month, to seek the revival of real religion, and the extension of Christ's kingdom in the world."[119] Interestingly, Fuller's subsequent comments from the entry record that he felt "very unhappy" for reason that his heart "should be no more in it."[120] That, "very little of the true spirit of prayer" followed the momentous occasion of corporate prayer may explain Fuller's gloomy outlook.[121]

Ryland records an entry only five days later, dated May 16, 1784, in which Fuller spent a morning, "tender in prayer, for the revival of religion and carrying on of a good work among our young people."[122] On July 9 we read, "Some serious tenderness of spirit, and concern for the carnality of my heart for some days past. Read to our friends, this evening, a part of Mr. Edwards's *Attempt to Promote Prayer for Revival of Religion*, to excite them to the like practice. Felt my heart profited, and much solemnized by what I read."[123] Two months hence, on July 13, Fuller records prayer and fasting in accordance with the Northamptonshire pastors' commitment, but unlike a previous experience (May 11?), he "found some tenderness and earnestness in prayer, several times a day."[124] Ryland's final entry, dated from December 6, 1784, reads, "An affecting meeting of prayer, this evening, for the revival

117. Ryland, *Fuller*, 86.

118. At this juncture, Fuller had no published writings, though the original manuscript of *Gospel Worthy* was completed in 1781, yet without intention to publish. His involvement with the Northamptonshire Association had exceed six full years with all its attendant theological and practical contributions. As noted, Fuller had altered his preaching style to address unconverted hearers in early 1779. Furthermore, he had read Jonathan Edwards's *Freedom of the Will*. With these considerations in mind, it is perhaps unsurprising to find Fuller heartened by the prospect of spiritual renewal.

119. Ryland, *Fuller*, 96.

120. Ryland, *Fuller*, 96.

121. Ryland, *Fuller*, 96. There is strong evidence that Fuller suffered from clinical depression throughout his life. This is discussed in some detail in Ryland, *Fuller*, 271–77.

122. Ryland, *Fuller*, 96.

123. Ryland, *Fuller*, 97.

124. Ryland, *Fuller*, 98. The entry includes: "Wrote a few thoughts on the desirableness of the coming of Christ's kingdom."

of real religion: found much pleasure in singing, and freedom with God in prayer: prayed against my late skeptical feelings."[125]

After a run of revival-themed entries from 1784, Ryland records a longer account from May 2, 1785 in which Fuller reflects on another monthly prayer meeting in which he, "felt tender all the time of the prayer-meeting for the revival of religion" but upon hearing deacon Beeby Wallis pray for him, "was overcome" on account of Wallis', "having a better opinion of me than I deserve."[126] Evidently, this encounter moved Fuller to private prayer during which, he found his mind "engaged more than usual" in praying for revival.[127] However, Fuller's subsequent comments are noteworthy as they disclose transparency about his doubts: "I had felt many skeptical thoughts; as though there were room to ask—What profit shall I have if I pray to God?—for which I was much grieved."[128] Of course, Fuller was troubled by this incredulous disposition, yet, his recourse is to acknowledge that subjectively, there is "great satisfaction in these monthly prayer meetings" and objectively, "even supposing our request should not be granted, yet prayer to God is its own reward."[129]

From these seemingly commonplace entries, several observations may give further insight into Fuller's theology of revival. First, Fuller continues steadfast in prayer for revival despite internal languish on a subjective level. This is clear from candid evaluations of his prayer life that, though judged by Fuller as often anemic, did not preclude ongoing persistence. Consequently, the efficacy of prayer is not constrained by a supplicant's mere apprehension. Fuller does not stop praying for revival merely because he felt his prayers were ineffectual. Second, Fuller longs for the affections to coincide with the act of prayer. Herein lies a paradox. Prayer derives its efficacy from God's gracious action alone; the degree of one's zeal and passion is secondary. Nonetheless, prayer, as an act of communion ought to encapsulate the full extent of human faculties in its wake.[130] Andrew Fuller

---

125. Ryland, *Fuller*, 103.

126. Ryland, *Fuller*, 107. For discussion on textual variance between Ryland's entry and the original diary manuscript, see *Complete Works of Andrew Fuller Volume 1*, 126n192.

127. Ryland, *Fuller*, 107.

128. Ryland, *Fuller*, 107.

129. Ryland, *Fuller*, 107.

130. Like Isaac Watts, Fuller longed for passion and duty to be united. cf. John Owen's definition of communion as, "[God's] communication of himself unto us, with our return unto him of that which he requires and accepts, flowing from that union, which in Jesus Christ we have with him" (*Communion with the Triune God*, 94). Fuller defines prayer as "Ascending of the heart to God," in *On Spiritual Declension* in *WAF*, 3:620.

was not content to remain in a cold or disinterested state, but longs that feelings would accompany his faith. Fuller acknowledges finding "great satisfaction" in the monthly prayer meetings and is troubled by his own skepticism. Lastly, the most earnest prayerful pursuits remain subservient to a God who is entirely free in his sovereignty. Fuller concedes that the Northamptonshire Association's requests may simply not be answered. Yet, this is not attributed to human inadequacy or divine impotence. Whatever is perceived internally, or transpires externally—nothing is in vain, if God is prayer's "own reward."

Revival at Shepshed

Considering the Northamptonshire Associations impassioned pursuit of revival, any firsthand experience by Fuller and his friends deserves attention. John Ryland Jr., in correspondence with John Sutcliff, shared of a revival that occurred in the village of Shepshed, Leicestershire under the ministry of a certain William Guy (1739-1783).[131] Ryland verifies its genuineness, noting that though Guy is "the plainest rough-hewn preacher you ever saw or heard," yet, ". . .3 sabbaths back 24 gave in their experience there, the Church meeting lasted from 4 in the afternoon to 12 at night." After Sutcliff visited Shepshed himself, he acknowledged, "God is with him [i.e. Guy] I am persuaded."[132] Guy pastored Shepshed Baptist Church from 1774 till his death in 1783, and revival began shortly after he took the pastorate. Speaking at the Shepshed Baptist church after their pastor's death, John Ryland commented that the pastor had an "alarming ministry," used powerfully by God for the conversion of sinners.[133] The Shepshed revival was unusually powerful in scope, spreading to various villages in Leicestershire. In an 1807 correspondence with a Welsh Baptist pastor John Williams (1767-1825), who immigrated to America, Ryland wrote,

> We seldom seem to fish with a net, as you have often done in America. It is very uncommon I mean for an awakening to run through a town or village. The most similar case to those I have read of, in your country, was the awakening in Sheepshead in

---

131. This account is drawn from Haykin, *One Heart and One Soul*, 83–84. Shepshed was spelled "Sheepshead" in the eighteenth century.

132. Ryland, Letter to Sutcliff, August 26, 1777 (American Baptist Historical Society Archives). Cited in *One Heart and One Soul*, 83.

133. Ryland, *Seasonable Hints*, 57.

Leicestershire near 30 years ago, when my friend Guy was first settled there."[134]

This account is illuminating for several reasons. First, it reveals to extent to which the Shepshed revival personally impacted Ryland, and Sutcliff. Second, William Guy, an otherwise obscure, inexperienced Baptist pastor was the instrument of a powerful work of God. Last, Ryland concedes that the Shepshed revival was the nearest equivalent English Particular Baptists had to the Great Awakening in America. For the Northamptonshire Baptist Association, Andrew Fuller included, revival would not manifest in the likeness of Connecticut River Valley Awakening or Whitefield's American tour of the 1740s.[135] Yet pursuit of revival would lead these pastors beyond Northampton and carry the gospel far from England's shores.

William Carey and the Baptist Missionary Society

Though Andrew Fuller did not personally experience an awakening such as wrought through Jonathan Edwards, or even revival in the likeness of Shepshed, his legacy and influence would eventually assure the gospel be preached across the globe, in large part due to the missionary activity of William Carey.[136] As noted, Fuller served as founding secretary of the Baptist Missionary Society in 1792 till his death in 1815.[137] The year prior to its founding at Clipstone in April 1791, Fuller preached, *The Instances, Evil, and Tendency of Delay, in the Concerns of Religion* a sermon that reveals a conviction that the gospel be preached to all nations. Referencing Matt 28:19–20 in the sermon, Fuller wrote,

---

134. Ryland, Letter to John Williams August 28, 1807 (American Baptist Historical Society Archives) (*One Heart and one Soul*, 84).

135. Fuller himself maintained correspondence with John Williams, and in an 1807 letter echoed Ryland's approbation of God's work in America. Notwithstanding, his judgement that the the spiritual condition of Particular Baptist churches in England was "low in general," is attributed to the removal of its best pastors including William Carey, John Ryland, Samuel Pearce, Webster Morris, and Thomas Blundel. See American Baptist Historical Society Archives, Rochester, New York. Cited in *Armies of the Lamb*, 193. See Fuller's hope that revival would begin in England and spread abroad in a 1791 diary entry. See n449.

136. On Carey's life, see Carey, *Memory of Carey*; Carey, *William Carey*; Belcher, *William Carey*; Drewrey, *Carey: Shoemaker and Missionary*. For a popular-level introduction see George, *Faithful Witness*.

137. For the early history of the BMS, see Stanley, *History of the Baptist Missionary Society 1792–1992*, 1–29; Cox, *History of the Baptist Missionary Society, from 1792 to 1842*.

> When the Lord Jesus commissioned his apostles, he commanded them to go teach "all nations" and preach the gospel to "every creature"; notwithstanding the difficulties and oppositions that would lie in their way. The apostles executed their commission with assiduity and fidelity; but, since their days, we seem to sit down half contented that the greater part of the world should remain in ignorance and idolatry. Some noble efforts have been made; but they are small in number, when compared with the magnitude of the object.[138]

Though Fuller did not explicitly say that the "Great Commission" was binding on all believers through the ages, the conclusion was implied.[139] Fuller supported his claim by arguing that advances in technology, particularly maritime navigation, made viable unprecedented oceanic travel. Under such conditions, "it deserves to be considered whether this is not a circumstance that renders it a duty particularly binding on us."[140] Further in the Clipstone sermon, Fuller employs another distinctive theological motif, saying, "We pray for the conversion and salvation of the world, and yet neglect the ordinary means by which those ends have been accomplished. It pleased God, heretofore, by the foolishness of preaching, to save them that believed; and there is reason to think it will still please God to work by that distinguished means."[141] Fuller asks why fellow believers are not presently contributing resources to missionary endeavors considering Scripture's pronouncement that "whoever shall call upon the name of the Lord shall be saved."[142] Fuller follows the Apostle Paul's development of Rom 10:14–15 to it rhetorical crescendo: "how shall they preach except they be sent?"[143]

The Clipstone sermon discloses concrete applications of Fuller's theology. "Means" are human instruments, and/or structures that Christians can employ for accomplishing God's will revealed in Scripture. Duty is the divine obligation, a responsibility to appropriate whatever might achieve that end. The gospel should be preached to all nations as the Bible commands, and the provision for accomplishing this mission comes through sundry arrangements—print, travel, labor—all of which tend towards proclamation. The importance of the message for founding the BMS is demonstrated in

---

138. Fuller, *Pernicious Consequences of Delay* in *WAF*, 1:147.

139. Morden, *Life and Thought*, 116. Carey was, in fact, first among his colleagues to express this conviction in his *Enquiry into the Obligations for Christian to use Means for the Conversion of the Heathen*. See George, *Faithful Witness*, E.1–E.8.

140. Fuller, *Pernicious Consequences of Delay*, in *WAF*, 1:147.

141. Fuller, *Pernicious Consequences of Delay*, in *WAF*, 1:148.

142 Fuller, *Pernicious Consequences of Delay*, in *WAF*, 1:148.

143. Fuller, *Pernicious Consequences of Delay*, in *WAF*, 1:148.

that all major accounts of its founding record the Clipstone sermon.[144] After dinner that evening, Carey proposed that a missionary society be established. Yet, it was not until October 2, 1792, several months after *Enquiry* was published that an iconic sermon by Carey on Isa 54:2–3, "Expect Great Things; Attempt Great Things," hastened the official Founding of the BMS.[145]

As its title suggests, *An Enquiry into the Obligations of Christians to use Means for the Conversion of the Heathens* employs the language of Edwardsean evangelical Calvinism; the theology Fuller, Ryland, and others heartily endorsed.[146] Brian Stanley, in his *History of the BMS* agrees that some of Carey's language corresponds closely to Fuller's 1791 Clipstone sermon.[147] Ryland records that he, along with Fuller and Sutcliff, had read Carey's *Enquiry*, approved of its content and actually urged Carey to publish.[148] Peter Morden's conclusion that Carey likely drew on Fuller's Clipstone sermon to some extent, is a sound summary of the relationship between these documents.[149]

Andrew Fuller's zeal and devotion to the BMS cause never waned as a brutal travel schedule—he was regularly away from Kettering three months a year—and twelve-hour work days, attest. The sheer distance he covered throughout the isles renders Fuller's generally attained goal of "a pound a mile" remarkable.[150] Fuller's fundraising provided Carey with several co-laborers including Joshua Marshman (1768–1837) and William Ward (1764–1823), whose contribution to the mission alongside Carey would

---

144. Adding to the intrigue is John Sutcliff's sermon on 1 Kgs 19:10, "Jealousy of the Lord of Hosts Illustrated" preached the same day. The only extant sermon from Sutcliff, it can be found in Haykin, *One Heart and Soul*, 355–65. For the impact of Sutcliff's message, as originally preached, see Ryland, *Fuller*, 149. See Morris, *Memoirs*, 103. Cf. Morden, *Life and Thought*, 117.

145. For discussion on the disputed longer title of Carey's most famous sermon, see Payne, "John Dyer's Memoir of Carey," 326–27; Smith, "Spirit and Letter of Carey's Catalytic Watchword," 226–37. Ryland, *Fuller*, 150 has the longer title. Unfortunately, Carey's full manuscript has been lost.

146. Morden, *Life and Thought*, 118.

147. Stanley, *History of the Baptist Missionary Society*, 12.

148. Ryland, *Fuller*, 238–39. Though the Clipstone sermon preceded the publication of Carey's *Enquiry*, it is unclear when Fuller and others first read the pamphlet. Thus, determining who drew from whom is unclear. Fuller did opine that insufficient efforts had been made "for the propagation of the gospel in the world" (*Pernicious Consequences of Delay* in *WAF*, 1:147–48).

149. Morden, *Life and Thought*, 119.

150. See Stanley, *History of the Baptist Missionary Society*, 20; Modern, *Life and Thought*, 164. Fuller visited Ireland (1804), Wales (in 1812) and Scotland in 1799, 1802, 1805, 1808, and 1813.

earn them the sobriquet "the Serampore trio."[151] Recalling a conversation with "a confidential friend" John Ryland recollected Fuller saying the following in reference to establishment of the *BMS*:

> Our undertaking to India really appeared to me, on its commencement, to be somewhat like a few men, who were deliberating about the importance of penetrating into a deep mine, which had never before been explored. We had no one to guide us; and while we were thus deliberating, Carey, as it were, said, 'Well, I will go down, if you hold the rope'. But before he went down...he, as it seemed to me, took an oath from each of us, at the mouth of the pit, to this effect that 'while we lived, we should never let go of the rope.'[152]

Conclusion

The chapter has focused on Andrew Fuller's personal and theological development as it provided the context in which he came to understand revival. Prominent events, persons, and compositions converged to establish his ministerial trajectory. Fuller's conversion experience as a youth at Soham and his personal struggle with high Calvinist dogma, namely, finding the "warrant of faith," and the antinomian tendencies at Soham set an early course away from this distinctive theology. Membership in the Northampton Baptist Association exposed Fuller to a community of lifelong friends who introduced him to influential authors such as Jonathan Edwards. Edwards's natural-ability, moral-inability dichotomy presented in *Freedom of the Will* served to answer conceptual difficulties that vexed Fuller for years, namely, how orthodox Calvinism be maintained, and Christ be offered freely to all. Under Edwards's definition of the will—which Fuller adopted—a faculty acts on what is most desirable, and any person in bondage to sin can only change if Christ becomes an object of love, adoration, and reverence. Consequently, by a sovereign, supernatural work of regeneration alone is the moral ability to "choose Christ" possible. Because of natural ability,

---

151. "Serampore" derived from the missionaries' base of operations from 1800 onwards. Though India would be the primary focus on the *BMS* during Fuller's lifetime, Jacob Grigg and James Rodway were sent to pioneer a mission in Sierra Leone in 1795 and work in the Caribbean would commence in 1813/14. See Fuller, letter to William Carey, October 11, 1796 (Morden, *Life and Thought*, 162). On Baptist missions in India see Potts, *British Baptist Missionaries in India 1793–1837*; Laird, "William Carey and Bengal," 47–54.

152. Ryland, *Fuller*, 157. Gilbert Laws drew from this metaphor the title to his book: *Andrew Fuller: Pastor, Theologian, Ropeholder*.

resistance to belief cannot be attributed to innate factors as intellectual incomprehension, or external constraints. Human subjects who reject Christ choose freely to do so.

Fuller's appropriation of two biblical texts to warrant approaching God for grace led to his conversion and confirmed in Fuller an essential Biblicism. Fuller's break with high Calvinism is encapsulated in *The Gospel Worthy of All Acceptation*, a synthesis of Edwardsean philosophical categories, Puritan writers, and biblical exegesis, that represents evangelical Calvinism in its Enlightenment form. From Owen, and especially Edwards, Fuller employed the concept of "means" as an intellectually satisfactory presentation of compatibilism for a contemporary audience. The ordained methods, or processes by which God accomplishes his expressed purpose for the church will be applied to preaching, evangelism, and missions.[153]

Though Fuller does not explicitly define revival, it was not his intent to give systematic treatment on the subject. Fuller and others in Northamptonshire swam in the current of revival and their abundant references to it suggests their audience understood what was meant by the term. Nevertheless, as has been shown, an inferential, provisional definition can be given based on textual evidence. As argued here, Fuller's theology of revival is best understood as compatibilist in nature. Revival is something only God can enact, yet divine revelation provides the proper response incumbent on human agents for this end. Thus, Fuller can write that, ". . .whatever design or mercy might exist in the mind of God, that could not become a ground of hope till revealed by the word of God."[154]

The exceptional nature of the Shepshed revival reveals that Fuller and his friends did not experience an awakening in the likeness of 1740s New England. The long-term outcome of Fuller's contributions to revival, prompted by the Prayer Call of 1784, would be the formation of the Baptist Missionary Society in 1792.[155] While Particular Baptists did grow numerically during Fuller's lifetime, the sending of William Carey to India was the catalyst for evangelicalism's global expansion—an unprecedented "extension of Christ's Kingdom around the world."[156]

---

153. William Carey's claim that "Fervent prayer" would precede an "Outpouring of the Spirit" on the basis of Zech 12 and 13 follows Edwards's argumentation in *Humble Attempt to Extraordinary Prayer* (*Enquiry*, E.52–E.57).

154. Fuller, *Excellency and Utility of the Grace of Hope*, in *WAF*, 3:310.

155. Fuller, in an 1807 letter to John Williams acknowledged that "we consider the mission to Bengal as the most favourable symptom attending our denomination." See Letter to John Williams, American Baptist Historical Society Archives, Rochester, New York. Cited in Haykin, *Armies of the Lamb*, 194.

156. See Young, "Place of Andrew Fuller in the Developing Modern Missions

Chapter Four

"Use of Means"
Fuller and The Fruit of Revival

IT IS THE INTENT of this chapter to explore Andrew Fuller's praxis for pursuing revival within the scope of his overarching theological project. Fuller employed the term "means" with frequency and fluidity to denote appropriate measures and applications for spiritual renewal. Two documents will be the focus of this section: a 1785 circular letter, *Causes of Declension in Religion, and Means of Revival*, and an essay, *On Spiritual Declension and the Means of Revival*.[1] As has been argued throughout this book, Andrew Fuller's theology of revival is best understood as compatibilist in nature. Consequently, "means," though not by nature an essential component to spiritual renewal, were judged effectual on basis of divine revelation concerning this explicit telos—revival of religion.[2] These writings offer practical application of various means, and additionally emphasize the importance, respectively, of individual and corporate holiness as requisite to revival's commencement, and as the genuine fruit produced by it.

Movement." For a brief summary, Young, "Andrew Fuller and the Modern Missionary Movement," 17–27.

1. See Fuller, *WAF*, 3:318–24, 615–34.

2. Cf. Fuller's comments in *Causes of Declension*, in *WAF*, 3:626. Fuller insisted that salvation—and by soteriological virtue, revival—is accomplished by the sovereign God alone. For, he writes, "...though the way of salvation is in itself so glorious, that a man must be an enemy to God, to mankind...yet I believe the pride, ignorance, enmity, and love to sin in men, is such that they will not come to Christ for life; but, in spite of all the calls and threatenings of God, will go on, till they sink into eternal perdition. Hence I believe, arises the necessity of an almighty work of God the Spirit, to new-model the whole soul, to form in us new principles or dispositions as the Scriptures call it, to give us, 'a new heart and a right spirit'" (Fuller, *Last Remains*, 209–17).

Circular Letter: Causes of Declension in Religion and Means of Revival

As noted in chapter three, Fuller gives a summary of the spiritual condition of several congregations with whom he had correspondence in a 1785 circular letter, *Causes of Declension in Religion and Means of Revival*. This letter is notable for its early composition—published the same year as *Gospel Worthy*—and its denomination-wide dissemination. Understandably, it is relatively succinct compared to the five essays in *Spiritual Declension and Means of Revival*, comprising only six pages in the Sprinkle edition. Notwithstanding, its status as the earliest of the two revival writings mentioned, several thematic motifs are shared. In the letter, Fuller enumerates causes for spiritual decline with several positive counterproposals. Included among doctrinal and practical patterns predominant in Particular Baptist churches, and inimical to their flourishing is contentment with a mere, "superficial acquaintance with the gospel," namely, assent to doctrinal positions that are only seriously considered in polemical contexts.[3] This approach is fundamentally flawed for its failure to, "influence the heart and life." For to maintain proper doctrine but not, "*feel* the grace therein discovered," is to miss the mark.[4] Christian doctrine, rightly understood, enlivens and moves the believer. Spiritual lethargy cannot be attributed to theological substance, but to a human subject's failure to grasp the proper meaning and implication of such truths. Fuller explains,

> Christ's words are spirit and life to them who hunger and thirst after them, or have a heart to live upon them; and could we but more thoroughly enter into this way of living, we should find the doctrines of the gospel, instead of being dry, to be what they were in the days of Moses, who declared, "My doctrine shall drop as the rain, my speech shall distill as the dew; as the small rain upon the tender herb, and as the showers upon the grass." Deut. xxxii. 2.[5]

---

3. Fuller, *Causes of Declension*, in *WAF*, 3:319. From this circular letter Michael Haykin distills five principle ways Baptists could seek revival. These include, in order of frequency: prayer, cultivation of Christianity in the home, witnessing to unbelievers, honest examination of character, and the development of spirit of generosity to those in need (*Armies of the Lamb*, 69). I've used some of these headings for purpose of structure.

4. Fuller, *Causes of Declension*, in *WAF*, 3:319. One hears echoes of Jonathan Edwards and a "spiritual sense." For further discussion see Williams, "Enlightenment Epistemology and Eighteenth-Century Evangelical Doctrines of Assurance," 345–74.

5. Fuller, *Causes of Declension*, in *WAF*, 3:319.

Fuller proposes a corollary source of declension, stemming from a complacent attitude, namely, one that is indifferent to holy living.[6] Such professors eagerly claim the glory of God as the supreme goal of their lives, yet disregard the ordinances and church membership, claiming they have no bearing on salvation. They are in error for the precise reason that they are asking the wrong questions.[7] He senses fear that, "the old puritanical way," of devoting, "bodies, gifts, time, property. . .to serve is widely neglected.[8] The remedy, says Fuller, is an entire change of disposition by which believers will be led to ask not, "what *must* I do for God? but rather, what *can* I do for God?"[9] He advises his readers to pursue a course of action that includes, "earnest and constant," private prayer, times designated particularly for the, "effusion of the Holy Spirit," doctrinal instruction among families, evangelism with neighbors and associates, and funds designated for charitable donations.[10] Each of these is worthy of consideration in detail.

Prayer

As a pastor and theologian, prayer was a major component in Andrew Fuller's life as documentary evidence attests. Unsurprisingly, he placed high value for its relation to revival.[11] The Northamptonshire Baptist Association's Prayer Call, embodied in a sermon Fuller preached at its institution in 1784 reveals this conviction.[12] Fuller asked for an "outpouring of God's Spirit" within the denomination and extending to, ". . .all that in every place call upon the name of Jesus Christ our Lord. . ."[13] Insight into Fuller's private

---

6. Fuller, *Causes of Declension*, in *WAF*, 3:320.

7. Fuller, *Causes of Declension*, in *WAF*, 3:320. Adding perspective to these observations, during Fuller's Kettering pastorate, of the large majority who attended services on a given Sunday—sometimes upwards to 1,000—only 174 joined the church. See Ryland, *Fuller*, 374, 246. Cf. Morden, "Andrew Fuller: A Biographical Sketch," 16.

8. Fuller, *Causes of Declension*, in *WAF*, 3:319.

9. Fuller, *Causes of Declension*, in *WAF*, 3:319. In William Carey's iconic sermon "Attempt Great Things," one can hear echoes of Fuller. But although Carey likely would have read the circular letter, I have found no explicit evidence of literary dependence.

10. Fuller, *Causes of Declension*, in *WAF*, 3:320. Fuller advises frequent "watches." Treatment on the Holy Spirit and revival will be the subject of ch. 5. Note that Fuller echoes John Howe's belief in the importance of the Holy Spirit's outpouring, yet he offers his hearers concrete actions to perform in the meantime.

11. See *Spiritual Declension*, in *WAF*, 3:620–23.

12. Fuller, Diary and Spiritual Thoughts, May 11, 1784, cited in Ryland, *Fuller*, 96.

13. Fuller, *Nature and Importance of Walking by Faith* in *WAF*, 1:131. The influence of the Northamptonshire Association prayer meetings extended to Particular Baptist churches in Warwickshire and Western Associations in 1786 and 1790, respectively

devotional practices are attested in letters written to missionaries overseas. To Jabez Carey (1793–1879), son of William Carey, Fuller advised, "it will be a matter of great consequence that you be much in prayer (dear Sutcliff said near his end, "I wish I had prayed more!")[14] To missionaries James Chater (1806–1829) and William Robinson (1784–1853), Fuller explained his own pattern of prayer and scripture reading,

> I find it advantageous to read a part of the Scriptures to myself, before private prayer, and often turn it into prayer as I read. Do not read the scriptures merely as preachers, in order to find a text…but read them that you may get good to your own souls.[15]

Fuller could testify to his own experience and practice of prayer. Moreover, his sermons expressed zeal that families engage in this spiritual discipline, demonstrating his belief in the vital connection between faithfulness in private prayer and that performed corporately.[16] Fuller's desire that parents' prayer lives be worthy of imitation aligns with a second prerequisite for revival: "cultivation of Christianity in the home."

Cultivation of Christianity in the Home

Within successive generations of Dissent, catechisms composed intentionally for families by figures within the tradition reveal the importance of piety in the home. Isaac Watts and Philip Doddridge wrote respective catechisms that were widely-disseminated, as did figures in the Baptist tradition such as Benjamin Keach.[17] Jonathan Edwards, in his works on revival, noted the prominent role of young people in Northampton's awakenings. John Wesley,

---

(Morden, *Life and Thought*, 115). In "Jealousy of the Lord of Hosts," 15–16, John Sutcliff claimed that when Christ's people pray and evangelize, "The empire of Jesus shall advance, his kingdom arise, and the crown flourish upon his head" (cited in Haykin, *One Heart and One Soul*, 209). See ch. 3, n. 144.

14. Morden, *Offering Christ*, 172. Adding to this letter's poignancy is the fact that Fuller himself died only a year after Sutcliff.

15. Morden, *Offering Christ*, 172. See Ryland, *Fuller*, 161–62.

16. An excerpt from a sermon preached on July 1, 1800 reads, "The godly parent has a very solemn and important charge, and he feels it to be such. It has been remarked more than once, where a child has been born and added to a family, 'Now we have another body to provide for, but a soul to pray for' Oh for the parent to be able to say, on his dying bed, 'be ye followers of me as I have been of Christ!' Oh for the parent to be able to say to his family, when taking leave of life, "'The things that you have heard in me and seen of me, do,'" (*Importance of Union of Public and Private Interests* in *WAF*, 1:472).

17. E.g., Watts, *Divine and moral songs, attempted in easy language*. Keach, *Baptist Catechism*.

upon visiting Yorkshire in 1780, inquired as to what had become of a, "lovely class of little girls, most of them believers," whom he had met three years previous. He discovered that those, "who had pious parents remain to this day, but all of them whose parents did not fear God are gone back into the world."[18] Too astute a student of revival, Andrew Fuller did not overlook the essential component of familial piety. He admonishes his readers to,

> cherish a greater love to the truths of God—pay an invariable regard to the discipline of his house—cultivate love to one another, frequently mingle souls by frequently assembling yourselves together—encourage a meek, humble, and savory spirit."[19]

Though it is arguable that Fuller's ministerial workload compromised duties to his own family, anguish over his son Robert's rebellion discloses relentless passion that even his wayward eldest child attain salvation.[20] To summarize, Fuller's emphasis on discipleship in the home presents a holistic understanding of revival as broadly encompassing familial and ecclesial spheres.

---

18. *Wesley's Journal*, in *WJW*, 6:273. For discussion on the parental piety and revival, see Watts, *Dissenters*, 421–28.

19. Ryland, *Fuller*, 107.

20. Though unconverted in adolescence, Fuller hoped Robert would be saved and even become a pastor. Fuller did his best to secure work for young Robert, though the latter was unstable and perpetually transient. He confessed in his diary that he did not know what to do with his son (Diary and Spiritual Thoughts, July 1796 in *WAF*, 1:70–73). Four years later on July 21, 1800, an entry reads "The sorrows of my heart have been increased. . .to a degree almost insupportable." After Robert's departure to the Marines (the last of several attempts) in 1805, Fuller wrote his son, "Do not despair. Far as you have gone, and low as you are sunk in sin, yet if from hence you return to God by Jesus Christ, you will find mercy. Jesus Christ came into the world to save sinners, even the chief of sinners. If you had been ever so sober and steady in your behavior towards men, yet without repentance towards God and faith in Christ, you could not have been saved. And if you return to God by him, though your sins be great and aggravated, yet you will find mercy" (Fuller, Letter to Robert Fuller, December 1808 in Ryland, *Fuller*, 302). As Peter Morden has recently argued, it is plausible that Robert Fuller was finally converted shortly before his death off the coast of Portugal in 1809. Andrew Gunton Fuller, the eldest son from his father's second marriage, believed Robert was saved before he died (Fuller, *Men Worth Remembering*, 73). The evidence derives from a series of letters (now lost) that Robert wrote to his Father and half-sister, as well as Gunton Fuller's testimony that a certain Mr. Waldy—whom Gunton met in 1845—claimed to have been on the same ship as Robert and called him, "a very pleasing, nice youth, and [who] became a Christian man (Morden, *Life and Thought*, 161). That Gunton Fuller titled Andrew Fuller's biography *Men Worth Remembering* helps balance our picture of him as a father.

Witnessing to Unbelievers

Andrew Fuller's journey from high, to evangelical Calvinist, summarized in the previous chapter, came through his decisive rejection of a "warrant," as prerequisite to faith and repentance. Fuller believed the theologically-correct, and enduring motivation for evangelism came through acknowledging God's sovereign freedom to use human means for the conversion of sinners, which would inevitably, "stir up" ministers to preach the gospel, "to every creature." Even, "private Christians, situated in this or that dark town or village," would, "use all means" to announce the good news, "by a meek and unblemished conversation."[21]

Though Fuller's pulpit served as his primary evangelistic platform, this did not preclude witnessing to individuals outside the ecclesiastical context.[22] Fuller's correspondence with friends and relatives reveal an earnest compassion for their salvation.[23] Though ministries intentionally targeting children and youth were not common in Fuller's day, the spiritual condition of this demographic was considerably important.[24] Fuller himself would preach a sermon to the young congregants of Kettering each New Year's Day. One message in 1799, drawn from Ps 90:14, was aimed at what Fuller called, "the rising generation."[25] That some younger members in the con-

---

21. Fuller, *Causes of Declension*, in *WAF*, 3:323. For an overview of village preaching ministry, including a 1796 "experiment," in Cornwall, funded by the BMS, and of whose preachers Fuller maintained correspondence, see Brewster, "Out in the Journeys: Part I," 5–11; Brewster, "Out in the Journeys: Part II," 5–14. The assiduous records kept by these itinerant preachers record 27,500 total hearers.

22. Evidence includes a letter Fuller wrote to the "son of an intimate friend" inquiring if this young man had yet come to Christ. Fuller asks, "That you have sins to repent of, you yourself know. And have you, my dear, repented?" See Ryland, *Fuller*, 512–13. Another letter, "To an elder relative," was a stirring plea to trust Christ by faith (Ryland, *Fuller*, 498–500). A diary entry from 1791 recalls a "religious concern," among five or six young people to which Fuller acted by proposing, "to meet them once a week at the Vestry to talk and pray with them" (*Complete Works of Andrew Fuller Volume I*, 181).

23. In an era when letter writing was a premier art form, one can detect within the context of polite discourse, intentionality. Cf. Hindmarsh, *John Newton*, 244–47.

24. A surprising case to the contrary comes from John Newton (1725–1807). To draw children into his parish for catechetical instruction, Newton distributed what he termed, "little donatives," in the form of catechisms, sermons, and later, modest monetary gifts. In a matter of months, children who attended surpassed 200 (Hindmarsh, *John Newton*, 196–99). Catechesis among families was particularly important to Richard Baxter (1615–1691), although the practice of preaching sermons specifically to youth, as Fuller did, was uncommon. On Baxter and catechesis see: *Reformed Pastor*, 172–89.

25. "O satisfy us early with thy mercy, that we may rejoice and be glad all our days." Fuller, *Advantages of Early Piety*, in *WAF*, 1:422.

gregation had died unexpectedly the previous year added to its poignancy. John Ryland Jr. commented that Fuller would, "pour out all his heart. . .exhorting and charging every one, as a Father [sic.] doth his children."[26] An excerpt from the message reveals Fuller's passion and urgency.

> What shall I say more? Will you, dear young people, will you drink and be satisfied at the fountain of mercy; a fountain that is wide open and flows freely through our Lord Jesus Christ? You cannot plead the want of sufficient inducements. Ministers, parents, Christians, angels, the faltering voice at death, the solemn assurance of a judgment to come, and, above all, the sounding of the bowels of Jesus Christ, all say, Come.[27]

For Fuller, evangelism was not merely preached, but modeled. As his life and ministry proved, gospel proclamation had existential significance. Fuller employed all possible means through voice and pen to make Christ known. Revival, though the sovereign prerogative of God, would be spread instrumentally through the bold witness of the local church.

Charitable Giving to the Poor

Pastoring in a disenfranchised denomination with firsthand experience of poverty, Andrew Fuller was conscious of his responsibility to the poor in his midst and convinced that a spirit of generosity was evidence of saving faith, and thus, proximate to revival.[28] A central role for Fuller as secretary of the BMS was fundraising. Hence, personal visits to congregations throughout the British Isles made him keenly aware of attitudes towards giving and its connection to spiritual vitality. As he will do in another sermon on revival,

---

26. Ryland, *Fuller*, 359–60.

27. Fuller, *Advantages of Early Piety*, in *WAF*, 1:425–26.

28. A sermon Fuller preached from Jas 1:27 on March 27, 1800 reveals his attitude towards the poor, specifically widows and orphans. "[What] The Apostle here speaks [of] is not to be considered as a definition of religion, including the whole of it, but as a declaration of some of its essential branches, some of the essential parts of religion, and some of its first fruits. . . ." The passage, claims Fuller, reveals that, "It was suitable and desirable that the apostle should insist on those fruits, to such persons and at such a time, when they substituted theory for practice" (*Characteristics of Pure Religion* in *WAF*, 1:398). Fuller also wrote a circulating letter, *The Situation of the Widows and Orphans of Christian Ministers Etc.* in which he encourages Christian ministers to provide for orphans and widows through careful planning. He writes, "The trust that we are called to place in our heavenly Father does not however preclude the exercise of prudent foresight, either in ourselves, or in the friends of Christ towards us for his sake" (*WAF*, 3:365). Cf. 363–66. His concluding essay in *Spiritual Declension* lists generosity as a prerequisite to revival (*WAF*, 3:632).

Fuller celebrates generosity in the primitive church recorded in the book of Acts. Drawing from Jesus's words on the cross that the Apostle John care for Mary, Fuller makes a grand pronouncement in a sermon on Jas 1:27 that,

> There was not in the world, at least so far as I have been able to ascertain, either an hospital, or a charity-school, or a society for the relief of the distressed; none of these were known in the world till Christianity founded them: it is the gospel that has softened the hearts of those that embraced it; and it is often known that it has provoked to emulation those that had not.[29]

Fuller's exhortation suggests that, "Pure and undefiled religion promotes general good will in the hearts of those that believe it. . ." and in such cases, "their generosity shall provoke to generosity to those who do not."[30] Fuller was ever aware that poorer congregations would be tempted to forego giving, leaving this responsibility to the rich. In a sermon on the beatitudes, he reminds his hearers that, "It is taken for granted that the disciples of Christ were in the habit of giving alms; and this notwithstanding they generally consisted of persons who labored for their subsistence." These early Christians, though possessing meager means, "would deny themselves many comforts for the sake of being able to relieve [the poor]."[31] Revival is no more evident than in the Acts of the Apostles, and thus Fuller is wont to draw applications for his own audience.

The Necessity of Self-Examination

Fuller expresses confidence that upright conduct, characterized by meekness and love will better, "recommend religion" to the world,[32] but laments that the majority of congregants are apathetic and unreflective of their actual state."[33] A crucial component to holiness, vital for recognition of what must change in a believer's life, is the practice of self-examination. For this reason, it is not surprising that Fuller considers a third source of religious declension making "the religion of others," a standard in place of God's word.[34] When comparison to others in religious matters is primary,

---

29. Fuller, *Characteristics of Pure Religion*, in *WAF*, 1:403.
30. Fuller, *Characteristics of Pure Religion*, in *WAF*, 1:404.
31. Fuller, *Almsgiving and Prayer*, in *WAF*, 1:575.
32. Fuller, *Causes of Declension in Religion*, in *WAF*, 3:320.
33. Fuller, *Causes of Declension in Religion*, in *WAF*, 3:321.
34. Fuller, *Causes of Declension in Religion*, in *WAF*, 3:321. Fuller writes, "So if the question turns on *any particular piece of conduct*, whether it be defensible or not,

numerous ills arise. Included among them is increasing dullness to, "a sense of...vast and constant defects," namely, unrepentance that inexorably leads to vanity and spiritual pride.[35] Congregants whose concern is conformity to the religious status quo—not to Christ and his word—will merely attain an inadequate standard of piety, thereby becoming imitators with successive moral digressions.[36] Considering its prominence in Fuller's writing, it would behoove the reader to consider the nature and application of self-examination as he understood it.

Being part of a tradition deeply indebted to the Puritans of the seventeenth century, Andrew Fuller embraced, for the purpose of spiritual discipline, a pattern of rigorous self-examination. As noted, his diary served to this end.[37] Taken at face value, entries from the early 1780s disclose despondence and severity, with Fuller even questioning his own salvation.[38] For example, an entry from November 1784 speaks of "carnal mindedness," a "perpetual tendency to depart from God," and, "one continual disposition to do evil."[39] As noted, he experienced profound personal tragedy in

---

instead of searching the Bible, and praying to be led in the narrow way of truth and righteousness, how is it to hear such language as this—Such and such good men do so; surely, therefore, there can be no great harm in it! In short, great numbers appear to be quite satisfied if they are but about as strict and holy as other people with whom they are connected."

35. Fuller, *Causes of Declension in Religion*, in *WAF*, 3:321.

36. Fuller, *Causes of Declension in Religion*, in *WAF*, 3:321.

37. For a description of the fastidious and methodical devotional practices of Whitefield, Wesley, and early Methodism, see Hindmarsh, *Spirit of Evangelicalism*, 7–44. Authors and especially editors made clear that pious writings would serve as means of spiritual inspiration for future generations. *The Life and Diary of David Brainerd* exemplifies this pattern. In his preface, Jonathan Edwards explains his purpose for publishing Brainerd's diaries: "I am persuaded every pious and judicious reader will acknowledge, that what is here set before him is indeed a remarkable instance of true and eminent Christian piety in heart and practice tending greatly to confirm the reality of vital religion, and the power of godliness, that it is most worthy of imitation, and many ways calculated to promote the spiritual benefit of the careful observer" (*The Life of David Brainerd*, in *WJE*, 7:97).

38. An entry from 1780 reads, "Very much in doubt respecting my being in a state of grace...The Lord have mercy on me, for I know not how it is with me. One thing I know, that if I be a Christian at all, real Christianity in me is inexpressibly small in degree. O what a vast distance is there between what I ought to be, and what I am! If I am a saint at all, I know I am one of the least of all saints, I mean, that the workings of real grace are so feeble, that I hardly think they can be feebler in any true Christian...I think of late, I cannot in prayer, consider myself a Christian, but as a sinner casting myself at Christ's feet for mercy" (Ryland, *Fuller*, 78). It should be noted that no extant evidence reveals that Fuller explicitly doubted his salvation after 1784.

39. "Diary and Spiritual Thoughts," November 29, 1784 in Ryland,*Fuller*, 96.

his family, which included the deaths of several children, and additionally, mental illness that plagued his first wife, Sarah.[40]

Fuller's own diary entries, while illuminating, do not give a systematic method to apply self-examination. For such purposes, *The Backslider: His Nature, Symptoms and Recovery* is a reader's best source, though various principles are expounded in other revival writings. *The Backslider* begins with an ambivalent judgment on the spiritual condition of his era, a sentiment echoed elsewhere. On one hand, "...there are some eminently zealous and spiritual [people], perhaps as much so as at almost any former period." However, "it is no less evident that others are in a sad degree conformed to this world...[.] Even those who retain a decency of character, many are sunk into a Laodicean lukewarmness."[41]

In his final chapter, Fuller advises eight "Means of Recovery." Among these, diligent scripture reading, particularly that accompanied by prayer, as doing so allows the mind to be, "more at liberty for reflection," and provides opportunity to, "apply the subject to your case."[42] Advantages to this commonsense method are made explicit: "Solemn approaches unto God are adapted to impress the mind with a sense of sin, and to inspire us with self-abhorrence on account of it."[43] Sounding every bit the Puritan, Fuller advises,

> Reflect on the aggravating circumstances of Thine offences, or on those things which render it *an evil and bitter thing* to have departed from the living God, and to have sinned against him in the manner thou hast done. Every return to God begins with reflection.[44]

Fuller's third prescription is to, "reflect on the Goodness of God in having hitherto borne with thee," the fourth, to, "reflect on the state and

---

40. Fuller, Letter to Mr. Gardiner, August 25, 1792, speaks of his wife's "hysterical affections," and "wild despair." On one occasion, Sarah fled the house and was found in a graveyard scratching the dirt and grass off the tombstones of her deceased children. Sarah eventually died giving birth to a daughter, Bathoni, who perished after three weeks (Fuller, *Memoir* in *WAF*, 1:59–62).

41. Fuller, *Backslider* in *WAF*, 3:635; 635–59. cf. A similar judgment is found in *On Spiritual Declension* which reads, "...the bulk of Christians in the present age are very deficient in spirituality, and come far short of the primitive Christians in a close walk with God" (*WAF*, 3:615). Ancient Laodicea as an archetype of spiritual insipidness is repeated at several places in Fuller's revival writings.

42. Fuller, *Backslider*, in *WAF*, 3:654.

43. Fuller, *Backslider*, in *WAF*, 3:655.

44. Fuller, *Backslider*, in *WAF*, 3:656.

exercises of thy mind in former times."⁴⁵ A providential interpretation of history that renders lessons for his contemporary audience is a recurring motif in Andrew Fuller's theology.⁴⁶ Fifth, Fuller recommends set-apart times for fasting and prayer.⁴⁷ His final three precepts advise watchfulness and humility in pursuing holiness. Believers should not become complacent, but expect spiritual opposition.⁴⁸

Though self-examination is necessary and good, Fuller acknowledged the pitfalls of its excesses. With firsthand experience of the anguish at feeling unworthy of salvation, he reminds his hearers that though they are sinners, "the door of mercy is open," and they are welcome in.

> Let your past character be then what it may, and let your conversion be ever so doubtful, if you can from this time relinquish all for Christ, eternal life is before you.⁴⁹

Whatever zeal and assiduousness a supplicant possesses, the sovereign mercy of Christ is the only means of hope. Self-examination must always lead back to this place.

In discussing the various sources of declension juxtaposed with the aforementioned remedial measures, Fuller cites a problematic tendency among believers to underestimate the consequences of their, "good and evil conduct."⁵⁰ By this is understood a proclivity towards sloth, stemming from a faulty conviction that spiritual disciplines such as prayer and corporate worship have little bearing on God's redemptive work in the world. Fuller considers an "atheistical spirit," not the proper application of Calvinistic doctrine, as the essential source of such perspectives.⁵¹ Like dutiful soldiers, each Christians should act, "as if the whole issue of the battle depended

---

45. Fuller, *Backslider*, in *WAF*, 3:657.

46. In *Causes of Declension*, Fuller encourages believers to, "recollect the best periods of the Christian church, and compare them with the present; and the best parts of our own life, if we know when they were, and compare them with what we are now" (*WAF*, 3:323). Fuller devotes space to praising the early church in several places (*Why Christians in the Present Day Possess Less Joy*, in *WAF*, 3:325–31).

47. Fuller, *Backslider*, in *WAF*, 658. Fuller claimed that, "A day devoted to God in humiliation, fasting and prayer, occasionally occupied with reading suitable parts of the holy scriptures, may, by the blessing of the Holy Spirit, contribute more to the subduing of sin, and the recovery of a right mind, than years spent in a sort of half-hearted exercises."

48. Fuller, *Backslider*, in *WAF*, 658–59.

49. Fuller, *Backslider*, in *WAF*, 659.

50. Fuller, *Causes of Declension*, in *WAF*, 3:322.

51. Fuller, *Causes of Declension*, in *WAF*, 3:322.

upon *his* conduct."⁵² Thus, from a religious perspective, successes occur, "when everyone is concerned to act as if he were the only one that remained on God's side."⁵³ With emphatic locution, Fuller eviscerates an anemic understanding of God's action in the world, specifically in relation to prayer.

> Have done with that bastard humility, that teaches you such a sort of thinking low of your prayer and exertions for God as to make you decline them, or at least be slack and indifferent in them! Great things frequently arise from small beginnings. Some of the greatest good that has ever been done in the world has been set a going by the efforts of an individual. Witness the Christianizing of a great part of the heathen world by the labours of *Paul*, and the glorious reformation from popery began by the struggles of a *Luther*.⁵⁴

With a compatibilist echo, Fuller summarizes his preceding argument, reminding readers that, "Though there is nothing in our doings from which we could look for such great things," yet, "God is pleased frequently to crown our poor services with infinite reward."⁵⁵ Throughout Christian history, God has blessed the efforts of his servants, particularly in missionary endeavors. Obedience to the divine command and the appropriation of the ordained means ought, "stir-up" ministers and private Christians.⁵⁶ The completion of Fuller's letter provides brief salutary, "means"—antitheses to religious declension—that he claims will pave the way for "a happy revival."⁵⁷

Means to Revival

The actual measures proposed by Fuller in this section of the circular letter are surprisingly brief, though as noted, several "means," are interspersed among the sources of decline. Fuller essentially proposes two applications. The first, a historically-oriented proposition is to, "Recollect the best periods of the Christian church," in comparison to the present state, and likewise, "the best parts of our own life," contrasted with one's current

---

52. Fuller, *Causes of Declension*, in WAF, 3:322.
53. Fuller, *Causes of Declension*, in WAF, 3:322.
54. Fuller, *Causes of Declension*, in WAF, 3:322.
55. Fuller, *Causes of Declension*, in WAF, 3:323.
56. Fuller, *Causes of Declension*, in WAF, 3:323.
57. Fuller, *Causes of Declension*, in WAF, 3:323.

spiritual condition.[58] Fuller cites noteworthy periods of church history in a hagiographic spirit not atypical of nineteenth-century evangelical historiography.[59] Speaking of the early church, he exhorts his readers to consider the primitive Christians', "disinterestedness, zeal and godly simplicity,"[60] and additionally, the Protestant Reformers who serve as models of, "fervent zeal and holy piety."[61] With characteristic pride in a Dissenting heritage, Fuller asks readers to reflect on, "the spirit and conduct of our Puritan and Non-Conforming ancestors," who, "served God at the expense of all that was dear to them in this world, and laid the foundation of our churches in woods, and dens, and caves of the earth!"[62]

A corollary transition draws Fuller's audience from the distant history of the church to the intimacy of personal religious experience, taking for his second point, a direct citation from Rev 2:5 "*Do thy first works.*" Essentially a subsidiary-application of his first point, Fuller exhorts his hearers to return to an, "earnestness and constancy," that once marked their pursuit of salvation.[63] With encouragement to live faithfully in the various civic and familial spheres, Fuller advises them to continue, "seeking to promote by all means, for the present and eternal welfare of those around you."[64] Fuller's return to the subject of prayer forms an *inclusio* to the letter that reflects his theological understanding of revival and its relation to means:

> Our need of God's Holy Spirit to enable us to do any thing, and every thing, truly good, should excite us. . . . Without his blessing all means are without efficacy, and every effort for revival will be in vain. Constantly and earnestly, therefore, let us approach his throne. Take all occasions especially for *closet prayer*; here

---

58. Fuller, *Causes of Declension*, in *WAF*, 3:323.

59. Several evangelicals composed ecclesiastical histories that stressed succession with previous periods of Christian history. This includes Erasmus Middleton (1739–1805), one of six students expelled from Oxford for Methodism, who authored *Biographica Evangelica* a four-volume work. Joseph Milner composed *History of the Church of Christ*. The Victorian Anglican J.C. Ryle's *Christian Leaders in the Past Century* also fits this genre. For discussion on these figures and early evangelical successionist understandings of history see Stewart, "Did Evangelicalism predate the Eighteenth Century?," 135–53.

60. Fuller, *Causes of Declension,* in *WAF*, 3:323. See also Fuller, *Joy and the Primitive Disciples* in *WAF*, 3:325–31.

61. Fuller, *Causes of Declension,* in *WAF*, 3:323.

62. Fuller, *Causes of Declension,* in *WAF*, 3:323.

63. Fuller, *Causes of Declension,* in *WAF*, 3:324.

64. Fuller, *Causes of Declension,* in *WAF*, 3:324.

if any where, we shall get fresh strength, and maintain a life of communion with God.[65]

On Spiritual Declension and the Means of Revival

Andrew Fuller's most extensive treatment on spiritual renewal, *On Spiritual Declension and the Means of Revival*, expounds several familiar themes along with some new material in five separate essays. Though date and context are not given, these five essays almost certainly postdate his 1785 circular letter. The work is distinctive for its penetrating questions and confessional emphases. The piece begins with a lament typical of Fuller. "It is a matter of complaint too common. . . .. that the bulk of Christians in the present age are very deficient in spirituality." Notwithstanding, complaints "will not effect a cure," therefore, successive essays are given, three of which focus on the sources of decline, and two propose salutary measures.[66]

The Want of a Proper Regard to the Word of God

Perhaps unsurprising for a Particular Baptist, Fuller begins with the Bible, of whose neglect he attributes, "almost all the remarkable declensions in the church of God." Conversely, in times of revival and reformation, the Scriptures have been "the grand means of their being brought about."[67] He expounds three subpoints, the first attributes declension to a neglect of reading, meditation, and prayer over the word.[68] The second involves a failure to read the "ends and purposes" for which the Bible was written, by which Fuller means an erroneous disposition toward Scripture. Some despise the word of God who set their own reason above it, whereas others read without an "an intention and determination" to form their "conduct by it."[69] On the opposite spectrum are those who rely on "dreams, visions, or supposed immediate revelations from heaven," and these Fuller calls "enthusiasts" as they

---

65. Fuller, *Causes of Declension*, in *WAF*, 3:324.
66. Fuller, *On Spiritual Declension*, in *WAF*, 3:615.
67. Fuller, *On Spiritual Declension*, in *WAF*, 3:616.
68. Fuller, *On Spiritual Declension*, in *WAF*, 3:617.
69. Fuller, *On Spiritual Declension*, in *WAF*, 3:618. See also Fuller, *Calvinistic and Socinian Systems Examined*, in *WAF*, 2:108–234. For a comparative analysis of Fuller and noted Deists and Socinians in the eighteenth century see Hoselton, *Love of God Holds Creation Together*. Fuller cites the example of reading a chapter once or twice a day to one's family "merely for the sake of decency" and without "an intention of complying with what shall be found to be the mind of God" (*WAF*, 3:618).

do not abide by the "plain meaning of the word of God." His conventional interpretive guidance is to evaluate any scriptural "impressions" by the rule that such texts contain the same meaning independent of that impression.[70]

Fuller's third subpoint laments those with "a low opinion of the truths contained in [the Bible]," judging them dry and uninteresting.[71] Ever the evangelical Calvinist, Fuller contends that, "Doctrinal, experimental, and practical religion are all necessarily connected together; they have no existence apart from each other." From his standpoint, "The influence of truth upon the mind is the source of all our spiritual feelings, and those feelings are the springs every good word and action."[72] Like John Howe in *The Prosperous State of the Christian Interest*, Fuller judges the prevailing low regard for the word of God as a kind of spiritual chastisement for sin, likened to the removal of the Holy Spirit—"the sum of every spiritual good."[73] A corollary reason for indifference to the Scriptures is what Fuller deems "a natural consequence of sin."[74] In the above instances, adverse effects result actively, in the form of divine censure, and passively, as consequence of the moral order of creation. Fuller concludes the section with a warning to pastors that exponential harm results from dereliction to scriptural devotion.[75]

---

70. *On Spiritual Declension*, in *WAF*, 3:618. cf. Jonathan Edwards's analysis of impressions in *Religious Affections*, Part II sec. v, 71, "That [religious affections] come with Texts of Scripture is no Sign" where he writes, ". . .affections may arise on occasion of the Scripture, and not properly from the Scripture, as the genuine fruit of the Scripture and by a right use of it; but from abuse of it. All that can be argued from the purity and perfection of the Word of God, with respect to experiences, is this, that those experiences which are agreeable to the Word of God are right, and cannot be otherwise; and not that those affections must be right which arise on occasion of the Word of God coming to the mind." To balance the perspective, Fuller did claim a qualified enthusiasm in contrast to Socinian Joseph Priestly when he wrote, ". . .if it be enthusiasm to think and feel concerning ourselves as to the Scriptures represent us, and concerning Christ as he is there exhibited, let me live and die an enthusiast." Cited in *Calvinistic and Socinian Systems Examined* in *WAF*, 2:213. See also: 206–14.

71. Fuller, *On Spiritual Declension*, in *WAF*, 3:618.

72. Fuller, *On Spiritual Declension*, in *WAF*, 3:619.

73. Fuller, *On Spiritual Declension*, in *WAF*, 3:619. Drawing from Ezek 39:29, "I will no more hide my face," Howe writes, ". . .that till the time of this eminent effusion there was a very displeased hiding of God's face, and a great retraction and holding back of the Spirit. Other scriptures, that I relate as I conceive to the same eminent season, intimate also the dreadful foregoing desolation." Sermon 15:2.

74. Fuller, *On Spiritual Declension*, in *WAF*, 3:619. Drawing a wisdom application from Ps 1, devotional adherence to the word benefits the reader who heeds its counsel. However, it is "From want of religious principle proceeds a more than ordinary liability to *errors in judgment*. . ." for, "once the truths of God sink into disteem" do errors in judgment lead to "errors in spirit and conduct."

75. Fuller, *On Spiritual Declension*, in *WAF*, 3:619. He writes, "It becomes us to

The Manner in Which We Attend to the Duty of Prayer

This essay shares with each of Fuller's revival writings the importance and necessity of prayer, which he defines as "the ascending of the heart to God." Prayer is the ordinary means by which we communicate with him, and of which "our spiritual prosperity will bear some proportion to the degree of fervor and constancy with which this duty is attended."[76] This section on prayer is unique for its extensive analysis posed in the form of seven questions, specifically the "manner" by which prayers are performed. The first asks whether a supplicant genuinely desires what he or she prays for. Opposing approaches stem from the same error. Those who pray in a strictly formal manner, and others who pray unreflectively extempore are alike tempted to forget the God whom they approach, and therefore, share the mistake of "repeating words without meaning."[77]

At this juncture, Fuller distinguishes between praying for mercies God has not bound himself to bestow and those he has, in the following ponderous question: "Are we not apt to be less earnest in matters wherein we should take no denial, than in others wherein it would become us to be submissive?"[78] Two Old Testament figures, David and Jabez, are representative of those whose offered respective prayers for something not promised to them by God. Jabez's request was granted, David's was not, yet both submitted to the divine decision. Categorically, Fuller distinguishes two kinds of mercies. The first being "all our earthly comforts, and some things in the religious life; of the latter are those spiritual blessings essential to salvation."[79] Fuller's distinction offers insight into his theology of revival since the duty to pray depends on a pronouncement via divine revelation of a certain outcome. David and Jabez were not obligated to pray for their requests, whereas "in respect to spiritual and eternal blessings, God has bound himself to grant the desire of the righteous, and to perfect that which concerns his praying people."[80] In other such instances, pertaining to certain prophetic texts, Fuller believed God had obligated himself to answer

---

tremble, and to inquire whether the defections among our people be not owing in part to the wholesome truths of God being withheld from them, or delivered in a languid and careless manner."

76. Fuller, *On Spiritual Declension*, in *WAF*, 3:620.
77. Fuller, *On Spiritual Declension*, in *WAF*, 3:620.
78. Fuller, *On Spiritual Declension*, in *WAF*, 3:621.
79. Fuller, *On Spiritual Declension*, in *WAF*, 3:620.
80. Fuller, *On Spiritual Declension*, in *WAF*, 3:621.

particular prayers. In two writings, he will give detailed explanations for the connection between prayer, the millennial kingdom, and spiritual renewal.[81]

Fuller's third query centers on the telos of individual prayers. Though general requests for provision or success are permissible, they may actually be for the purpose of "sensual gratification." Those who pray thus, should not expect God to hear them.[82] Question four touches on a recurring theme included among the five means for revival in Fuller's 1785 circular letter, namely, self-examination. The specific concern is disingenuous confessions of sin in which no actual resolve is made to forsake such sins. Fuller concedes that the act of confession may be present, while "godly sorrow" is absent.[83] Question five returns to the relationship between Scripture and prayer, whether the supplicant intends to "follow the dictates of God's word" and be "led in all truth," or simply follow a predetermined course, hoping that the Bible will "affirm an existing inclination.[84]

Fuller's sixth, and perhaps most interesting, question asks, "Are we not greatly wanting in what may be called religious public spirit in our prayers?" The subject is a Christian whose primary concern is "poring over" whether they are a genuine believer and who therefore, lack robustness in their spiritual life. Fuller speaks from firsthand experience as one who spent excessive time "recollecting former evidences" to determine the veracity of his own faith. At this juncture, he explicitly warns against the preoccupation with self-examination to acquire assurance.[85] For, however necessary it may be to find assurance of salvation, if this is a believer's primary focus, and other spiritual duties are neglected, he or she will fail to attain the object. "Like reputation, and some other things, to pursue it as an end is the way to lose it."[86] The means by which a person comes to know they are a Christian is to seek Christ's kingdom first, after which a vibrant spirituality invariably follows. The concluding inquiry, an apt summary of the previous six considerations, asks whether requests are done "wholly in the name of Christ?"

---

81. Fuller, *On Spiritual Declension*, in *WAF*, 3:621.

82. Fuller, *On Spiritual Declension*, in *WAF*, 3:622.

83. Fuller, *On Spiritual Declension*, in *WAF*, 3:622. Note his emphasis on the affections in which the believer ought, "feel [their] hearts go out against the sin, as to return to the Lord with all [their] soul."

84. Fuller, *On Spiritual Declension*, in *WAF*, 3:621.

85. The "primitive Christians," notes Fuller, "did not seem to have been so much troubled with these thoughts as with as with their want of conformity to Christ. Christ taught his disciples to approach daily to God as their Father; and by the accounts we have, it would seem they generally did so; but such sweet freedom is now rarely found, even among the godly" (Fuller, *On Spiritual Declension*, in *WAF*, 3:623).

86. Fuller, *On Spiritual Declension*, in *WAF*, 3:623.

A genuine "persuasion of...utter unworthiness" serves as a reminder that to ask blessings in the name of Christ is to pray for the sake of his glory, not our own.[87]

Sin of Lying on the Conscience Unlamented

Fuller's third and final essay on the sources spiritual declension draws from the second epistle to the Corinthians the Apostle Paul's fear that upon his coming, he will find, "many who have sinned already, and have not repented of their deeds."[88] Fuller prefaces that,

> Sin, if not habitually lamented, and removed by repeated applications to the cross of Christ, is like poison in the bones; it rankles within us, and is destructive of our soul's prosperity. So long as sin remains unlamented, so long as we have an habitual liking to it...God has a controversy with us.[89]

Presented in first-person plural form, the essay is Fuller's most intentionally individual application of self-examination. Several listed "evidences" suggest unlamented sin. Among them, a "particular evil" that persists in an individual's life because ongoing confession of sin is not matched by forsaking it. Mere "prudential considerations" restrain such transgressions, as is evident in persons of whom "past evils are remembered with pleasure and approbation."[90] True repentance means possessing a "holy abhorrence" by which one wishes all sins were "annihilated."[91] Fuller concludes this essay by noting that unrepentance, "weakens and enervates our graces," consequently, hindering "usefulness."[92] Communion with God is severed, which in turn gives Satan a great advantage among those who no longer

---

87. Fuller, *On Spiritual Declension*, in *WAF*, 3:623.

88. 2 Cor 12:12 (AV) "And lest, when I come again, my God may humble me among you, and that I shall bewail many of which have sinned already, and have not repented of their uncleanness, and fornication and lasciviousness which they had committed."

89. Fuller, *On Spiritual Declension*, in *WAF*, 3:624.

90. Fuller, *On Spiritual Declension*, in *WAF*, 3:624. Fuller explains that guilt by small degrees is more likely to go unlamented, because "being contracted a little at a time, it has obtained a place in the heart almost unnoticed." Fuller cites John Owen (without reference to the work), God's repudiation of a kind of man "who opposes nothing to the seduction of evil in his own heart, but fear of shame among men, or hell from God, is sufficiently resolved to do that evil if there were no punishment attending it."

91. Fuller, *On Spiritual Declension*, in *WAF*, 3:624. Note Fuller's comment that "...things are never safe till the soul, dissolved in grief, lies prostrate at the feet of Jesus."

92. Fuller, *On Spiritual Declension*, in *WAF*, 3:624.

resist.[93] "Secret sins" will likely become "manifest and open."[94] An attentive reader, following the progression of probing questions may express concern about their standing with God. Echoing central themes from *The Backslider*, Fuller affirms that while "no true Christian will ever seek into apostacy," unlamented sin is, "the same road" trod by those who have apostatized.[95]

To summarize, Fuller's three sources of declension pertain respectively, to the denigration of Scripture, the insincerity of prayer, and pseudo-repentance. Fuller's metaphor of the individual soldier, dutifully obedient to orders, and acting as if the battle's outcome is contingent on his conduct alone, encapsulates Fuller's conviction that the spiritual quality of individuals is the key to whether the church experiences lethargy or revival flourishing.

Means

Three preliminary points preface Fuller's exposition on means for revival, each bearing broad conformity to his theology. As noted, means, claims Fuller, should be considered as precisely that, nothing more. Believers "should place no dependence on them, but entirely upon the Spirit of God as the first cause." The two successive propositions, ethical in tone, implore backsliders to renounce idolatry by putting away any idols "without reserve,"[96] and third, demonstrate a sincere desire to return to God. With this noted proviso, Fuller proceeds to other "Scriptural directions," centered on the sobering reality of sins committed after conversion. Though most dissimilar from other points in Fuller's revival writings, post-conversion/post-baptismal sins are a theological dilemma found in the early writings of the Apostolic Fathers and which has prompted diverse remedial measures throughout church history.[97]

The first of Fuller's four subpoints asserts that sins done after conversion constitute a violation of "solemn vows and covenant engagements that subsist in the act of repentance." Interestingly, this section bears thematic similarities to the Puritan covenant renewals common in the late

---

93. Fuller, *On Spiritual Declension*, in *WAF*, 3:625.

94. Fuller, *On Spiritual Declension*, in *WAF*, 3:626. "It is not in human nature to be able for a long continuance to conceal the ruling bias of the heart. It will come out in some way or other, and it is fit it should. A wise Providence has so ordered it that the heart and conduct shall not be at perpetual variance."

95. Fuller, *On Spiritual Declension*, in *WAF*, 3:626.

96 Fuller, *On Spiritual Declension*, in *WAF*, 3:626.

97. The issue of forgiveness for post-baptismal sins was a concern early in the second century as the *Shepherd of Hermas* attests. For discussion see Gonzalez, *History Christian Thought*, 2:86–90, 94.

seventeenth century, particularly those in New England that preceded the First Great Awakening by over half a century.[98] In conveying the solemnity of covenant, Fuller draws a similitude between the so-called "covenant of redemption" between the Father and Son in eternity, and a covenant "between Christ and his people in time."[99] Additionally, he finds the marital metaphor appropriate to describe conversion. Believers who are thus "married," should return to Christ their spouse.[100]

Fuller's sermonic appeal from sundry Old Testament texts reminds his hearers that departure from God has no justification, for he is a Father, neither "churlish," nor a "hard master." Subpoint three, echoing, the first, judges post-conversion sins to be "attended with circumstances of peculiar and horrible ingratitude."[101] In consistent hermeneutical form, Fuller makes typological connection to ancient Israel, acknowledging that though his hearers never possessed the geographical land of Canaan, they live in a nation where the gospel privileges transcend any earthly inheritance, and therefore render, "greater obligations." Fuller hopes such sober realizations will "deeply wound" those who've, "slighted and dishonoured a God of such love as this."[102] Sins committed after conversion, writes Fuller, express "the most extreme and singular folly." Likening eighteenth-century England to ancient Israel in the time of Jeremiah whom the prophet denounced for forsaking allegiance to Yahweh for other gods, Fuller warns that "departing from God," is a foolish exchange of liberty, peace, and joy, for drudgery, slavery, anguish, and bitter remorse.[103]

Fuller's concluding essay, second of the two proposed means, echoes *Causes of Declension and Means of Revival* in its drawing typological application from the book of Revelation. Appropriating the warnings given to the seven ancient churches recorded in Revelation chapters two and three,

98. Crawford mentions Increase Mather's claim that "it is a known principle. . . . *That renewal of covenant is the way to attain Church Reformation,*" and Nathaniel Leonard of Plymouth who believed ill-conduct such as, "Impiety, prophaneness, Sabbath-breaking, Gaming, Tavern-hunting, Intemperance, and other evils" must cease before "reformation" could commence (*Seasons of Grace*, 180–83). See also Miller's belief that revival in New England represented the culmination of covenant renewal (*Errand into the Wilderness,* 153–66).

99. Fuller, *On Spiritual Declension*, in WAF, 3:627.

100. Fuller, *On Spiritual Declension*, in WAF, 3:627. In a mystical, albeit sober tone, Fuller continues, "Conversion is a marriage wherein (with reverence be it spoken) Christ resigns up himself, with all he is and has, to us, and we resign ourselves, with all we are, and have, to him."

101. Fuller, *On Spiritual Declension*, in WAF, 3:628.

102. Fuller, *On Spiritual Declension*, in WAF, 3:628.

103. Fuller, *On Spiritual Declension*, in WAF, 3:629.

Fuller addresses several topics previously discussed. Like his circular letter, he attributes religious declension to a "neglect of the word of God,"[104] and furthermore, cites the early church as a model of exemplary conduct. Generosity, charity, "soundness of faith" render a "lovely picture of primitive Christianity" that should be "closely reviewed."[105] Furthermore, the "doctrines which the generality of Reformers held," which Fuller concedes cannot be proven to possess "Divine origin," are nonetheless worthy of notice for "their moral tendency."[106]

Fuller has in mind the courage with which early Reformed churches "threw off the yoke of popery" by committing to the ordinances in "primitive simplicity" despite persecution.[107] Though it was the "right of private judgement" over and against the authority of Rome that led to the Reformation, many in Andrew Fuller's context have made poor use of religious liberty, whose primary purpose ought serve as a "means" for obtaining truth, not an end.[108] Religious liberty, "however equitable and valuable it is in itself, is certainly of no further use *to us* than as it is applied to the discovery of truth, and the practice of righteousness."[109]

With a return to introspection and self-examination, Fuller asks his readers to consider God's past work in their lives compared to the present—anticipating a negative answer. The remedial prescription is repentance, for "if ever there be any true revival of religion it must originate in this."[110]

---

104. Fuller, *On Spiritual Declension* in *WAF*, 3:629. He continues, ". . .it will ill become me, in writing on the means of returning to him, to forget to make use of that unerring guide. Hence it is that I have endeavored, as much as possible, to introduce some particular part or parts of the word of God, as the ground of what has been advanced on every subject."

105. Fuller, *On Spiritual Declension*, in *WAF*, 3:630. Fuller writes, "If there be any considerable revival in the church, or in the souls of individuals, it will be when diligence, disinterestedness, tenderness of conscience, generosity and faithfulness of those times are imitated" (*On Spiritual Declension*, in *WAF*, 3:632).

106. Fuller, *On Spiritual Declension*, in *WAF*, 3:630. For the listing of these doctrines see ch. 2, 100, n130. Fuller's central thesis in *The Gospel its Own Witness*, an apologetic piece against Deism, is that the latter does not "tend" toward virtue and morality (*WAF*, 2:1–233).

107. Fuller, *On Spiritual Declension*, in *WAF*, 3:630.

108. Fuller, *On Spiritual Declension*, in *WAF*, 3:631. For Philip Doddridge's similar comments on religious liberty, see ch. 2, 97–98.

109. Fuller, *On Spiritual Declension*, in *WAF*, 3:631.

110. Fuller, *On Spiritual Declension*, in *WAF*, 3:631. Fuller weighs the objection common among high Calvinists, that no obligation exists to "love Christ and divine things." To which he proceeds to argue a familiar *reductio ad absurdum* that if no duty exists apart from Divine superintendence, then, "it must follow that we are not obliged to do any good thing whatever" (*On Spiritual Declension*, in *WAF*, 3:632).

With ongoing focus on the centrality of holiness from the Revelation text, Fuller juxtaposes ancient Laodicea and eighteenth-century Britain, recognizing in the Asia Minor city a lukewarm character that, "bears too near a resemblance" to the churches of his day. By excelling in trade, both have ". . .produced riches; and riches, like pride, indifference, and spiritual wretchedness."[111] Fuller's principle counsel, to "deal with Christ," is followed by three specifics to invigorate "real religion:" spiritual riches, spiritual beauty, and spiritual discernment.[112] It is not enough to "be once interested in pardoning and justifying grace." On the contrary, "if we would be rich in the sight of God, we must be dealing with Christ as guilty, self-condemning sinners for forgiveness and acceptance."[113] Fuller has in mind concrete efforts to maintain holiness in opposition to mere verbal assent to spiritual poverty, or a weak desire for sanctification, when he claims that "daily dealing with Christ" is necessary for the mortification of sin. Awareness of antinomian tendencies within Particular Baptist churches leads him to confront confessions of doctrinal rectitude incompatible with lived practice.

In dialectical form, Fuller returns to the section's dominant motif: "dealing with Christ," whose meaning is described in detail as a kind of sapiental knowledge brought by "an unction from the Holy One," and through intimate communion with Christ.[114] For only through an increasing acquaintance with him will one's sins appear "the more bitter, unnatural, disingenuous, and shameful. . ."[115] Fuller draws the essay to a close with a sermonic *meditatio* calling hearers to consider the sacrifice of Christ and comprehend his intrinsic worth. Like Isaac Watts, Fuller intends his discourse to arouse the rational faculties as well as passions, thereby bringing full persuasion, as is evidence in his claim that if "any of the foregoing

---

111. Fuller, *On Spiritual Declension*, in *WAF*, 3:632. Fuller has Britain as his subject without qualification, but later in the sentence cites "British churches," therefore, I've provided brackets for clarity.

112. Fuller, *On Spiritual Declension*, in *WAF*, 3:632. Fuller's usage "spiritual beauty" bears the marks of Jonathan Edwards, notably *The Nature of True Virtue* but also echoes aesthetic themes in other works. Virtue, writes Edwards, "is the beauty of the qualities and exercises of the heart, or those actions which proceed from them," 2; Whereas, ". . .secondary beauty differs from a sensation of primary and spiritual beauty, consisting in a spiritual union and agreement" (*Ethical Writings* in *WJE*, 8:33).

113. Fuller, *On Spiritual Declension and the Means of Revival*, in *WAF*, 3:633.

114. Fuller, *On Spiritual Declension* in *WAF*, 3:633. Aware of the charge of fideism, Fuller counters, "we are not abandoning either thinking, reasoning, or on all occasions even disputing." He seems to have in mind something akin to Jonathan Edwards's "sense of the heart," a deep spiritual dependence on Christ, both immediate and intuitively compelling, as articulated in *A Divine and Supernatural Light* in *WJE*, 17. See also Walton, *Jonathan Edwards, Religious Affections*.

115. Fuller, *On Spiritual Declension*, in *WAF*, 3:634.

papers, should be the means of reclaiming any from the error of their ways, either mental or practical. . ... I shall enjoy the satisfaction of not having written in vain.[116]

Conclusion

In *Evangelicalism in Modern Britain*, David Bebbington argued for conversion as one of four distinguishing marks of evangelicalism. As an evangelical Calvinist, Andrew Fuller understood the importance of personal transformation, and his writings extend this corporately to the sphere of revival. Considering reliance on pragmatic endeavors to initiate and sustain revival in two successive centuries after his death, a reader may be modestly surprised how impractical Fuller's "means" are. Though he affirmed the importance of witnessing to unbelievers, of cultivating Christianity in the home, even of caring for the poor, Fuller's dominant emphasis is on repentance, confession, and personal holiness. Perhaps it would be best to describe Fuller's means as practical, yet not pragmatic.

The efficacy of means depended first, on the sovereign, gracious will of God, and subsequently, the spiritual quality of the individual persons who comprised the collective body of Christ.[117] Although the initiative and approbation of the divine is requisite, Fuller never advocated a kind of Moravian stillness, apt to paralyze those who had not acquired full assurance of salvation. As an initiator of the 1784 Call to Prayer and secretary for the BMS, Fuller believed in the application of means. And yet, when reading his revival writings, one cannot escape the iteration that a person "deal with Christ." Several of the early evangelical figures heretofore mentioned, who drew from the Gospel of Luke the account of Mary and Martha, were fond to draw a conversion application from the words of Jesus, "Only one thing is needful."[118] To this Fuller would surely assent.

---

116. Fuller, *On Spiritual Declension*, in *WAF*, 3:634.

117. See John Howe's comments in the eighth sermon of *The Prosperous State*: "Therefore let us learn, what our own present business must be, to labour to have the causes of common calamity wrought out from ourselves, and the causes of common felicity and prosperity inwrought into ourselves. We cannot tell how to mend the state and condition of the world, and our duty reaches not so far, but we have each of us a work to do at home, in our own bosoms" (Sermon 8:7).

118. Philip Doddridge's widely-disseminated, *The Care of the Soul Urged as the One Thing Needful*, is the earliest usage of this passage to stress conversion. John Wesley preached on this text more than fifty times as did Jonathan Edwards and George Whitefield (Hindmarsh, *Spirit of Evangelicalism*, 1–3); see 280 for endnote.

Broadly considered, the essence of Fuller's means constitute not a set of tools for a task, but a plea to a devoted life. Thus, the sermonic nature of his revival writings possessed a pathos of their own, drawing the listener to respond in action. It is fitting that Fuller saw in the book of Acts the purest embodiment of revival Christianity. Not on sole account of miracles, communal generosity, or emboldened evangelism, did the first generation of Christians serve as a paradigm of revival. Rather, it was the Holy Spirit's power gifted to the Apostles at Pentecost—which Fuller suggestively contextualized as "a prayer meeting." For him, it would be equally true to consider the fruit of revival as a necessary product preceding revival's commencement, as would the judgment that such fruit was the very effect of revival.

Chapter Five

"The Promised Spirit"
Fuller on The Work of The Holy Spirit in Revival

IN SEEKING TO UNDERSTAND Andrew Fuller's theology of revival, this book has discussed Fuller's theological development, personal and literary influences, experiences of revival, and consequent application of means to that end. As explored in chapter three, the Northamptonshire Baptist Association's institution of the 1784 Call to Prayer was heavily indebted to Jonathan Edwards's *Humble Attempt to Extraordinary Prayer*.[1] Considering the enduring outcomes of the Prayer Call, and *Humble Attempt*'s contribution to the theology of the Northamptonshire Association's pastors, Andrew Fuller included, examination of the treatise warrants attention.[2] Several works by Fuller parallel notable themes contained in Edwards's succinct book on prayer.

Fuller's understanding of the Holy Spirit's relationship to revival is connected to several eschatological motifs drawn from Edwards. Though

---

1. The degree of *Humble Attempt*'s impact on Ryland, Sutcliff, and Fuller becomes clear when considering that the Call to Prayer was established in April 1784, only days after these pastors read the book. At the time of its first publication in 1747, *Humble Attempt* bore a lengthy 145-word title. The 1784 publication, though significantly shorter than in 1747, and still long by modern standards, reads: *An Humble Attempt to promote an explicit agreement and visible union of God's people through the world, in extraordinary prayer, for the revival of religion and the advancement of Christ's kingdom on earth, pursuant to Scripture promises and prophecies concerning the last time*(Edwards, *Apocalyptic Writings* in *WJE*, 5:309–436).

2. The Prayer Call became a denominational catalyst for overseas missions that saw its culmination in the evangelistic work of William Carey. In several respects, *Humble Attempt* prompted and sustained the Modern Missions Movement. This is argued by Young, "Andrew Fuller and the Modern Missionary Movement," 17–27. See also, Piggin, "Expanding Knowledge of God," 266–96.

a generally optimistic view concerning a spiritualized earthly millennial reign of Christ was shared by Puritan predecessors such as John Howe, Fuller's views derive primarily from the New England divine. An essential belief that the millennial reign of Revelation 20 was imminent inspired the Northamptonshire Association to pray fervently for revival.[3] Two works by Fuller encapsulate his understanding of revival and the activity of the Holy Spirit: an 1810 circular letter, *On the Promise of the Spirit* and undated sermon, *A Few Persuasives to 'A General Union in Prayer' for the Revival of Religion*.[4] As in other works on the subject, compatibilist patterns undergird Fuller's theology of revival.

Jonathan Edwards, The Concert of Prayer, and *Humble Attempt*

The magnitude of the revivals that unfolded during Jonathan Edwards's ministry, particularly the years 1740–42, were unprecedented in American history up to that time. Traditionally termed the "Great Awakening," some recent historians have argued that religious stirrings in the middle colonies and the southern frontier in the 1750s and 60s should be given placement alongside New England's revivals.[5] The Awakening's origins, however, are widely accepted, and Jonathan Edwards was at the forefront.[6] As a young

---

3. Thomas Kidd observes that although New England pastors like Edwards believed the millennium recorded in Rev 20 would be preceded by an increase in wickedness and expansion of the true church, most rarely agreed on the fine point of eschatology and frequently shifted their views. He therefore judges any equation of eighteenth-century millennial thought with either post or pre-millennial theological camps "fruitless," see Kidd, "Very Vital Breath of Christianity," 28. See also, 19–33. Edwards firmly believed that all great historic outpourings of the Spirit were accompanied by prayer and the "Concert of Prayer" in *Humble Attempt* is the product of this conviction.

4. Fuller, *A General Union of Prayer for the Revival of Religion* in WAF, 3:666–70; Fuller, *Promise of the Spirit and the Grand Encouragement in Promoting the Gospel* in WAF, 3:359–66.

5. If such premises are acceptable, periodic revivals formed a continuous series that extended beyond the Revolutionary period. By implication, the term "Second Great Awakening" is misleading. Rather, one finds a "long First Great Awakening," a long-term turn toward Baptist and Methodist piety from the American Revolution to the Civil War, punctuated by new revivals like one at Cane Ridge, Kentucky, in 1801. This view is espoused by Erik Seeman, who argues that revivals in the 1760s form a continuity (*Pious Persuasions*, 174–77), and Kidd, *Great Awakening*, 252, 321). By contrast, historians such as Noll (*America's God*, 161–63) and Butler (*Awash in a Sea of Faith*, 223–24), consider the late eighteenth century a period of spiritual decline for evangelicals.

6. Packer, *Quest for Godliness*, 309–28. David Bebbington finds it noteworthy that

pastor, Edwards witnessed what became known as the Northampton and Connecticut Valley Awakenings in 1734-35.[7] Among towns where the grandchildren and great grandchildren of English Puritans had lost the religious zeal that distinguished their ancestors, local pastors witnessed a newfound conviction over sin, and a renewed interest in preaching.[8]

The revivals of 1734-35 were a prelude to what would occur less than a decade later. Through the fiery preaching of the British evangelist George Whitfield, tens of thousands of New Englanders were converted. Scores of men and women during this time including Edwards's wife, Sarah, experienced powerful, and unusual manifestations of the Holy Spirit.[9] The Awakening was not without its critics—some of whom were a part of Edwards's own household. Bizarre and erratic behavior among some participants impugned the reputation of the Awakening, and consequently, its defenders.[10] As a moderate, Jonathan Edwards devoted extensive thought to

as early as 1775 twelve of Edwards's published works in America pertained to revival ("Remembered Around the World," 181).

7. Edwards recounts the 1734-1735 revival in *Faithful Narrative* (in *WJE*, 4:99-205). Edwards's other revival works can be found in *The Great Awakening* vol. 4.

8. Edward's grandfather, Solomon Stoddard longed for revival in his lifetime, and did experience periodic small-scale movements under his ministry at Northampton. In late 1727, when Edwards was transitioning as Stoddard's successor, a powerful earthquake shook New England, leading to an immediate spiritual shift, with many congregants claiming conversion experiences. Stoddard did not live to see revivals the extent of which would accompany his grandson's ministry (Marsden, *Jonathan Edwards*, 114-24). On Stoddard see Miller, "Solomon Stoddard," 298.

9. In *Some Thoughts*, Edwards made veiled reference to Sarah's mystical experiences that began with the 1735 Northampton revivals, and with increasing intensity after 1739. At various times, her body would go limp, sometimes for hours. She would speak of heavenly visions and of an overwhelming peace. Such occurrences happened during church services and at home. Although his own experiences did not match his wife's, Jonathan never questioned the genuineness of the experiences, or the veracity of Sarah's faith. See also Edwards, *Thoughts Concerning Revival* in *WJE*, 4:331-32, 341; and Marsden, *Jonathan Edwards*, 139-52.

10. An infamous character who embodied the revivalist excesses for a brief time, James Davenport (1716-1757) excoriated local pastors, especially those critical of revival, instigated a book burning, and even encouraged burning clothes to signify renunciation of worldliness. Davenport later renounced his actions in *Davenport's Confession and Retraction*. For an extended account of Davenport's life and ministry see Goen, *Revivalism and Separatism*, 17-27. Davenport was not the sole radical of the time. Others included itinerant preachers James and Daniel Rogers and Andrew Croswell (Kidd, "Daniel Rogers' Egalitarian Great Awakening," 111-35). The instantaneous healing of Mercy Wheeler in 1743—two years after Whitefield—substantiates claims of the miraculous that could not easily be dismissed as psychological manipulation (Kidd, *Great Awakening: The Roots of Evangelical Christianity in Colonial America*, 162-63). In scholarly circles, the Great Awakening is no less disputed (Lambert's *Inventing the "Great Awakening."*)

an array of factors, natural and spiritual, employing painstaking efforts to rightly discern what experiences signified regeneration. He concluded that the effects accompanying a genuine work of the Holy Spirit as an "increase of sweetness, rest and humility," and "delight in singing praises to God and Jesus Christ."[11] Against "Old Lights" such as Charles Chauncy, he defended the revivals until his death, and a famous outburst—"If this be distraction, I pray God that the world of mankind may all be seized with this benign, meek, beneficent, glorious distraction"—captures Edwards's ethos.[12]

In response to naysayers, Edwards published *A Treatise on Religious Affections*, a remarkable and penetrating work of religious psychology.[13] In *Religious Affections*, Edwards seeks to defend the evangelical revivals, but only after proposing a careful and comprehensive thesis that "true religion, in great part, exists in holy affections."[14] His astute analysis seeks to account for the variegated outcomes of the Awakening. Rather than simply acknowledge the spuriousness of individual conversions, Edwards sought to explain why, and even how this happens. In Part III, he devotes attention to distinguishing the Holy Spirit's work in regenerate and unregenerate, respectively.[15] To describe the revival to which he was intimately acquainted, Edwards employs an arboreal metaphor.

> It appears plainly to have been in the visible church of God, in times of great reviving of religion from time to time, as it is with the fruit of trees in the spring; there are a multitude of blossoms, all of which appear fair and beautiful, and there is a promising of young fruits; but many of them are of short continuance; they

---

11. Edwards, *Great Awakening* in *WJE* 4:334; 337 and *Distinguishing Marks* in *WJE* 4:214–88. See also, Jenson, *America's Theologian*, 75.

12. See Edwards, *Great Awakening*, in *WJE*, 4:341. Chauncy (1705–1787) was a vocal critic of Edwards and the New Lights throughout Edwards's lifetime. Chauncy's 1743 publication, *Seasonable Thoughts on the State of Religion in New England* was a rebuttal to Edwards's own work published the same year, *Thoughts Concerning the Present Revival* in New England. For Chauncy's activity in the 1740s, see Gaustad, *Great Awakening*, 80–101 and Noll, *Rise of Evangelicalism*, 129–30. Opinions varied from superficial and emotion-centered commitments, to psychological manipulation—even the device of Satan himself.

13. Edwards, *Religious Affections*, in *WJE*, vol. 2.

14. Edwards, *Religious Affections*, in *WJE*, 2:23.

15. Edwards, *Religious Affections*, in *WJE*, 2:124–65. Edwards concedes that unregenerate individuals can be filled with the spirit and thereby outwardly exhibit seemingly authentic signs. His keen analysis leads to a distinction between the saints, of whom the Spirit is "a vital principle in their souls" and thus "exerts and communicates himself in his own proper nature." As for hypocrites, the Spirit, may act in ways, "agreeable to His nature, yet may not at all communicate Himself in His proper nature, in the effect of that action" (*Religious Affections*, in *WJE*, 2:28–29).

soon fall off, and never come to maturity. . .for though there never will, in this world, be an entire purity, either in particular saints, in a perfect freedom from mixtures of corruption.[16]

For Edwards, blame lies not in revival itself, but ". . .the mixture of counterfeit religion with true, not discerned and distinguished," for which reason, ". . .the devil has had the greatest advantage against the cause and kingdom of Christ all along hitherto."[17] In the years following New England's Awakening, religious lethargy returned to the churches. Yet this declension did not dampen Edwards pastoral and evangelistic passion, nor his disillusionment with revival. Rather, he longed to see it again, not just in New England, but around the world. At this juncture, in 1747, he composed *An Humble Attempt for Extraordinary Prayer*.[18]

Humble Attempt: The Proposal

Though Edwards wrote *Humble Attempt* only six years after Whitfield's monumental preaching tour, his assessment of New England's piety is strikingly bleak—in his own words, "lamentable." In Puritan fashion, and a posture later adopted by Andrew Fuller, Edwards contrasts his generation's religious indifference with the piety of their forbearers. He blames ministers and churches who have neglected the ordinances or failed to discipline errant members. Furthermore, the conduct associated with Davenport and others he deemed, "gross delusions of the devil." He perceives a tragic irony that such claimants would indulge in antinomian excesses under the guise of spiritual purity and zeal.[19]

Reflecting on revival, Edwards acknowledges a broad-spectrum of error inside and outside the church.[20] For a source of remedial inspiration, Edwards looked to several Scottish pastors who committed to concerted prayer beginning in 1740.[21] In 1744, the Scottish clergy conducted a

16. Edwards, *Religious Affections*, in *WJE*, 2:88

17. Edwards, *Religious Affections*, in *WJE*, 2:88.

18. *Humble Attempt* was not released until 1748. See Marsden, *Jonathan Edwards*, 334; Murray, *Jonathan Edwards*, 295.

19. Edwards, *Humble Attempt*, part II, sec. vii in *WJE*, 5:357–58.

20. Edwards speaks in further detail on the topic of discrimination and the need for scripture as criterions of judgment in *Thoughts Concerning Revival*, in *WJE* 4:293–347.

21. There was precedent within the Scottish tradition of revival going back to 1630, notably at Kirk O' Shotts. Yet most important were the small "praying societies" established in 1630 which placed specific focus on conversion. These continued into the eighteenth century. See Drummond and Bullock, *Scottish Church*, chs. 1–3. Also, Mitchell, "Jonathan Edwards's Scottish Connection," 222–47. Fawcett, *Cambuslang*

two-year "experiment" uniting various prayer societies with a singular focus on revival. The designated times were Saturday evening, Sunday morning, and the first Tuesday of each quarter.[22] The salutary effects of the experiment warranted a published account titled, *Memorial*, which called for prayer in churches worldwide. Five-hundred copies were sent to Boston, one of which Edwards acquired. He admired the tract for several reasons, including its anonymity, and potential to mobilize Christians for prayer. Edwards believed that in composing *Humble Attempt*, he could provide the theological basis for the *Memorial*'s vision.[23]

Edwards divided *Humble Attempt* into four major sections. Part One is a response to the *Memorial* itself. Part Two Discusses the promises for latter-day glory, that is, the millennial reign of Christ.[24] Part Three reviews motives for united prayer. Part Four answers objections to the Prayer Call. Edwards gives a brief preface to each section outlining the proposed direction. Eschatology is the heartbeat of *Humble Attempt*, and Zech 8:20–22 is its central text. The Authorized Version reads,

> Thus saith the Lord of hosts, It shall yet come to pass, and there shall come people, and the inhabitants of many cities; and the inhabitants of one city shall go to another saying, 'Let us go speedily to pray before the LORD, and to seek the LORD of hosts: I will go also. Yea, many people and strong nations shall come to seek the LORD of hosts in Jerusalem, and to pray before the LORD.

The hermeneutical hinge on which Edwards's exegesis turns is found in the typological nature of prophetic fulfillment.[25] Edwards asserts that Zechariah 8 is "a prophecy of a future glorious advancement of the church of God, wherein it is evident that something further is intended than ever

---

Revival, 54–74, and Robe, *Faithful Narrative*.

22. David Bryant, introduction to *Humble Attempt*, 16. Bryant of the PCUSA did more than any other leader to promote Edwards's concerts of prayer as a practice in American evangelicalism. See Bryant, *With Concerts of Prayer*. Cf. Smart, "Edwards's Revival Instinct," 133–63.

23. Bryant, *With Concerts of Prayer*, 17.

24. Davidson, *Logic of Millennial Thought*. On Puritan views of the millennium see Gribben, *Puritan Millennium*; Murray, *Puritan Hope*.

25. See Stein, "Quest for the Spiritual Sense," 99–113. David Barshinger advocates the broader, descriptive label: "redemptive historical" in "Making the Psalter One's 'Own Language,'" 28. Cf. Abernathy, "Jonathan Edwards," 815–17. For early history of typology, see Goppelt, *Typos* and Danielou, *From Shadows to Reality*. See Holmes, *God of Grace*, 99–123 for discussion and synopsis of Edwards's use of typology.

was fulfilled to the Jewish nation under the Old Testament."[26] Like many interpreters of the history of the church, Edwards believed scripture abounds with various "types" and "shadows" that signify past, present, or future realities, particularly ancient Israel's correspondence with the New Testament church..[27] Edwards stood in the American colonial Puritan tradition whose very self-understanding as the "New Israel" resulted in application prophecies to national life, not just the history of redemption.[28] Beyond typology, Edwards's philosophy of history, or properly, his theology of history, was grand in scope, with Christ's redemption being central. Only a vision of such magnitude could warrant a work Edwards never completed: *A History of the Work of Redemption*.[29] Thus, the minutest event in history was meaningful in the overarching scheme.[30] Nothing was accidental or insignificant. Every dimension of life, including eighteenth-century New England was worthy of investigation.[31] Robert Jenson's insight is apt: "the history of the

26. Edwards, *Humble Attempt*, Part I, in *WJE*, 5:312. Edwards explains the application of this text: ". . .we have an account how this future glorious advancement of the church of God should be brought on, or introduced; viz., by great multitudes in different towns and countries taking up a joint resolution and coming into an express and visible agreement, that they will, by united and extraordinary prayer, seek to God that he would come and manifest himself, and grant the tokens and fruits of his gracious presence" (Edwards, *Humble Attempt*, 5:314). Note the similarities to John Howe's hermeneutic, exegesis, and even application in *Prosperous State* (1678). See ch. 1.

27. Edwards's repeated concern for the visibility of the church is connected with language of glory. Thus, Holmes concludes, "in the church the beauty of God, which is the presence of the Holy Spirit, should be seen, and so there is a need for harmony and consent amongst the members of the Church. If the Church, that is, is to reflect God's own beautiful nature back to Him, then it must be beautiful" (*God of Grace and God of Glory*, 194).

28. Holmes notes that though Samuel Mather's standard *Manual Figures or Types of the Old Testament* insisted on defining typology as "some outward or sensible thing ordained of God under the Old Testament to represent and hold forth something of Christ in the New," the rules were often broken (*God of Grace and God of Glory*, 104). Kidd cites several New England preachers in the 1760s whose millennial expectations and/or prophecies placed America at its forefront. Among these were Samuel Buell (1716–98) and the radical Jacob Johnson (1713–97) of Groton, CT (*Great Awakening: The Roots of Evangelical Christianity in Colonial America*, 276–87).

29. In *WJE*, vol. 9.

30. Indicative of Edwards's ambitious quest is "Concerning the End for which God Created the World," in *Ethical Writings*, in *WJE*, vol. 8. For a recent sympathetic evaluation of Edwards's metaphysical proposals for creation see Schultz, "Metaphysics of Edwards's End of Creation," 339–59.

31. Notebooks recording personal thoughts reveal a young Edwards's fascination with eschatology and the book of Revelation in particular. Living in New York City as an interim pastor in 1722, Edwards would absorb the latest news from abroad and seek to connect current events with prophecies in the Apocalypse. Reflecting on his

world, as Edwards tells it, just *is* the history of the church on its way from sin to deification. . . .. [a]t every step, great and small, God's pragmatism is to triumph through adversity, by 'remarkable outpourings of the spirit.'"[32]

Jonathan Edwards believed God providentially guided history to a definitive telos. *Humble Attempt* challenges the reader to take prophecies such as Zechariah 8 seriously, and Edwards's reading of such texts leads him to conclude that their fulfillment has yet to be accomplished. Thus, he can write, "There never happened anything, from the time of the prophet Zechariah to the coming of Christ, to answer this prophecy."[33] Edwards maintains that neither historical events in ancient Israel, nor future fulfillment at the eschaton, properly account for this text. If the prophet's words speak of a blessedness yet experienced, then why, he reasons, can it not be accomplished through Christ's church today—specifically through the modicum of prayer?

Reflecting on ancient Israel's Babylonian captivity coupled with their return to Canaan, Edwards transitions from the original historical context in the book of Zechariah to a typological, spiritual, and plausibly, superior interpretation for the Christian church.

> We find it common in the prophecies of the Old Testament, that when the prophets are speaking of divine favours and blessings on the Jews—attending or following their return from the Babylonish captivity—the Spirit of God takes occasion thence to speak of the incomparably greater blessings on the church, that shall attend and follow her deliverance from spiritual or

---

days in New York, Edwards later recalled, "If I heard the least hint of any thing that happened in any part of the world, that appeared to me, in some respect or other, to have a favourable aspect on the interest of Christ's kingdom, my soul eagerly catched at it; and it would much animate and refresh me. I used to be earnest to read public newsletters, mainly for that end; to see if I could not find some news favorable to the interest of religion in the world (*Letters and Personal Writings* in *WJE*, 16:797). See Marsden, *Jonathan Edwards*, 48. Edwards ministered in New York only two years after Theodore Frelinghuysen (1691–1747)—considered by many as a forerunner and catalyst of the First Great Awakening—preached his inaugural sermon. On Frelinghuysen's life, see Beeke and Pronk, biographical introduction to Beeke, *Forerunner of the Great Awakening*, vii–xxxviii. For a comprehensive annotated bibliography of sources, see 335–39.

32. Jenson, *America's Theologian*, 178.

33. Edwards, *Humble Attempt* in *WJE*, 5:312. Again, among eighteenth-century New England pastors, Edwards's hermeneutic was not anomalous. Reflecting on New England's revivals, Samuel Buell could ask how skeptics could maintain that, "the influences of the Holy Spirit were confin'd to the Apostolick Age, and are not now to be expected. . . .The days are not very far off, when such Outpourings of the Spirit will become more frequent and general among the Lord's people: And in the Process of Time, the world Over" (*Faithful Narrative*, 42).

mystical Babylon, of which those were a type, and then speaks almost wholly of these latter and vastly greater things, so as to seem to forget the former.[34]

Herein lies part of the unique appeal of *Humble Attempt*. It draws readers to pray toward a goal. A glorious and fruitful period of world history can be attained through the concerted prayer of the saints. Edwards's optimistic, even triumphant vision, though tepidly received in New England, would be received eagerly, and applied concretely by Ryland, Sutcliff and Andrew Fuller three decades after Edwards's death.

Reception of Humble Attempt by Northamptonshire Association

As noted previous, the vision of concerted prayer in *Humble Attempt* did not take root in New England during Jonathan Edwards's lifetime, though a concert of prayer was initiated by Princeton students in 1758.[35] *Humble Attempt* was introduced to the English context upon republication by John Sutcliff 1789.[36] Sutcliff's enthusiastic promotion of Edwards's treatise stemmed from personal experience; he and fellow ministers of the Northamptonshire Baptist Association had adopted the book's principles five years earlier, instituting their own concert of prayer for revival and global extension of Christ's kingdom.

Only months after reading *Humble Attempt*, Andrew Fuller was scheduled to preach at the Northamptonshire Association meeting in June 1784. In a sermon from 2 Cor 5:7 titled *The Nature and Importance of Walking by Faith*, Fuller exhorted his hearers to unite in earnest prayer for the cause of Christ around the globe. Correlation between the tenor of Fuller's sermon and the content of *Humble Attempt* has been noted, particularly Fuller's appeals that hearers engage in "earnest and united prayer" for an "outpouring of God's Spirit," not only among Particular Baptists—"those only of our own

---

34. Edwards, *Humble Attempt*, in *WJE*, 5:314.

35. Bryant, *With Concerts of Prayer*, 19. The university did experience periodic awakenings during the next 100 years. Some references to these accounts can be found in Moorhead, *Princeton Seminary*.

36. On Sutcliff's life and work see Haykin, *One Heart and Soul*. On his involvement in the 1784 Call to Prayer and promotion of *Humble Attempt* see 152–71. See Hindmarsh, "Reception of Jonathan Edwards," 201–21. *Humble Attempt* was adopted and promoted by William Carey as a catalyst for global missions. It also served to inspire participants in subsequent revivals, particularly in nineteenth-century America.

connexion"—but upon, "all that in every place call upon the name of Jesus Christ our Lord, both theirs and ours (1 Cor 1:2)."[37]

After preaching the *Walking by Faith* sermon, the invigorating effects of *Humble Attempt* on Fuller and the Northamptonshire Association's pastors, is evident from a diary entry one month later in May 1784.[38] Several subsequent entries substantiate this positive perspective.[39] Jonathan Edwards's optimism concerning the future prospect of the church on earth enlivened the English Particular Baptist denomination, fanning the flames of evangelistic fervor. The Northamptonshire Association interpreted *Humble Attempt* in the precise manner Edwards intended: as a theological justification for concerted prayer. In his introduction for Section Two Edwards draws from the Zechariah 8 text a rationale for churches across the globe to join in concerted prayer for the advance of Christ's kingdom and therefore, receive "the tokens and fruit of his gracious presence."[40]

John Sutcliff's 1789 republication of *Humble Attempt* included in the preface a narration of the 1784 Prayer Call. Though brief, the preface describes the formation of prayer meetings in Northampton and Leicester counties, and their growth to adjacent regions in 1786. Sutcliff notes that such meetings could not be deemed sectarian as they included paedobaptist churches. Their expressed focus was the expansion of Christ's kingdom, not denominational advancement. In Sutcliff's own words, "The republication of the following work is with the avowed design of promoting the above agreement and practice."[41] Sutcliff's endorsement of *Humble Attempt*, however, was not the result of blind and unbridled enthusiasm. In his preface, Sutcliff renders a mild, but definite disclaimer pertaining to some of Edwards's prophetic interpretations, something Andrew Fuller would also

---

37. Haykin, *One Heart and Soul*, 163. See Fuller, *Nature and Importance of Walking by Faith*, in *WAF*, 1:131. Fuller's concern that the concerted prayer include believers of other "connexions" (i.e. denominations), is consistent with John Howe's own vision that an effusion of the Spirit would include a visible union between churches.

38. "Read to our friends this evening, a part of Mr. Edwards's Attempt to Promote Prayer for the Revival of Religion, to excite them to the like practice. Felt my heart profited, and much solemnized by what I read." See also, Ryland, *Fuller*, 97.

39. A diary entry from December 6, 1784 reads, "had an affecting meeting of prayer" ("Diary and Spiritual Thoughts," in Ryland, *Fuller*, 103). March 7, 1785 reads, "enjoyed divine assistance at the monthly prayer meeting, in speaking on continuing in prayer, and in going to prayer, though I felt wretchedly cold before I began" (Ryland, *Fuller*, 105).

40. Edwards, *Humble Attempt*, in *WJE*, 5:314.

41. Sutcliff, "Preface by a Former English Editor" May 4, 1789 in *Humble Attempt*, 29.

do.⁴² Though he does not disavow Edwards's hermeneutical method, nor minimize the difficulty in interpreting Old Testament prophetic passages, Sutcliff, offers the following cautious, if not prosaic comment:

> In the present and imperfect state, we may reasonably expect a diversity of sentiments upon religious matters. Each ought to think for himself, and everyone has a right, on proper occasions, to show his opinion. Yet all should remember that there are but two parties in the world, each engaged in opposite causes; the cause of God and of Satan; of holiness and sin; of heaven and hell.⁴³

As noted, *Humble Attempt*'s impressions on Fuller's preaching are evident in his sermon *The Nature and Importance of Walking by Faith*. The influence of this work, however, extends deeper, contributing unique aspects to Fuller's theology of revival. His corpus, particularly sermons and scriptural commentary share with Jonathan Edwards a markedly optimistic eschatology, particularly as relates to a spiritualized millennial reign.⁴⁴ Edwards spoke glowingly of the church's worldwide advancement propelled by concerted prayer. Andrew Fuller embraced the vision that an unprecedented period of gospel flourishing was imminent. Corporate intercession would function as the obedient response to the divine will revealed in scripture. For Fuller and Edwards, a most certain end—the church's global expansion, and essential human means—prayer and preaching, were fully compatible.

Circular Letter: On the Promise of the Spirit

The Promise of the Spirit the Grand Encouragement in Promoting the Gospel, a circular letter written by Fuller in 1810, provides crucial insight into Andrew Fuller's pneumatology. Its intended purpose, expressed in the self-descriptive title shares several motifs with *Humble Attempt* including Christ's millennial reign, Old Testament prophecy, revival, and corporate prayer—with the Spirit's work identified as the unifying element.⁴⁵ The the-

---

42. Sutcliff states: "By republishing the following work, I do not consider myself as becoming answerable for every sentiment it contains. An author and editor are very distinct characters. Should any entertain different views respecting some of the prophecies in the inspired page, from those that are here advanced, yet such may, and I hope will, approve of the general design" ("Preface," 30).

43. Sutcliff, "Preface," 30.

44. For a detailed analysis on *Humble Attempt* and its influencing Andrew Fuller's missiology, see Chun, *Legacy*, 66–83. Morden calls the similarities between the 1784 Call to Prayer and Humble Attempt, "striking" (*Offering Christ*, 124.)

45. Fuller, *Promise of the Spirit*, in *WAF*, 3:359–63.

sis of this text, perhaps best drawn from its concluding paragraph, is that "the time for the promulgation of the gospel is come; and, if attended to in a full dependence on the Spirit, it will, no doubt, be successful."[46] Though this work is not explicitly intended as a revival sermon, revival is within its purview as references to spiritual renewal attest. Furthermore, the Holy Spirit's role in revival, crucial in Andrew Fuller's theology, renders it worthy of examination.

Fuller beings the letter with praise for his audience, pastors of the Northamptonshire Association, who appointed designated times of prayer eighteen-years earlier for the sake of overseas missions, and interprets the sending of these missionaries and their consequent success as a sign of divine approbation.[47] Fuller stresses throughout, that the Holy Spirit's work to advance the gospel draws believers away from two extreme, erroneous positions, namely that, "converting the heathen is either extremely easy or absolutely impossible."[48] He proceeds with examples from the biblical text where God's people were preserved despite religious apostasy and political disarray. He acknowledges the Spirit's work in those times, but, like John Howe, perceives a more powerful manifestation yet to come upon the church. Hence, we read,

> Consider, brethren, the dispensation under which we live. We are under the kingdom of the Messiah, fitly called, "the ministration of the Spirit," because the rich effusions of the Holy Spirit are reserved for his reign, the great accessions to the church from among the Gentiles ordained to grace his triumphs. It was fit that the death of Christ should be followed by the outpourings of the Spirit, that it might appear to be what it was, its proper effect; and that which was seen in the days of Pentecost was but an earnest of what is yet to come. To pray under such a dispensation is coming to God in good time.[49]

---

46. Fuller, *Promise of the Spirit*, in *WAF*, 3:363. Reliance on the Holy Spirit is a noteworthy detail, and his led historians such as Thomas Kidd to add to David Bebbington's Quadrilateral a fifth element—the importance of the Holy Spirit—to the standard classification of evangelicalism as biblicism, conversion, crucentricism, and activism.

47. Alluding to the founding of the BMS, Fuller notes that, "It was in prayer that the late undertakings for spreading the gospel among the heathen originated. We have seen success enough attend them to encourage us to go forward" (*Promise of the Spirit* in *WAF*, 3:359, 362).

48. Fuller, *Promise of the Spirit*, in *WAF*, 3:360. Fuller writes, "Those who disown" the Holy Spirt, apply its work to the miraculous gifts given to the Apostolic period alone, and now assume that men can be converted "by the mere influence of moral suasion" (*Promise of the Spirit*, in *WAF*, 359).

49. Fuller, *Promise of the Spirit*, in *WAF*, 362. Compare similar comments found

Fuller returns to the promise that Christ's spiritual presence in the church today is a surety of success. He cites various passages including God opening the heart of Lydia in Acts 18. Additionally, 2 Cor 2:14, "God always causeth us to triumph," and 10:4, "the weapons of warfare are mighty through God to the pulling down of strongholds." Fuller even contextualizes The Pentecostal event, noting that, "It was from a prayer-meeting, held in an upper-room, that the first Christians descended, and commenced that noble attack on Satan's kingdom in which three thousand fell before them."[50] Fuller proceeds from New Testament examples to Church history. Drawing from Daniel seven, he describes the four powers: Babylonian, Persian, Greek, and Roman, with the last "subdivided into ten kingdoms, and the little papal horn growing up among them."[51] Throughout his life, Fuller was unequivocal in insisting that the Roman Catholic Church is Babylon of Revelation 18 and that the Pope is antichrist. He draws much confidence from any declension in predominantly Catholic nation-states, including an overall numerical decrease. Such events, in Fuller's interpretive framework, were a prelude to nascent millennial blessings.[52] Fuller concludes by exhorting the church to press onward with confidence and alacrity, noting that the advancement of Christ's kingdom may go unnoticed—even at times by believers—for extended periods.[53]

Returning briefly to *Humble Attempt*, when Jonathan Edwards composed this work, he believed himself to be situated in a historically-unique time for Protestant Christianity, a notion shared by many contemporaries.[54] Major sections of *Humble Attempt* contain citations in direct reference, or allusion to, gospel advancement in the last days. Part II shares several

throughout John Howe's *Prosperous State*.

50. Fuller, *Promise of the Spirit*, in *WAF*, 3:360.

51. Fuller, *Promise of the Spirit*, in *WAF*, 3:362. Fuller's views on Catholicism and the papacy in particular is typical of most Protestants since the Reformation, particularly those of the eighteenth century.

52. Fuller, *Promise of the Spirit*, in *WAF*, 3:362. Commenting on the supposed decline of Catholicism in his day, Fuller writes, "We have seen his rise, and, in a considerable degree, his downfall" (*Promise of the Spirit*, in *WAF*, 362). At various junctures, and prior to the Napoleonic Wars, Fuller ascribes the French Revolution to this end (*Times of the Millennium* (1815), in *WAF*, 1:608–12).

53. Fuller, *Promise of the Spirit*, in *WAF*, 3:363.

54. Edwards, *Great Awakening*, in *WJE*, 4:215–23, esp. 215, 216, 217. William Cooper of Brattle Street Church deemed the present "evangelical dispensation" as "the brightest day that ever shone," and claimed that, "The dispensation that we are now under is certainly such as neither we nor our fathers have seen; and in such circumstances so wonderful, that I believe there has not been the like since the extraordinary pouring out of the spirit immediately after our Lord's ascension" (Marsden, *Jonathan Edwards*, 235–36).

themes and patterns with Fuller's *Promise of the Spirit* sermon. In Section One, "The latter-day glory not yet accomplished," Edwards reasons that, "It is natural and reasonable the world should finally be given to Christ, as one whose right it is to reign, as the proper heir of him is originally the King of all nations, and possessor of heaven and earth." Edwards perceives the Trinitarian missions, and particularly Christ's mediatorial office, make certain his kingly triumph. As "heir of the world"—the Messianic conqueror of Psalm two—Christ has been promised the nations as his inheritance.[55] Fuller agreed with Edwards on this point, considering his own era as unprecedented in redemptive history.[56]

In section five of *Humble Attempt*, "Precepts, Encouragements, Examples," Edwards explains why the church should be hopeful that their present prayers will be answered. He posits that their confidence lay in the compatible arrangement between God's sovereign decrees and duties incumbent on his servants. In a separate work, Edwards maintains that although God is not "properly moved or made willing by our prayers" he often appears "as though he were prevailed on by prayer."[57] He reasons that scriptural promises serve to encourage believers towards faithful intercession. Paradoxically, prayer remains a duty in so much that it is the means preceding, and accompanying, the ordained end.[58] This, asserts Edwards, affords believers "the strongest assurances that their prayers will be *successful.*[59] Fuller agreed with Edwards on this point, grounding confidence and

---

55. Edwards, *Humble Attempt*, in *WJE*, 5:330. Edwards cites Heb 1:2 and 2:8 as well as Ps 2:6–8. Fuller will cite Ps 2 as being fulfilled through the kingdom's advancement (*Promise of the Spirit a Grand Encouragement in Promoting the Gospel*, in *WAF*, 3:668). Edwards does note the comprehensive e nature of kingdom—its consummation being fulfilled in the last judgment, but also sees the church's dominion extending across the globe preceding the eschaton.

56. Fuller, *Promise of the Spirit*, in *WAF*, 3:362.

57. Edwards, *Most High a Prayer-Hearing God*, in *WJE*, 2:116. In *Freedom of the Will*, Edwards labors extensively to prove that contingency cannot properly apply to God and is incompatible with sovereignty (sec. 3, "Concerning the Meaning of the Terms Necessity, Impossibility, Inability, Etc., and of Contingence," and sec. 12, "God's Certain Foreknowledge of The Future Volitions of Moral Agents, Inconsistent with Such a Contingence of Those Volitions, as is Without All Necessity" (*WJE* 1:149–55; 257–70). See also Fuller's comments that, "Though there is nothing in our doings from which we could look for such great things," yet, "God is pleased frequently to crown our poor services with infinite reward" (*Causes of Declension in Religion* in *WAF*, 3:323).

58. Recall John Owen's assertion that "The Holy Spirit so worketh *in us* as that he worketh *by us*, and what he doth in us is done by us. Out duty is to apply ourselves unto his commands, according to the conviction of our minds; and his work is to enable us to perform them" (*Pneumatalogia*, in *WJO*: 3:204). See ch. 1.

59. Edwards, *Humble Attempt*, in *WJE*, 5:351.

comfort in prayer from scripture's prophetic word concerning the future kingdom, whose efficacy is grounded in the sovereign will of God.[60] Alluding to Matt 28:20, Fuller writes that Christ's promise to be spiritually present with his church validates believers' confidence in "the great success which prophecy gives us to expect in the latter days."[61]

Sermon: *A Few Persuasives for the Revival of Religion*

In an early undated sermon, *A Few Persuasives to a 'General Union in Prayer' For the Revival of Religion*, preached on corporate prayer, Fuller places a bracketed preface that reads, "Addressed to all who love and long for the coming of Christ's blessed kingdom, and whose hearts may be inclined to unite in seeking its welfare."[62] Thus, it appears he has a broad audience in mind. The sermon contains seven points aimed at exhorting hearers to pursue ardent prayer based on historic deliverances, present events, and future prophetic fulfillments. The message bears affinity to the *Promise of the Spirit* circular letter, with parallel themes, notably the imperative to pray for the outpouring of the Holy Spirit.

Fuller begins by challenging his hearers to consider first, "Christ's readiness to hear prayer, especially on these subjects," and second, "what the Lord has done in times past, and that in answer to prayer."[63] Third, that the majority of people around the globe have never heard the gospel should move them to action, and fourth, Scriptural reasons why God has promised to abundantly bless his church in a forthcoming millennial reign.[64] Fuller makes his fifth point eminently practical, proposing that Baptists pray for fellow countrymen, "connexions" and friends. Point six is simply that his

---

60. Hence, we read in *The Most High a Prayer-hearing God* that when God's people pray, "it is the effect of his intention to show mercy, therefore he pours out the spirit of grace and supplication" (Edwards, *WJE*, 2:116). On the theological complexities of prayer as enjoined with a traditional doctrine of God, see Woznicki, "Is Prayer Redundant?," 333–48.

61. Fuller, *Promise of the Spirit*, in *WAF*, 3:361.

62. Fuller, *A Few Persuasives* in *WAF*, 3:666. See also, 666–70. Joseph Belcher, editor for the Sprinkle Edition of Fuller's Works, notes that the sermon was Fuller's first publication, but does not give its date. Morris and Babcock claim the sermon was given in 1784 and published in 1786. https://books.google.com/books?id=QuEKAAAAYAAJ (80, 83). Mullen gives June, 1784 as the date preached (*Complete Works of Andrew Fuller Volume I*, xxii).

63. Fuller, *Few Persuasives* in *WAF*, 3:666.

64. Fuller, *A Few Persuasives*, in *WAF*, 3:668.

hearers consider that "what is requested is very small," while the seventh proposal, echoed elsewhere in Fuller's writings, encourages his audience that even if they do not perceive their prayers being answered, "It will not be in vain, whatever be the immediate and apparent issue of it."[65] Each of the above points will be noted with respective parallels to *Humble Attempt*.

As for Christ's willingness and ability to answer his people's prayers, Fuller reminds his audience that, ". . .so far is he from being reluctant to grant us these requests, that he is pleased in these matters not only to command us to ask, but to represent himself as waiting to be gracious; yea, as being at our command, as ready to bestow these mercies whenever we shall earnestly pray for them."[66] The person and work of Christ serve to model steadfastness and perseverance in evangelism and missionary endeavors, for he is "pleased to look upon the conversion of sinners as reward enough for all his sorrows."[67] By analogy, the kingdom's present advancement, though demanding arduous labor from its subjects, is a worthwhile sacrifice.

At this juncture, it is appropriate to examine several parallels to the content of Fuller's *Promise of the Spirit* sermon in *Humble Attempt*. In Part II, titled, "Promises for the Latter-Day glory," Edwards presents his third subpoint whose description reads: "How much Christ prayed and labored and suffered, in order to the glory and happiness of that day." He recounts the Trinitarian act of redemption in which Father sends the Son, and both persons send the Holy Spirt. A relationship of unbroken eternal communion between persons is communicated to the church, the object of Triune love.[68] A subsequent subpoint speaks of God's "respect to the prayers of his saints in all his government of the world," and as Christ "standing ready to be gracious to his church," language similar to that found in Fuller's sermon.[69] Edwards even renders an allegorical reading of Song 4:16 as a descriptor of the Holy Spirit's outpouring and the coming of Christ.[70]

---

65. Fuller, *A Few Persuasives*, in *WAF*, 3:668. A diary entry from 1785 in which Fuller, reflecting on the results of their prayer meetings, claims, "even supposing our request should not be granted, yet prayer to God is its own reward" (Ryland, *Fuller*, 107). Like John Howe, Fuller possessed sufficient foresight to understand that later generations often inherit the spiritual blessings of their predecessors.

66. Fuller, *A Few Persuasives*, in *WAF*, 3:668.

67. Fuller, *A Few Persuasives*, in *WAF*, 3:666.

68. Edwards, *Humble Attempt*, in *WJE*, 5:341. These themes were developed in his first published sermon on July 8, 1731: "God glorified in Man's Dependence," in *WJE*, vol. 45.

69. Edwards, *Humble Attempt*, in *WJE*, 5:341.

70. "When the spouse prays for the effusion of the Holy Spirit, and the coming of Christ, by granting the tokens of his spiritual presence in the church, "Awake, O north wind, thou south, blow upon my garden, that the spices thereof may flow out; let my

Edwards, like Fuller, understood the work of Christ, notably, his prayers and sufferings as endured for the sake of future effusions of the Spirit. Employing scriptural language from Hebrews chapter five, Edwards vividly describes Christ's eternal resolve to give his life, "offering up strong crying and tears, and his precious blood to obtain it." On such a basis, he draws the conclusion that, "...surely his disciples and members should also earnestly seek it, and be much in prayer for it."[71] Fuller employs a similar progression of arguments in his *Revival of Religion* of sermon. The redemptive work of Christ performed centuries ago is applicable to the prayer-life of the church, and the prayers of his people should, in fact, reflect his own prayers. Edwards and Fuller were compelled that Christ foresaw what would be accomplished though the church in their own day. This being certain, Fuller can nonetheless plead with his hearers, "let us not be backward on our part."[72]

Fuller's second point in his *Revival of Religion* sermon, a challenge to "Consider what the Lord has done in times past, and that in answer to prayer" echoes the sentiment of Jonathan Edwards, evident in seventeenth-century Puritan discussions on the subject.[73] As the writings of Abraham Cheare and especially John Howe argue, the people of God frequently experience adversity prior to deliverance. Fuller shares a similar perspective when he writes that,

> The church of God was reduced exceedingly low just before the coming of Christ, but what was the conduct of those few who were on God's side? Some of them are distinguished by the character of those who "looked for redemption in Jerusalem," and other are said to have "continued in prayer night and day." At length through the tender mercy of God, their prayers were answered, and "the day-spring from on high visited them![74]

---

beloved come into his garden, and eat his pleasant fruits;" there seems to be an immediate answer to her prayer..." (Edwards, *Humble Attempt*, in *WJE*, 5:353).

71. Edwards, *Humble Attempt*, in *WJE*, 5:345. This is a citation from Heb 5:7 (AV), "who in the days of his flesh, when he had offered up prayers and supplications, with strong crying and tears unto him that was able to save him from death, and was heard in that he feared." Edwards also draws deeply from the Gospel of John, specifically 12:23–32, where Jesus expresses anguish at his impending death, and anticipation of future blessings provided therein. Christ serves therefore, as a model for his church in this regard.

72. Fuller, *A Few Persuasives*, in *WAF*, 3:667.

73. Fuller, *A Few Persuasives*, in *WAF*, 3:667.

74. Fuller, *A Few Persuasives*, in *WAF*, 3:667.

Fuller drew encouragement from the condition of Christ's disciples prior to Pentecost. Though discouraged and downcast, the Apostles waited in prayerful expectation, after which God answered in a powerful and decisive manner. Fuller was convinced that something of a similar nature would happen in his day.[75]

As noted, Fuller's pneumatology as it pertains to his theology of revival is distinctive for its eschatological orientation. The importance of biblical prophecies to foreshadow an outpouring of the Spirit that inaugurates the millennial reign of Christ is likewise, a prominent motif in *Humble Attempt*. In addition to Zechariah 8, a broad-spectrum of passages from the book of Isaiah are interpreted as predicting widespread conversions across the globe.[76] Edwards places particular focus on Isa 45:23, ". . .unto me every knee shall bow." Though the passage should rightly be understood "in so comprehensive a sense as to extend to what shall be accomplished at the day of judgment," yet the wider context suggests fulfillment through the "spreading the gospel of salvation, and the power of grace."[77]

In evaluating Edwards's detailed analysis of Old Testament prophecies, an important consideration is that under his hermeneutic, most predictions in Scripture were believed to have been fulfilled by the eighteenth century. Under such an interpretive scheme, only a brief period preceded the millennial reign of Christ. Andrew Fuller shared the conviction that most prophecies had already been fulfilled in church history.[78] This is most apparent

---

75. Edwards was not discouraged by spiritual declension but rather perceived a pattern that would, paradoxically, anticipate a great work of the Spirit. Fuller himself, drawing from Dan 2:35, says, "Let us not imagine that God has yet done all he intends to do for his church; or that Christ has yet seen of the travail of his soul as to be satisfied. Besides the various promises referred to in the foregoing pages, the first setting up of Christ's kingdom is compared to a little stone, cut out of a mountain without hands, but with which should in time break in pieces all the rest, and become great mountain and *fill the whole earth*" (Fuller, *A Few Persuasives*, in *WAF*, 3:668).

76. These include 45:12, 49:23, 55:12, and 60:16. The entirety of Isa 45:23 reads, "I have sworn by myself, the word is gone out of my mouth in righteousness, and shall not return, that unto me every knee shall bow." Again, note the similarities to John Howe in the *Prosperous State* on citations from Isaiah.

77. Edwards, *Humble Attempt* in *WJE*, 5:330. These subsequent quotations include: "all the ends of the earth look to him that they may be saved," and that they come to him in "righteousness and strength, that in him they might be justified, and might glory." That is, Isa 45:22 and 45:24, respectively.

78. Eschatologically, Edwards maintained preterist views. In *Humble Attempt*, he sees in the apostles' question to Christ prior to his ascension: "*will thou at this time restore the kingdom of Israel?*" (Acts 1:6) as answered in the person of Constantine (272–337 AD). Edwards believed Constantine's conversion to Christianity is a fulfillment of the fifth seal in Rev 6, an answer to the plea, "How long, Lord, holy and true, dost thou not judge and avenge our blood on them that dwell on the earth?" (Chun,

when reading his *Expository Discourses on the Apocalypse*.[79] Fuller, in his *Revival of Religion* sermon asks his audience that, "the present religious state of the world be considered to this end," that is, the church's advancement across the globe. Echoing Edwards's twofold understanding of Isaiah 45, with its respective historical and eschatological fulfillments, Fuller saw the millennial reign as accomplished through worldwide evangelization. Scores of unreached peoples served as impetus to missions. The following is representative of Fuller's perspective on the spiritual state of the world:

> Christianity has not yet made its way, even in name, over one-fifth part of the world. Out of about one thousand millions, who are supposed to inhabit our globe, not above one hundred and seventy millions profess the Christian name; all the rest are heathens, Jews, or Mahomedans; and, of those who profess it, the far greater part are either of the apostate Church of Rome or of the Greek Church, which is nearly as corrupt.[80]

In a diary entry dated July 12, 1784, Fuller records having read part of a poem by John Scott (1730–1783) "on the cruelties of the English in the West Indies," particularly their "causing artificial famines."[81] His ethical concern, evident in the following prayer, provides a clue into Fuller's response to the problem of evil: "My heart felt most earnest desires, that Christ's kingdom might come, when all these cruelties shall cease."[82] The coming of Christ's millennial kingdom functions, in part, as an eschatological theodicy. This entry is illuminating as it shows Fuller's sincere concern for the unjust

---

Legacy, 72–76). Fuller also adopted this interpretation as read in his *Discourses on the Apocalypse*, in *WAF*, 3:227–35.

79. Fuller gives detailed historical explanations of types, symbols, and various referents in *Discourses*, in *WAF*, 3:201–307.

80. Fuller, *A Few Persuasives*, in *WAF*, 3:668.

81. Ryland, *Fuller*, 98. Scott was a Quaker poet and humanitarian know for several works among which *Poetical Works* (1782) had *Serim: or, the Artificial Famine. An East-Indian Eclogue*, the poem referenced by Fuller which highlighted the theme of forced famines in India by the British (*Diary of Andrew Fuller*, 61n171).

82. Ryland, *Fuller*, 98. The remainder of the entry reads, "O for the time, when neither the scepter of oppression, nor heathen superstition, shall bear sway over them! Lord Jesus, set up thy glorious, peaceful kingdom all over the world! Found earnest desire, this morning, in prayer, that God would hear the right, as to them, and hear our prayers, in which the churches agree to unite, for the spread of Christ's kingdom" (Ryland, *Fuller*, 98). While eschatological claims about the eradication of evil can often ring hollow, Fuller's belief that the reign of the millennial kingdom was imminent should give pause to such criticism. Fuller believed and taught that the millennium was temporally proximal to his own day. For this reason, believers could expect cruelty such as mentioned to soon be gone, possibly within their lifetime.

treatment of non-European peoples by his fellow Britons, and a confidence that the millennial kingdom will eradicate such evils.

Spiritual conditions notwithstanding, the church should not be disheartened as prophecy discloses unprecedented gospel advancement. Fuller's confidence that evangelical missions will achieve final victory leads him to exclaim, "Surely it is high time for us to awake out of sleep, and to send our united cries to heaven in behalf our fellow creatures."[83] Fuller's fourth point in *Revival of Religion* enjoins the doctrine of God's sovereignty with the practice of prayer: "Consider what God has promised to do for his church in times to come." Rather than hinder a passion for intercession, Fuller's patently-Reformed response posits the opposite,

> For an absolute impossibility we can have no hope, and for what God hath declared shall never come to pass we can have no warrant to pray; but when we pray for the spread of Christ's kingdom, our object is clogged with neither of these difficulties. On the contrary, it is accompanied with the strongest assurances of success.[84]

This succinct passage accurately encapsulates Andrew Fuller's theology of revival. The inviolable divine will enlivens the contingent human will, drawing it to obedient response. Fuller continues with demonstration of several Old Testament prophetic texts awaiting future fulfillment.[85] In a prophecy drawn from Daniel two, Fuller perceives a description of Christ's kingdom, gradually filling the earth, but whose beginnings are likened to leaven and a mustard seed in the Gospels.[86] The church's advancement through the centuries would be by means of gospel proclamation, and because the Christian message has yet to be universally-disseminated, the millennium has not commenced. This was, however, soon to be accomplished.

Citing Ps 2:8 Fuller speaks of its Messianic fulfillment in a global context, conceding that "Forlorn as the state of the heathen world is," nonetheless, "our Lord Jesus has asked them for his inheritance, and he will have them, even the uttermost parts of the earth for his possession."[87] Such a "blessed period," in which, "Jew and Gentile, the Fair European and

---

83. Ryland, *Fuller*, 98.

84. Fuller, *A Few Persuasives*, in *WAF*, 668.

85. These include, in addition to Dan 2, Isa 19, 62, Hos 3, and Ezek 36.

86. Fuller, *A Few Persuasives*, in *WAF*, 668. Mark 4:30–32; Matt 13:31–32; Luke 13:18–19.

87. Fuller, *A Few Persuasives*, in *WAF*, 3:668.

the sunburn African, with men of every other description, shall all unite to serve the Lord," is an impetus to missionary activity.[88]

An intriguing dimension of Fuller and Edwards's eschatology, shared by many Protestant contemporaries, was the conviction that a widespread conversion of Jews would precede Christ's bodily return.[89] Moreover, that a Jewish diaspora would be restored to the Holy Land prior to the millennium was expected.[90] Speaking on the olive tree metaphor from Rom 11:15, Fuller sees Jewish settlement in Palestine as fulfilling Isa 19:23, 25, 62:6,7, and Psalm 87.[91] Jewish evangelism and a general interest in their welfare is expressed at various junctures in Fuller's writings. In the appendix to *The Gospel its Own Witness*, Fuller dedicates a sermonic exhortation "To the Jews."[92] In this address, he mentions their return to the Holy Land as an eschatological harbinger. Fuller devotes a series of sermon expositions and general letters that claim prophetic passages predict widespread Jewish conversions to Christianity. He does not, however, espouse unconditional divine approbation on account of Palestine's requisition.[93]

For Fuller, Jewish conversion was not an historical or theological abstraction. In his *Memoir*, a diary entry from September 23, 1802, describes Fuller's conversation with a Jewish man in Scotland. While riding in a carriage together, Fuller and his interlocutor, of whose name we are given only initials, discuss a variety of subjects including biblical prophecy, the Pentateuch, claims of Christ, and even settlement of Palestine.[94] This intrigu-

---

88. Fuller, *A Few Persuasives*, in *WAF*, 3:668.

89. Edwards believed the defeat of the antichrist, namely the destruction of the papacy, would be accompanied by widespread Jewish conversion. His basis is Dan 2 and 7 and the entirety of Revelation. Drawing from Rom 9 Edwards explains that ". . .after the national conversion of the Jews, *which shall be as life from the dead to the Gentiles, and the fullness of both Jews and Gentiles shall be come in*" (*Humble Attempt* in *WJE*, 5:333–34).

90. Emphasis on mass Jewish conversion had roots in Theodore Beza's notes on Romans 9–11, widely-popularized in 3rd edition of the *Geneva Bible* (1599) and picked-up by William Perkins in England. See Crawford Gribben, "Evangelical Eschatology and the 'Puritan Hope,'" in Haykin, *Emergence of Evangelicalism*, 387.

91. Fuller, *A Few Persuasives*, in *WAF*, 3:668.

92. See Fuller, *The Gospel its Own Witness*, in *WAF*, 2:102–05.

93. Fuller, *Gospel its Own Witness*, in *WAF*, 2:104. Furthermore, he writes, ". . .the same prophets that have foretold your return to Canaan have also foretold that you must be brought to 'repent of your sins, and to seek Jehovah your God, and David your King.' Your holy land will avail you but little unless you be a holy people." The texts Fuller cites include, among others, Ezek 37, Isa 11 (*Conversion of the Jews*, in *WAF*, 1:592–608).

94. Fuller recounts a candid, yet genial dialogue that ended with Fuller's promise to send the man a New Testament. Additionally, he appropriated a copy of *The Gospel*

ing account, coupled with efforts to evangelize Jews, and speculation about occupation of Palestine, demonstrates the degree of seriousness to which Fuller regarded the millennial reign of Christ and its concrete implications.[95]

Eschatological Optimism: An Impetus for Pursuing Revival

In evaluating Andrew Fuller's divergence from Jonathan Edwards's proposals in *Humble Attempt*, the work of Chris Chun represents the most recent comprehensive scholarly contribution to this subject. Chun explores the apocalyptic dimensions of eschatology where he argues that optimism drove Fuller's missionary efforts.[96] Edwards and Fuller had a shared vision concerning the eschaton and its various implications for the church, of which the following excerpt for Edwards is indicative: "The world is made for the Son of God; his kingdom is the end of all changes that come to pass in the state of the world. All are only to prepare the way for this; it is fit, therefore, that the last kingdom on earth should be his."[97] Such conditions assure a period of unprecedented spiritual blessings that ought to lead the church to "encourage her, maintain her hope, and animate her faith and prayers, from generation to generation, that God has promised her cause should finally be maintained and prevail in the world."[98] From Edwards's perspective, the church's global triumph was imminent.

Though Andrew Fuller's post-millennial optimism never waned, he acknowledged that present spiritual labors may be his generation's prayerful contribution to future revival. Regardless of when it arrived, there would be no question of revival's instrumental source—the prayers of God's people. Fuller poses an honest and searching transitional question for his hearers: "Suppose we should never live to see those days, still our labour shall not

---

its Own Witness in Glasgow, as it possessed "an address to the Jews." Fuller wrote the following message: "A small token of respect from the author, to Mr. D.L.A, for his friendly attention to him on a journey from Glasgow to Liverpool, Sept. 23, 24, 25, 1802" (*Memoir*, in WAF, 1:80). See also, 78–81.

95. Fuller's views on Rev 20 are found in *Discourses on the Apocalypse*, in WAF, 3:291–97, and *Prophecies of the Millennium*, in WAF, 1:608–12.

96. Chun, *Legacy of Jonathan Edwards*, 71.

97. Edwards, *Humble Attempt*, in WJE, 5:337. Optimism would characterize much of Protestantism's ethos over the next century-and-a-half, yet postmillennialism would acquire a secular, and particularly rationalist trajectory, driven in part by the idea of historical progress.

98. Edwards, *Humble Attempt*, in WJE, 5:337.

be in vain in the Lord. God would be glorified; and is this of no moment?[99] As has been noted throughout this monograph, harmonizing the scriptural duty to pray with the sovereign freedom of God has been the laborious work of theologians and pastors through the ages. Yet, this is no less a concern among lay persons, who may wonder why they should diligently pray without guarantee of immediate, certain results. Fuller suggests that the wisdom of God arranges some to pray for spiritual harvest, others to reap, with each being rewarded according to his or her faithfulness.[100] Proceeding to answer his own question, Fuller writes,

> It should convey this piece of intelligence to the world, that God has yet some hearty friends in it, who will continue to pray in the darkest times. But this is not all: our petitions may prove like seed in the earth, that shall not perish, though it may be not spring up in our days. Thus the prophets labour, and the apostles entered into their labours (John 4:38): and what if we should be the sowers and our prosperity the reapers, shall we begrudge this?[101]

Divergence Between Fuller and Edwards: "Slaying of the Witnesses"

Revelation 11 stands among the most exegetically-challenging passages for biblical interpreters. In this apocalyptic narrative "two witnesses" are killed after prophetic denouncement of the earth's inhabitants, then miraculously restored to life. Most exegetes have traditionally understood these witnesses as symbolic representatives for the church, with their deaths signifying a period of intense persecution. Jonathan Edwards is unique in his belief that Revelation 11 is an event that had already taken place—in what he asserts was the lowest point in church history—just prior to the Reformation.[102] In Britain's eighteenth-century theological milieu, Anglican clergyman John Newton, and John Gill favored the majority interpretation, understanding

---

99. Fuller, *A Few Persuasives*, in *WAF*, 3:670.

100. See Fuller's sermon on 2 Thess 2:19, "if we are faithful ministers, we shall be of the same mind as Christ—and this is the reward which satisfied [Paul]. He endured all things for the elect's sake; and so shall we, if we be of his mind," and "If we be faithful, our loss will be made up in the approbation of God" (*Reward of a Faithful Minister*, in *WAF*, 1:543).

101. Fuller, *A Few Persuasives*, in *WAF*, 3:670.

102. Edwards, *Humble Attempt*, in *WJE*, 5:381.

Revelation 11 as a period of future tribulation for the church.[103] Edwards rejected this view, believing it would serve to hamper enthusiasm for the Concert of Prayer. In fact, he assures readers who would reason that the coming of Christ's kingdom (objection iv.) could not precede "a time of most extreme calamity to the church of God, and prevalence of her antichristian enemies against her," that such could not be the case.[104]

Chris Chun argues that Edwards's eschatological optimism influenced his interpretation of Revelation 11, and that Fuller followed suit.[105] Edwards admits that conceding to a period of future persecution would only be "a great damp to their hope, courage and activity, in praying for, and reaching after the speedy introduction of those glorious promised times."[106] In his *Discourses on the Apocalypse*, Fuller himself interpreted the slaughter of the witnesses as persecution of proto-Protestant sects such as the Waldenses, Albigenses and Bohemians.[107] The point of divergence for Fuller and Edwards is disagreement over commentator Moses Lowman's conclusions on Revelation 11.[108] Fuller's quotation from *Humble Attempt* in his *Discourses on the Apocalypse*—in which he quotes Edwards directly—evinces proof of literary dependence and originality of thought.[109] Notwithstanding, Fuller shares with Edwards the overarching theological vision of *Humble Attempt* namely, a markedly expectant eschatology. The coming millennial reign, initiated by an outpouring of the Holy Spirit, would provide confidence that the church's best days were ahead of her.

Conclusion

This chapter has sought to identify the pneumatological aspect of Andrew Fuller's theology of revival. Two compositions, *On the Promise of the Spirit*

---

103. Chun, *Legacy*, 79.

104. Edwards, *Humble Attempt*, in *WJE*, 5:378.

105. Chun, *Legacy*, 77. Chun carefully navigates the interpretations of Moses Lowman on the Apocalypse with those of Edwards and Fuller. Edwards and Fuller, unlike Lowman, are circumspect concerning the precise meaning of the 1,260 days of Revelation 11. Yet Edwards is more apt to speak of his time being the last days than Fuller.

106. Edwards, *Humble Attempt*, in *WJE*, 5:378.

107. Fuller, *Discourses on the Apocalypse*, in *WAF*, 3:248–49, 251.

108. A fellow Dissenter, Lowman (1680–1752) composed, *A Paraphrase and Notes on the Revelation of St. John*.

109. Fuller, *Discourses on the Apocalypse*, in *WAF*, 3:251. On the possibility that Fuller is indebted to Lowman over Edwards, Chun argues that Fuller explicitly cited Edwards for this insight, and second, that Lowman did not make a point of mentioning decrease in papal authority until the fifth vial (Chun, *Legacy*, 80).

and *A few Persuasives on the Revival of Religion* reveal the centrality of the Holy Spirit in his thought. Fuller spoke glowingly of a coming era in which "rich effusions" of the Spirit would be poured out, with the Protestant church increasing global influence. Fuller's biblicism provided certitude that prophetic passages had contemporary referents, pointing to a millennial kingdom whose inauguration was imminent. As has been noted, Andrew Fuller's theology bears the unmistakable marks of Jonathan Edwards's thought. *Humble Attempt*, the literary catalyst for 1784 Call to Prayer was the Northamptonshire Baptist Association's handbook for missional piety.

Phrases like "earnest and united prayer" and "an outpouring of God's Spirit on the churches" are not common to Fuller prior to 1784, yet the same year, in his *The Nature and Importance of Walking by Faith* sermon, distinctly Edwardsean language, tone, and emphases are evident. Fuller's eschatological views, though not identical to Edwards's in every detail, share critical similarities. Citing *Humble Attempt*, Fuller sides with Edwards's preterist interpretation of Revelation 11, affirming Chris Chun's claim of "missiological optimism." Spiritually bleak periods could be even understood as anticipatory for revival.[110] Like Edwards, Fuller did not insist that corporate prayer constituted a tool to leverage the divine will, thereby nullifying God's sovereign freedom.[111] A high view of Scripture joined with an eclectic hermeneutic united redemptive history with their own. Advances in the kingdom were an assured outcome. The Holy Spirit would guide the church and bless her labors, chiefly in prayer, for no other reason than that it was promised by God himself. Sharing with predecessors such as John Howe, the assured outpouring of the Spirit required nothing less than a disposition of hope. Genuine revival has always been judged a unique work of God, yet few in the church's history have expressed the confidence that a final divine visitation was proximate to their generation to the extent of Jonathan Edwards and Andrew Fuller.

---

110. The Napoleonic Wars did not hamper Fuller's eschatological enthusiasm as Hakyin notes, citing a selection from *Discourses on the Apocalypse* which reads, "We have seen enough, amidst all the troubles of our times, to gladden our hearts; and trust that our children will see greater things than these" (*WAF*, 3:202). See Haykin, "Evangelicalism and the Enlightenment," 44.

111. Though Edwards denied any compulsion on God's part to grant requests of supplicants, he did perceive the salutary effects of prayer on others. He explains, "Though it would not be reasonable to suppose that merely such a circumstance, as many people praying at the same time, will directly have on the prevalence of God; yet such a circumstance may reasonably be supposed to have influence on the minds of men" (*Humble Attempt*, in *WJE*, 5:374). Fuller follows Edwards on this point, ruling out contingency in God. See comments on *A Few Persuasives* in *WAF*, 3:668.

Conclusion

IN A LETTER WRITTEN in 1793, Andrew Fuller observed that "the Methodists of Mr. Wesley's connexions" had infiltrated Northamptonshire, and though he concedes that "there appear to be some religious people amongst them," expressed concern that ". . ..their labours have too great a tendency to mislead mankind by engaging them on slight and insufficient grounds to hope for eternal life."[1] As a pastor and theologian, whose writings, preaching, and activism drew British Baptists away from high Calvinism, and whose principle work *The Gospel Worthy of All Acceptation,* refuted the notion of a prerequisite, "warrant of faith," his ambivalence towards Arminian Methodism on such soteriological grounds is both revealing and ironic.

Fuller devoted much theological labor to preserving what he believed was a mysterious, yet compatible relationship between God's sovereignty and human responsibility, and though he never disavowed the formulations canonized at Dort,[2] and strenuously defended his theology as Reformed orthodox, his evangelical expression of Calvinism was sufficiently novel to earn the eponym "Fullerism."[3] Fuller understood his views as nothing

1. Andrew Fuller, letter of May 23, 1793, manuscript in Congregational Library. See also, Nuttall, "Methodism and Older Dissent," 273–74. Nuttall published this letter in a later journal article, identifying the recipient of the letter as a certain Josiah Lewis ("The State of Religion in Northamptonshire[1793]," 177–79). As noted in ch. 2, Fuller's own assessment of Northamptonshire Particular Baptist churches in 1814 disclosed that only four of 23 congregations were high Calvinist, most of which were planted after 1764.

2. On Dort's conclusion concerning the extent of the atonement, Fuller claims that he would not "wish for words more appropriate than the above to express my sentiments" (*Calvinism* in *WAF*, 2:712). John Ryland Jr. theologically distinguishes Particular Baptists as those who hold the Five Points (Ryland, *Fuller*, 3). See introduction n. 26.

3. See ch. 3, n. 119.

less than biblical Christianity in step with the doctrine articulated in the London Confessions of Faith of 1644 and 1689, and yet his theology was uniquely imbued with Enlightenment categories and concepts, due in large part to Jonathan Edwards. Compatibilism, articulated to various levels of sophistication by sundry pastors and theologians within the Reformed tradition, and expressed under Edwards's natural-ability, moral-inability schema, was applied by Fuller and others to various theological subjects. That he lived in the era of evangelicalism's genesis, a movement born out of revival, makes eighteenth-century patterns of thought understandable.

As has been argued previously, a compatibilist relationship best captures Andrew Fuller's theological understanding of revival. While a sovereign, gracious, and free act of God, spiritual renewal summons human response at every juncture in its chronological spectrum. Broadly understood, such a perspective is evident in several Puritans who have been examined here. As discussed in chapter one, the writings of John Owen, John Howe, and Abraham Cheare reveal the centrality of the Holy Spirit for vitality both within the hearts of believers, and outwardly, in the visible church. In Owen, we find terminology and theological patterns that would characterize Andrew Fuller's revival writings, including the notion of a human agent's duty to respond to revealed knowledge, and the application of means to accomplish a determinant end. In Cheare, radical dependence on the Spirit leads to a lament for the Spirit's absence, and where there is fervent prayer, confidence grows that an outpouring is at hand. Likewise, John Howe understood the dire necessity for an "effusion" of the same Spirit and possessed great confidence that a spiritualized millennial reign would bring unprecedented peace, unity, and conversions across the globe. Howe, like Fuller after him, believed predictive prophecy foretold that this period was imminent, a conviction that instilled greater urgency for prayer.

Chapter Two considered the theology of Gill and Brine as bearing responsibility for the spiritual stagnation of Particular Baptist life in the early eighteenth century, though with some exceptions within the denomination and Dissent as a whole. Andrew Gifford and Benjamin Francis preached evangelistic sermons whose spiritual fruit came through scores of conversions, yet they were exceptions among Baptist contemporaries, and the denomination steadily declined through mid-century. Isaac Watts and Philip Doddridge, aptly considered evangelicals before the revivals for their expressed desire for the Holy Spirit's influence, and emphasis on passionate preaching, mediated between doctrinal heterodoxy of Socinianism and Deism, and Crispian high Calvinism that refused to offer Christ to sinners. Watts and Doddridge's correspondence with revival figures in Britain and

North America, and promotion of their respective ministries, would enjoin Anglican Methodism and New Light Congregationalism to English Dissent.

Chapter three focused on Andrew Fuller's personal and spiritual development. His conversion, coupled with firsthand experience of antinomianism set an early divergent course from the theological system in which he was nurtured. As noted, Fuller believed and taught that faith and repentance were duties incumbent on all sinners, and that natural ability obviated any objections to contrary. Moral inability, however, explained why the Holy Spirit's sovereign work is necessary for conversion. Apart from a technical definition, Fuller's theological explanation of revival can be drawn from references to it interspersed throughout his works. Furthermore, Fuller's concrete application of revival included institution of monthly prayer meetings, a missionary sending agency, and funding itinerant village preachers. Several letters reveal that the Northamptonshire Baptist Association did not experience revival to the magnitude of that transpired in New England. However, the sending of William Carey and subsequent missionaries assured evangelicalism's global extension and long-term impact.

Chapter Four discussed a prominent theme in Fuller's discourse on revival: means. The gracious activity of the Holy Spirit is vital to revival, andunder a compatibilist framework, robust human response is appropriate. As Fuller understood them, means were variegated in nature, and appropriated to a wide range. Included were practical measures such as evangelism, prayer, and generosity; additionally, examination over the purity of intercession, and individual motives for revival. For revival to commence, the church must pursue holiness, with every believer striving to be set-apart for the divine task. If means were not intrinsically effectual, divine promises in Scripture provided grounds for their success.

Chapter Five weighed Andrew Fuller's pneumatology and its relation to revival. Wherever discussions on this subject are found, the Holy Spirit's presence and power occupy a central place in his writings. Optimism regarding the global Protestant church's near, and distant future was a hallmark of Jonathan Edwards's *Humble Attempt*, a work Fuller greatly admired. Belief that an outpouring of the Spirit was at hand prompted the formation of prayer meetings by Northamptonshire Baptist Association beginning in 1784. Such "concerts of prayer" served as a fitting response to Old Testament prophecies which Edwards and earlier figures such as John Howe, understood as foretelling the millennial reign of Christ. Compatibilism is no less evident in the belief that prayer meetings are the appropriate means to a divinely revealed outcome. However, even prayer meetings do not necessitate a divine response that revival commence immediately. Fuller would in fact note that such efforts may serve to increase communion with

God in the present, and possibly occasion an Awakening that commences in a later generation.

Eminent Victorian preacher Charles Spurgeon deemed Fuller the "greatest theologian" of the nineteenth century,[4] though Spurgeon himself ministered at a time when Calvinism as Fuller understood it, was at its nadir in Britain.[5] Furthermore, though Baptist historian Albert Henry Newman (1852–1933) could judge Fuller's impact on American Baptists as "incalculable," evangelicalism's predominant understanding of revival, particularly in North America, would increasingly resemble that of Charles Grandison Finney.[6] Consequent results have included adoption, even unconsciously, of philosophical pragmatism, and the usage of means unlike what Fuller meant by the term. Discontentment with mystery and paradox, an unmistakable mark of modernity, had serious consequences for nineteenth and twentieth-century evangelical Christianity. Such historical and theological developments may serve to temper the respective evaluations by Spurgeon and Newman.[7]

Fuller's reservations about Methodism in Northamptonshire suggest wariness of theological reductionism. From his perspective, high Calvinism and Arminianism were expressions of this same error, an unwillingness to affirm the tension between the God who is sovereign, and creaturely agents who exercise responsibility. While revival is not a human work, it beckons human participation. Conversely, revival is not of a nature that preparation of any kind, whether prayer or pursuit of holiness is irrelevant. The greatest threat to genuine revival is theological oversimplification, and its consequent

---

4. Laws, *Andrew Fuller*, 127.

5. Though it remained dogmatically-strong in places such as Yorkshire, by the late nineteenth century, Particular Baptist and the New Connexion denominations merged in 1891, believing that mission took precedent over traditional doctrinal distinctives. A concrete unification followed several decades of debate over election. Alexander McClaren's (1826–1910) comments that disputes over whether atonement is general or particular are fruitless when, "The whole world was asking is there any atonement at all," is indicative of the era's sentiment (Briggs, *English Baptists*, 155). For entire discussion see ch. 4, 96–157. By contrast, Fuller in several responses to the proposal of union with the established church and other Dissenters, was wary of doctrinal dilution for the sake of union. He espoused the principle that "Christian enlargement is not accomplished by extending our connexions but by confining them to persons with whom we can have fellowship, communion, and a mutual participation of spiritual interests" (*Decline of the Dissenting Interest*, in *WAF*, 3:488).

6. Newman, "Andrew Fuller," 409. Newman's judgment that it was due to Fuller, "more than any other individual, that the restoration of the Particular Baptist body to its original evangelical position," in *A Manual*, 687.

7. The theology of Baptists in America took an Arminian trajectory, particularly after 1830. See Hatch, *Democratization*, 130–39; 170–79.

applications. Thus, for evangelicals whose origins fit broadly within the Reformed tradition, Fuller's biblically-grounded and missions-oriented Calvinism make his understanding of revival worthy of consideration.

Bibliography

Abbey, C. J., and J. H. Overton. *The English Church in the Eighteenth Century*. London: Longman's Green, 1878.

Abernathy, Andrew T. "Jonathan Edwards as Multi-Dimension Bible Interpreter: A Case Study from Isaiah 40–55." *JETS* 56 (2013) 815–30.

Anderson, Clifford. "Seasons of Refreshing: Evangelism and Revivals in America." *JETS* 41 (1998) 656–57.

Aniol, Scott. "Was Isaac Watts Unitarian? Athanasian Trinitarianism and the Boundary of Christian Fellowship." *DBSJ* 22 (2017) 91–103.

Arnold, Jonathan. *The Reformed Theology of Benjamin Keach 1640–1704*. Oxford: Regent's College, 2014.

Ascol, Thomas Kennedy. "The Doctrine of Grace: A Critical Analysis of Federalism in the Theologies of John Gill and Andrew Fuller." PhD diss., Southwestern Baptist Theological Seminary, 1989.

Asty, John. "Memoirs of the Life of John Owen, D.D." In *A Complete Collection of the Sermons of the Reverend and Learned John Owen, D.D.* London: John Clark, 1721.

Augustine. *On Christian Doctrine*. Translated by D. W. Robertson Jr. Upper Saddle, NJ: Prentice Hall, 1958.

Barshinger, David. "Making the Psalter One's 'Own Language': Jonathan Edwards Engages the Psalms." *Jonathan Edwards Studies* 2 (2012) 28.

Bassinger, David, and Randall Basinger, eds. *Predestination and Free Will: Four Views of Divine Sovereignty and Human Freedom*. Downers Grove, IL: InterVarsity, 1986.

Baxter, Richard. *The Reformed Pastor*. Edited by William Brown. Repr. Carlisle, PA: Banner of Truth, 2007.

———. *Reliquiae Baxterianae*. Edited by M. Sylvester. London: n.d., 1696.

Bebbington, David. *Evangelicalism in Modern Britain: A History from the 1730's to the 1980's*. Winchester, MA: Unwin Hyman, 1989.

———. *Patterns of History: A Christian Perspective on Historical Thought*. Grand Rapids: Baker, 1990.

———. "Remembered Around the World." In *Jonathan Edwards at Home and Abroad*, edited by David Kling and Douglas Sweeney, 177–200. Columbia: University of South Carolina Press, 2003.

Beeke, Joel R. "The Age of the Spirit and Revival." *Puritan Reformed Journal* 2 (2010) 30–49.

———, ed. *Forerunner of the Great Awakening: Sermons by Theodorus Jacobus Frelinghuysen (1691–1747)*. Grand Rapids: Eerdmans, 2000.

Belcher, Joseph. *William Carey: A Biography*. Philadelphia: American Baptist Publication Society, 1853.

Bennett, G. V., and J. D. Walsh, eds. *Essays in Modern Church History*. London: A. & C. Black, 1966.

Beynon, Graham. "The Helpfulness of the Lesser-Known Work: Isaac Watts on the Passions." *Themelios* 42 (2017) 479–93.

———. *Isaac Watts: Reason, Passion and the Revival of Religion*. London: Bloomsbury; T. & T. Clark, 2016.

Boersma, Hans. *A Hot Pepper Corn: Richard Baxter's Doctrine of Justification in Its Seventeenth-Century Context of Controversy*. Repr. Vancouver, BC: Regent College, 2004.

Booth, Abraham. *The Works of Abraham Booth. . . With Some Account of his Life and Writings*. 3 vols. London: W. Button and Sons, 1813.

Box, Bart. "The Atonement in the Thought of Andrew Fuller." PhD diss., New Orleans Baptist Theological Seminary, 2009.

Brackney, William. "The Baptist Missionary Society in Proper Context. Some Reflections on the Large Voluntary Religious Tradition." *BQ* 34 (1992) 364–77.

Brewster, Paul. "Andrew Fuller (1754–1815): Model Pastor Theologian." PhD diss., Southeastern Baptist Theological Seminary, 2007.

———. *Andrew Fuller: Model Pastor-Theologian*. Nashville: B&H Academic, 2010.

———. "Out in the Journeys: Village Preaching and Revival Among 18th century Particular Baptists, Part I." *Andrew Fuller Review* 1 (2011) 5–11.

———. "Out in the Journeys: Village Preaching and Revival Among 18th century Particular Baptists, Part II." *Andrew Fuller Review* 2 (2012) 5–14.

Briggs, John H. Y., ed. *A Dictionary of European Baptist Life and Thought*. Studies in Baptist History and Thought 33. Colorado Springs: Paternoster, 2009.

———. *English Baptists of the Nineteenth Century*. Didcot, UK: Baptist Historical Society, 1994.

———. "The Influence of Calvinism on Seventeenth-Century English Baptists." *Baptist History and Heritage* 39 (2004) 8–24.

Brine, John. *The Certain Efficacy of the Death of Christ*. London: Aaron Ward, 1743.

———. *Preface to Treatise on Various Subjects*. London: John Ward, 1750.

Brown, Peter. *Augustine of Hippo*. Berkeley: University of California, 1969.

Brown, Raymond. "The Baptist Preacher in Early 18th Century England." *BQ* 31 (1985) 4–22.

———. *The English Baptists of the Eighteenth Century*. London: The Baptist Historical Society, 1986.

———. *Spirituality in Adversity: English Nonconformity in a Period of Repression, 1660–1689*. Milton Keynes: Paternoster, 2012.

Bryant, David. *With Concerts of Prayer Christians Join for Spiritual Awakening and World Evangelization*. Ventura, CA: Regal, 1984.

Buell, Samuel. *A Faithful Narrative of the Remarkable Revival of Religion*. Sag Harbor: Alden Spooner, 1808. https://books.google.com/books?id=ay2iixETVm4C.

Bunyan, John. *Grace Abounding to the Chief of Sinners*, 1666. Reprint. New York: Penguin, 1987.

———. *The Pilgrim's Progress*, 1678. Repr. Mineola, NY: Dover, 2003.

———. *The Works of John Bunyan: with an introduction to each treatise, notes, and a sketch of his life, times, and contemporaries*. 3 vols. Edited by George Offor. Glasgow: Blackie, 1861.

Burder, George, ed. *The Works of the Reverend and Learned Isaac Watts*. 2 vols. London: J. Barfield, 1810.

Burrage, Champlin. *The Early English Dissenters in Light of Recent Research*. New York: Russell and Russell, 1967.

Butler, Jon. *Awash in a Sea of Faith: Christianizing the American People*. Cambridge, MA: Harvard University Press, 1990.

Button, William. *Remarks on a Treatise Entitled the Gospel of Christ Worthy of All Acceptation*. London: J. Buckland, 1785.

Calamy, Edward. *Memoirs of the Life of the Late Rev. Mr. John Howe*. London: Westley and Davis, 1832.

Calvin, John. *Commentary on the Book of Psalms*. Volume 1. Translated by James Anderson. Calvin's Commentaries 4. Grand Rapids: Baker, 1996.

———. *Commentary on the Book of Psalms*. Volume 2. Translated by James Anderson. Calvin's Commentaries 5. Grand Rapids: Baker, 1996.

———. *Institutes of the Christian Religion*. Translated by Henry Beveridge. Grand Rapids: Eerdmans, 1989.

Capp, B. S. "Extreme Millenarianism." In *Puritans, the Millennium and the Future of Israel*, edited by Peter Toon, 66–90. Cambridge: James Clarke, 2002.

Carey, Eustace. *Memory of William Carey, D. D.* London: Jackson and Walford, 1936.

Carey, Samuel Pearce. *William Carey*. London: Carey, 1923.

Carson, D. A. *Divine Sovereignty and Human Responsibility: Biblical Perspectives in Tension*. Atlanta: John Knox, 1981.

Carwardine, Richard. *Popular Evangelicalism in America and Britain 1790–1865*. Carlisle, UK: Paternoster, 2007.

———. *Transatlantic Revivalism 1790–1865*. Westport, CT: Greenwood, 1978.

Champion, L. G. "John Robinson: A Pastor in Cambridge." *BQ* 31 (1986) 241–46.

Chauncy, Charles. *Seasonable Thoughts on the State of Religion in New England*. Repr. Hicksville, NY: Regin, 1975.

Cheare, Abraham. *Sighs for Sion*. London: Livewel Chapman, 1657.

———. *Words in Season*. London: Nathan Brookes, 1668.

Cheare, Abraham, and Henry Jessey. *A Looking-Glass for Children*. 3rd ed. London: Robert Boulter, 1673.

Cherry, Conrad. *The Theology of Jonathan Edwards*. Garden City: Doubleday, 1966.

Christianson, Paul. *Reformers and Babylon: English Apocalyptic Visions from the Reformation to the Eve of the Civil War*. Toronto: University of Toronto Press, 2016.

Chun, Chris. *The Legacy of Jonathan Edwards in the Theology of Andrew Fuller*. Boston: Brill, 2012.

———. "A Mainspring of Missionary Thought: Andrew Fuller on Natural and Moral Inability." *ABQ* 25 (2006) 335–55.

———. "'Sense of the Heart': Jonathan Edwards's Legacy in the Writing of Andrew Fuller." *Eusebia* 9 (2008) 117–34.

Cicero. *Selected Works*. Edited and Translated by Michael Grant. Baltimore: Penguin, 1960.
Clifford, Alan. "The Christian Mind of Philip Doddridge (1702–1751): The Gospel according to an Evangelical Congregationalist." *EQ* 56 (1984) 227–42.
Clipsham, E. F. "Andrew Fuller and Fullerism: A Study in Evangelical Calvinism." *BQ* 20 1–4 (1967).
———. "Andrew Fuller's Doctrine of Salvation." BD thesis, University of Oxford, 1961.
Clouse, Robert. "J. H. Alsted and English Millenariansim." *HTR* 62 (1969) 189–207.
Coffey, John. "Puritanism, Evangelicalism and the Evangelical Protestant Tradition." In *Emergence of Evangelicalism*, edited by Michael A. G. Haykin and Kenneth Stewart, 252–77. Nottingham: Apollos, 2008.
Coffey, John, and Paul Chang-Ha Lim, eds. *The Cambridge Companion to Puritanism*. Cambridge: Cambridge University Press, 2008.
———. *John Goodwin and the Puritan Revolution: Religion and Change in Seventeenth-Century England*. Woodbridge, UK: Boydell & Brewster, 2006.
Conner, R. Dwayne. "Early English Baptist Associations. Their Meaning for Baptist Connectional Life Today." *Foundations* 20 (1972) 163–85.
Cooper, Tim. *Fear and Polemic in Seventeenth-Century England: Richard Baxter and Antinomianism*. Burlington, VT: Ashgate, 2001.
———. *John Owen, Richard Baxter, and The Formation of Nonconformity*. Farnham, Surrey: Ashgate, 2011.
———. "Owen's Personality: The Man Behind the Theology." In *The Ashgate Research Companion to John Owen's Theology*, edited by Kelly M. Kapic and Mark Jones, 215–26. Burlington. VT: Ashgate, 2012.
Cooper, William. *The Works of William Cooper*. 4 vols. N.d.: Boston, 1743.
Copleston, Frederick. *A History of Philosophy: Medieval Philosophy*. New York: Doubleday, 1962.
Copson, Stephen. "General Baptists in the Eighteenth-century." In *Challenge and Change: English Baptist Life in the Eighteenth Century*, edited by Stephen Copson and Peter Morden, 29–56. Didcot, UK: The Baptist Historical Society, 2017.
Copson, Stephen, and Peter J. Morden, eds. *Challenge and Change: English Baptist Life in the Eighteenth Century*. Didcot, UK: The Baptist Historical Society, 2017.
Cox, F. A. *History of the Baptist Missionary Society, from 1792 to 1842*. London: T. Ward & Co./G. J. Dyer, 1842.
Cramp, J. M. *Baptist History: From the Foundation of the Christian Church to the Present*. London: E. Stock, 1871.
Crawford, Michael. *Seasons of Grace: Colonial New England's Revival Tradition in Its British Context*. New York: Oxford University Press, 1991.
Crisp, Oliver. *Deviant Calvinism: Broadening Reformed Theology*. Minneapolis: Fortress, 2014.
Crisp, Tobias. *Christ Alone Exalted; In the Perfection and Encouragements of the Saints, Notwithstanding Sins and Trials*. 2 vols. 4th ed. R. Noble: London: 1791.
Crosby, Thomas. *History of the English Baptists*. 2 vols. Repr. Lafayette, TN: Church History Research and Archives, 1978.
Cross, Frank Leslie, ed. *The Oxford Dictionary of the Christian Church*. New York: Oxford University Press, 1997.
Cuming, G. J., ed. *Studies in Church History*. 2 vols. London: Thomas Nelson, 1965.

Cunningham, William. "Calvinism and the Doctrine of Philosophical Necessity." In *The Reformers and the Theology of the Reformation*. Repr. Edinburgh: Banner of Truth, 1989.

Daniel, Curt D. "Hyper-Calvinism and John Gill." PhD diss., University of Edinburgh, 1983.

Danielou, Jean. *From Shadows to Reality: Studies in the Biblical Typology of the Fathers*. Translated by Wulstan Hibberd. London: Burns & Oates, 1960.

Davenport, James. *The Reverend Mr. Davenport's Confession and Retraction*. Boston: S. Kneeland and T. Green, 1744.

Davis, Arthur. *Isaac Watts: His Life and Works*. London: Independent, 1948.

Davidson, Bruce W. "Not From Ourselves: Holy Love in the Theology of Jonathan Edwards." *JETS* 59 (2016) 577–81.

Davidson, James West. *The Logic of Millennial Thought: Eighteenth Century New England*. New Haven, CT: Yale University Press, 1977.

Deacon, M. *Philip Doddridge of Northampton*. Northamptonshire: Northants Libraries, 1980.

Defoe, Daniel. *The Present State of the Parties in Great Britain: Particularly an Enquiry into the State of Dissenters in England*. London: J. Baker, 1712.

Doddridge, Philip. *The Care of the Soul Urged as the One Thing Needful: A Sermon Preached at Maidwell in Northamptonshire, June 22, 1735*. London: Richard Hett, 1735. Eighteenth-Century Collections Online. https://www.worldcat.org/title/care-of-the-soul-urged-as-the-one-thing-needful-a-sermon-preached-at-maidwell-in-northamptonshire-june-22-1735-by-p-doddridge-published-at-the-request-of-many-that-heard-it/oclc/642526649.

———. *The Family Expositor: or, A paraphrase and version of the New Testament with critical notes and a practical improvement of each section*. London: William Baynes & Sons, 1825.

———. *Free Thoughts on the Most Probable Means of Reviving the Dissenting Interest: Occasion'd by the late enquiry into the causes of its decay. Address'd to the author of that enquiry. By a Minister in the country*. London: Richard Hett, 1730. Eighteenth-Century Collections Online. https://quod.lib.umich.edu/e/ecco/004806452.0001.000/1:2?rgn=div1;view=fulltext.

Drewrey, Mary. *William Carey: Shoemaker and Missionary*. London: Hodder and Stoughton, 1978.

Drummond, A. L., and J. Bullock. *The Scottish Church 1688–1843*. St. Andrews: St. Andrews, 1973.

Duncan, Pope. *Hanserd Knollys: Seventeenth-Century Baptist*. Nashville: Broadman, 1981.

———. "The Influence of Andrew Fuller on Calvinism." PhD diss., Southern Baptist Theological Seminary, 1917.

Dutton, Benjamin. *The Superaboundings of the Riches of God's Free Grace*. London: J. Hart, 1743.

Dwight, Sereno. *Life of President Edwards*. Edited by Sereno Dwight. The Works of President Edwards, with a Memoir of His Life 1. New York: S. Converse, 1829.

Eddins, J. W., Jr. "Andrew Fuller's Theology of Grace." ThD diss., Southern Baptist Theological Seminary, 1957.

Edwards, Jonathan. *Apocalyptic Writings*. Edited by Stephen J. Stein. The Works of Jonathan Edwards 5. New Haven, CT: Yale University Press, 1977.

———. *A Call to United Extraordinary Prayer: An Humble Attempt*. Ross-shire, Great Britain: Christian, 2003.

———. *A Divine and Supernatural Light*. Edited by M. Valeri. The Works of Jonathan Edwards 17. New Haven, CT: Yale University Press, 1999.

———. *Ethical Writings*. Edited by Paul Ramsey. The Works of Jonathan Edwards 8. New Haven, CT: Yale University Press, 1989.

———. *Freedom of the Will*. Edited by Paul Ramsey. The Works of Jonathan Edwards 1. New Haven, CT: Yale University Press, 1957.

———. *The Great Awakening*. Edited by C. C. Goen. The Works of Jonathan Edwards 4. New Haven, CT: Yale University Press, 1972.

———. *The Life of David Brainerd*. Edited by Norman Pettit. The Works of Jonathan Edwards 7. New Haven, CT: Yale University Press, 1985.

———. *The Religious Affections*. Edited by John E. Smith. The Works of Jonathan Edwards 2. New Haven, CT: Yale University Press, 1957.

———. *The Works of Jonathan Edwards*. 2 vols. Repr. Peabody, MA: Hendrickson, 2005.

———. *The Works of Jonathan Edwards Online*, Jonathan Edwards Center, Yale University. Online: http://www.edwards.yale.edu.

Ella, George. "John Gill and the Charge of Hyper-Calvinism." *BQ* 36 (1995) 166–77.

———. *Law and Gospel: in the Theology of Andrew Fuller*. Eggleston: Go Publications, 1996.

Elwyn, T. S. H. *The Northamptonshire Baptist Association*. London: Carey Kingsgate, 1964.

Eifion Evans, "'The Power of Heaven in the Word of Life': Welsh Calvinistic Methodism and Revival." In *Pentecostal Outpourings: Revival and the Reformed Tradition*, edited by Robert Davis Smart et al., 7. Grand Rapids: Reformation Heritage, 2016.

Evans, John, et. al. "The Baptist Interest under George I." *Transactions of the Baptist Historical Society* (1911) 95–109.

Fairchild, Hoxie Neal. *Religious Trends in English Poetry*. New York: Columbia University Press, 1939.

Fawcett, Arthur. *The Cambuslang Revival: The Scottish Evangelical Revival of the Eighteenth Century*. London: Banner of Truth, 1971.

Feinberg, John. "God Ordains All Things." In *Predestination and Free Will: Four Views of Divine Sovereignty and Human Freedom,* edited by David Bassinger and Randall Basinger, 35–37. Downers Grove, IL: InterVarsity: 1986.

Ferguson, Sinclair B. *John Owen and the Christian Life*. Edinburgh: Banner of Truth, 1987.

Field, David. *"Rigide Calvinisme in Softer Dress": The Moderate Presbyterianism of John Howe*. Edinburgh: Rutherford, 2004.

Finn, Nathan A. "The Renaissance in Andrew Fuller Studies: A Bibliographic Essay." *SBJT* 17 (2013) 44–61.

Firth, Katherine R. *The Apocalyptic Tradition in Reformation Britain*. Oxford: Oxford University Press, 1979.

Fischer, Martin, and Mark Ravizza. *Responsibility and Control: A Theory of Moral Responsibility*. Cambridge: Cambridge University Press, 1999.

Fisk, Philip J. *Jonathan Edwards's Turn from the Classic-Reformed Tradition of Freedom of the Will*. Gottingen: Vandenhoeck & Ruprecht, 2016.

Flew, Antony, and Alasdair MacIntyre, eds. *New Essays in Philosophical Theology*. New York: Macmillan, 1955.
Flint, Thomas. "A Brief Narrative of the Life and Death of the Rev. Benjamin Francis, A. M." Annexed to *The Presence of Christ the Source of Eternal Bliss. A Funeral Discourse. . .occasioned by the Death of the Rev. Benjamin Francis, A.M.* by John Ryland Jr. Bristol: n.d., 1800.
Fountain, David. *Isaac Watts Remembered*. Worthing, UK: Gospel Standard Baptist Trust, 1974.
Frankfurt, Harry. "Alternate Possibilities and Moral Responsibility." *Journal of Philosophy* 66 (1969) 829–39.
———. *The Importance of What We Care About*. Cambridge: Cambridge University Press, 1988.
Fuller, Andrew. *The Complete Works*. 3 vols. Edited by Joseph Belcher. Repr. Harrisonburg, VA: Sprinkle, 1988.
———. *The Complete Works of Andrew Fuller Volume 1: The Diary of Andrew Fuller, 1780–1801*. Edited by Michael D. McMullen and Timothy D. Whelan. Boston: De Gruyter, 2016.
———. *The Complete Works of Andrew Fuller Volume 5: Apologetic Works*. Edited by Nathan Finn. Boston: De Gruyter, 2016.
———. *The Complete Works of Andrew Fuller Volume 4*: Memoirs of the Rev. Samuel Pearce. Edited by Michael A. G. Haykin. Boston: De Gruyter, 2016.
———. *The Gospel Worthy of All Acceptation*. Northampton: T. Dicey, 1785. Eighteenth Century Collections Online. http://www.galenet.galegroup.com.
———. *The Last Remains of the Rev. Andrew Fuller*. Edited by Joseph Belcher. Philadelphia: American Baptist Publication Society, 1856.
———. *The Works of Andrew Fuller*. Edited by Michael A. G. Haykin. Edinburgh: The Banner of Truth Trust, 2007.
Fuller, Gunton. *Men Worth Remembering: Andrew Fuller*. London: Hodder and Stoughton, 1882.
Fuller, John G. *A Brief History of the Western Association*. Bristol: I. Hemmans, 1843.
Garret, James Leo. *Baptist Theology: A Four-Century Study*. Macon, GA: Mercer University Press, 2009.
Garrison, Winfred Ernest, and Alfred T. DeGroot. *The Disciples of Christ: A History*. St. Louis: Bethany, 1948.
Gaustad, E. S. *The Great Awakening in New England*. New York: Harper, 1957.
George, Timothy. *Faithful Witness: The Life and Mission of William Carey*. Birmingham, AL: New Hope, 1991.
George, Timothy, and David S. Dockery, eds. *Theologians of the Baptist Tradition*. Nashville: Broadman, 2001.
Gibson, William, et al. *Religion, Politics and Dissent 1660–1832*. Burlington, VT: Ashgate: 2010.
Gifford, Andrew. *Eighteen sermons preached by the late Rev. George Whitfield, A.M. on the following subjects. . .Taken verbatim in short-hand, and faithfully transcribed by Joseph Gurney*. New York: John Tiebout, 1809. Eighteenth Century Collections Online. https://catalog.hathitrust.org/Record/008913083.
———. *The Living Water: or, the Work of the Spirit as the Sanctifier and Comforter of Believers in Jesus*. London: J. Lewis, 1746.

Gilbert, Alan D. *Religion and Society in Industrial England: Church, Chapel, and Social Change, 1740–1914.* New York: Longman, 1976.

Gill, John. *An Answer to the Birmingham Dialogue-Writers Second Part.* London: Aaron Ward, 1739.

———. *A Body of Practical Divinity.* London: George Keith, 1769.

———. *The Cause of God and Truth.* London: Aaron Ward, 1736. Online: https://archive.org/details/causegodandtrutoogillgoog/page/n9.

———. *A Collection of Sermons and Tracts.* 2 vols. London: George Keith, 1773.

———. *A Complete Body of Doctrinal and Practical Divinity.* London: George Keith, 1779.

———. *The Doctrines of God's Everlasting Love to His Elect. . . Stated and Defended. In a Letter to Abraham Taylor.* London: G. Keith, 1772.

———. *An Exposition of the Old Testament.* 4 vols. London: Matthews and Leigh, 1763–1765.

———. *An Exposition of the New Testament.* Volume 3. London: Aaron Ward, 1747.

Gillette, A. D. *Minutes of the Philadelphia Baptist Association from A.D. 1707, to A.D. 1807.* Philadelphia: American Baptist Publication Society, 1851.

Giradeau, J. L. *The Will in its Theological Relations.* Columbia, SC: Duffie, 1891.

Givens, J. M., Jr. "'And They Sung a New Song': The Theology of Benjamin Keach and The Introduction of Congregational Hymn-Singing to English Worship." *ABQ* 22 4 (2003) 406–20.

Goen, C. C. *Revivalism and Separatism in New England, 1740–1800.* New Haven, CT: Yale University Press, 1962.

Gonzalez, Justo L. *A History Christian Thought: From Beginnings to the Council of Chalcedon.* Volume 2. Nashville: Abingdon, 1969.

Goppelt, Leonhard. *Typos: The Typological Interpretation of the Old Testament in the New* Translated by Donald H. Madvig. Grand Rapids: Eerdmans, 1982.

Gough, Strickland. *An Enquiry into the causes of the decay of the dissenting interest: In a letter to a dissenting minister.* London: J. Roberts, 1730. Eighteenth-century Collections Online. https://quod.lib.umich.edu/e/ecco/004801828.0001.000/1:2?rgn=div1;view=fulltext.

Grant, Keith. *Andrew Fuller and the Evangelical Renewal of Pastoral Theology.* Milton Keynes: Paternoster, 2013.

Greaves, Richard L., and Robert Zaller, eds. *Biographical Dictionary of British Radicals in the Seventeenth Century.* Brighton, Sussex: Harvester, 1983.

Greenall, R. L. *The Kettering Connection—Northamptonshire Baptists and Overseas Missions.* Leicester: University of Leicester, 1993.

———. *Philip Doddridge, Nonconformist and Theologian.* Leicester: University of Leicester, 1981.

Gribben, Crawford. *Puritan Millennium: Literature and Theology 1550–1682.* Rev. ed. Milton Keynes: Paternoster, 2008.

Guelzo, Allen. *Edwards on the Will: A Century of American Theological Debate.* Middletown, CT: Wesleyan University Press, 1989.

Haakonssen, Knud, ed. *Enlightenment and Religion: Rational Dissent in eighteenth-century Britain.* Cambridge: Cambridge University Press, 1996.

Haldane, Alexander. *The Lives of Robert and James Haldane.* 3rd ed. London: Hamilton and Adams, 1853.

Hall, Basil. "Puritanism: The Problem of Definition." *Studies in Church History* 2 (1965) 283-96.

Haller, William. *Rise of Puritanism*. New York: Columbia University Press, 1938.

Hambrick-Stowe, Charles. *The Practice of Piety: Puritan Devotional Disciplines in the Seventeenth-Century New England*. Chapel Hill, NC: North Carolina University Press, 1982.

Hamilton, Thomas. *History of the Irish Presbyterian Church*. Edinburgh: T. & T. Clark, 1887.

Hanson, Brian L., and Michael Haykin. *Waiting on the Spirit of Promise: The Life and Theology of Suffering of Abraham Cheare*. Eugene, OR: Pickwick, 2014.

Harris, F. W. "Philip Doddridge and Charges of Arianism." *Congregational Historical Society Transactions* 20 (1965-1970) 267-72.

———. "Philip Doddridge: Eighteenth-Century Ecumenicist." *Foundations* 14 (1971) 251-70.

Harris, Howell. *A Brief Account of the Life of Howell Harris, Esq*. Travecka, UK: n.d., 1791.

Haste, Matthew. "Marriage and Family in the Life of Andrew Fuller." *SBJT* 17 (2013) 28-34.

Hatch, Nathan O. *The Democratization of American Christianity*. New Haven, CT: Yale University Press, 1989.

Hayden, Roger. *Continuity and Change: Evangelical Calvinism Among Eighteenth-Century Baptist Ministers Trained at Bristol Baptist Academy, 1690-1791*. Didcot, UK: Baptist Historical Society, 2006.

———. *English Baptist History and Heritage*. Oxfordshire, UK: Baptist Union of Great Britain, 2005.

———. "Evangelical Calvinism among Eighteenth-Century British Baptists, with particular reference to Bernard Foskett, Hugh and Caleb Evans and the Bristol Baptist Academy, 1690-1791." PhD diss., University of Keele, 1992.

Haykin, Michael A. G. "Andrew Fuller and the Defense of Trinitarian Communities." *ABQ* 32 (2013) 258-78.

———. "Andrew Fuller [1754-1815] and the Free offer of the Gospel." *Reformation Today* 183 (2001) 29-32.

———, ed. *The Armies of the Lamb: The Spirituality of Andrew Fuller*. Dundas, ON: Joshua, 2001.

———, ed. *"At the Pure Fountain of Thy Word": Andrew Fuller as an Apologist*. Studies in Baptist History and Thought 6. Carlisle, UK: Paternoster, 2004.

———. "The Baptist Identity: A View from the Eighteenth Century." *EQ* 67 (1995) 137-52.

———, ed. *The British Particular Baptists 1638-1910*. Volume 2. Springfield, MO: Particular Baptist, 2000.

———. *The Emergence of Evangelicalism: Exploring Historical Continuities*. Edited by Michael A. G. Haykin and Kenneth J. Stewart. Nottingham: Apollos, 2008.

———. "Evangelicalism and the Enlightenment: A Reassessment," in *The Emergence of Evangelicalism: Exploring Historical Continuities*, edited by Michael A. G. Haykin and Kenneth J. Stewart, 37-62. Nottingham: Apollos, 2008.

———. "'For God's Glory [and] for Good of Precious Souls': Calvinism and Missions in the Piety of Samuel Pearce (1766-1799)." *Puritan Reformed Journal* 2 (2010) 277-300.

———. "'The Glorious Work of Reformation': Andrew Fuller and the Imitation of Martin Luther." *Unio cum Christo* 3 (2017) 127–37.

———. "Great Admirers of the Transatlantic Divinity: Some Chapters in the Baptist Edwardsianism." In *After Jonathan Edwards: The Courses of New England Theology*, edited by Oliver D. Crisp and Douglas A. Sweeney, 197–207. Oxford: Oxford University Press, 2012.

———. "'A Great Thirst for Reading': Andrew Fuller the Theological Reader." *Eusebeia* 9 (2008) 5–25.

———. "A Habitation of God Through the Spirit: John Sutcliff (1752–1814) and the Revitalization of the Calvinistic Baptists in the Late Eighteenth Century." *BQ* 34 (1992) 304–19.

———. "A Historical and Biblical Root of the Globalization of Christianity: The Fullerism of Andrew Fuller's the Gospel Worthy of All Acceptation." *Puritan Reformed Journal* 8 (2016) 165–76.

———. "'He Went about Doing Good': Eighteenth-Century Particular Baptists on the Necessity of Good Works." *American Theological Inquiry* 3 (2010) 55–65.

———. "'The honour of the Spirit's Work': Andrew Fuller, Dan Taylor, and an eighteenth-century Baptist debate over regeneration." *BQ* (2016) 152–61.

———. "John Owen and the Challenge of the Quakers." In *John Owen: The Man and His Theology*, edited by Robert W. Oliver. Phillipsburg: P&R, 2002.

———, ed. *John Owen on the Christian Life: Living for the Glory of God in Christ*. Wheaton, IL: Crossway, 2015.

———. *The Life and Thought of John Gill (1697–1771): A Tercentennial Appreciation*. New York: Brill, 1997.

———. *One Heart and One Soul: John Sutcliff of Olney, his Friends and his Times*. Durham, England: Evangelical, 1994.

———. *Pentecostal Outpourings: Revival and the Reformed Tradition*. Edited by Robert Davis Smart et al. Grand Rapids: Reformation Heritage, 2016.

———. *Rediscovering our English Baptist Heritage: Kiffin, Knollys and Keach*. Leeds: Reformation Trust, 1996.

Hays, Richard. *Echoes of Scripture in the Letters of Paul*. New Haven, CT: Yale University Press, 1989.

Helm, Paul. "'Structural Indifference' and Compatibilism in Reformed Orthodoxy." *Journal of Reformed Theology* 5 (2011) 184–205.

———. "Synchronic Contingency in Reformed Scholasticism: A Note of Caution." *Nederlands Theologisch Tijdshrift* 57 (2003) 207–22.

Hill, Christopher. *Antichrist in Seventeenth-Century England*. London: Oxford University Press, 1971.

———. *Society and Puritanism in Pre-Revolutionary England*. London: Mercury, 1966.

Hillerbrand, Hans, ed. *Oxford Encyclopedia of the Reformation*. Oxford: Oxford University Press, 1996.

Hindmarsh, Bruce. "The Antecedents of Evangelical Conversion Narrative: Spiritual Autobiography and the Christian Tradition." *Crux* 38 (2002) 4–13.

———. *The Evangelical Conversion Narrative: Spiritual Autobiography in Early Modern England*. Oxford: Oxford University Press, 2005.

———. *John Newton and The English Evangelical Tradition*. Grand Rapids: Eerdmans, 1996.

———. "The Reception of Jonathan Edwards by Early Evangelicals in England." In *Jonathan Edwards at Home and Abroad*, edited by David Kling and Douglas Sweeney, 201–21. Columbia: South Carolina University Press, 2003.

———. *The Spirit of Evangelicalism*. Oxford: Oxford University Press, 2018.

Holmes, Geoffrey. "The Sacheverell Riots: The Crowd and the Church in Early Eighteenth Century London." *Past and Present* 72 (1976) 55–85.

Holmes, Stephen. *God of Grace and God of Glory: An Account of the Theology of Jonathan Edwards*. Edinburgh: T. & T. Clark, 2000.

Hopkins, Samuel. *The Life and Character of the Late Reverend Mr. Jonathan Edwards*. Boston: S. Kneeland, 1765.

———. *The Works of Samuel Hopkins, DD . . . With a Memoir* [by Edwards Amasa Park] *of his Life and Character*. 3 vols. Boston: Doctrinal Tract and Book Society, 1852.

Hoselton, Ryan P. *The Love of God Holds Creation Together: Andrew Fuller's Theology of Virtue*. Eugene, OR: Pickwick, 2018.

Howard, Kenneth W. H. "John Sutcliff of Olney." *BQ* 14 (1951) 304–9.

Howe, John. *The Works of John Howe*. Edited by Edmund Calumny. New York: John P. Haven, 1835.

———. *The Works of the Rev. John Howe, M.A.* 3 vols. Ligionier, PA: Soli Deo Gloria, 1990.

———. *Whole Works*. 8 vols. Edited by J. Hunt. London: 1827.

Hughes, Graham W. "Robert Hall of Arnesby: 1728–91." *BQ* (1941) 444–47.

Hupton, Job. *A Blow Struck at the Root of Fullerism*. London: L. J. Higham, 1804.

Hussey, Joseph. *God's Operations of Grace, But No Offers of Grace*. London: D. Bridge, 1707.

Idle, Christopher. *Philip Doddridge: Hymnwriter (1702–1751)*. London: Evangelical Library, 2002.

Ihalainen, Pasi. "The Enlightenment Sermon: Towards Practical Religion and a Sacred National Community." In *Preaching, Sermon, and Cultural Change in the Long Eighteenth Century*, edited by Joris van Eijnatten, 219–60. Leiden: Brill, 2009.

Ivimey, Joseph. *A History of the English Baptists*. n.d.: 1811.

———. *The Life of Mr. William Kiffin*. London: n.d., 1833.

Jackson, Samuel Macauley, ed. *The New Schaff Herzog Encyclopedia of Religious Knowledge*. 4 vols. New York: Funk and Wagnalls, 1929.

Jackson, Thomas, ed. *Lives of the Early Methodist Preachers*. 2 vols. London: Wesleyan Conference Office, 1872.

Jenson, Robert. *America's Theologian: A Recommendation of Jonathan Edwards*. New York: Oxford University Press, 1988.

Jewson, C. B. *The Baptists in Norfolk*. London: Carey Kingsgate, 1957.

Jones, R. Tudur. *Congregationalism in England 1662–1962*. London: Independent, 1962.

Jue, Jeffrey K. "Andrew Fuller: Heir of the Reformation." *Eusebeia* 9 (2008) 27–52.

Kane, Robert. *The Significance of Free Will*. Oxford: Oxford University Press, 1998.

Kapic, Kelly M., and Mark Jones, eds. *The Ashgate Research Companion to John Owen's Theology*. Burlington, VT: Ashgate, 2012.

Kapic, Kelly M., and Randall C. Gleason, eds. *The Devoted Life: An Invitation to the Puritan Classics*. Downers Grove, IL: InterVarsity, 2004.

Keach, Benjamin. *The Baptist Catechism, or A brief instruction in the principles of the Christian religion,: agreeably to the confession of faith put forth upwards of an hundred congregations in Great-Britain, July 3d, 1689; adopted by the General*

Association of Philadelphia September 22d, 1742, and now received by churches of the same denomination of the United States. : To which are added proofs form Scripture. Wilmington, DE: P. Brynberg, 1809.

———. *The Glory of a True Church, and its Discipline Display'd.* London: n.d., 1697.

———. *Gospel Mysteries Unveil'd: Or An Exposition of the Parable and Many Express Similitudes Contained in the Four Evangelists Spoken by Our Lord and Saviour Jesus Christ where also Many things are Doctrinally Handled, and Practically Improved by Way of Application.* London: R. Tookey, 1701.

———. *Sion in Distress or the Groans of the Protestant Church.* Second Edition. London: George Larkin, 1682.

———. *Troplogia: A Key to Open Scripture Metaphors, in Four Books.* London: Collingridge, 1856.

Keeble, H. H., ed. *John Bunyan: Conventicle and Parnassus. Tercentenary Essays.* Oxford: Clarendon, 1988.

Kent, John. *Holding the Fort: Studies in Victorian Revivalism.* London: Epworth, 1978.

Kidd, Thomas. "Daniel Rogers' Egalitarian Great Awakening." *Journal of the Historical Society* 7 (2007) 111–35.

———. *George Whitfield America's Spiritual Founding Father.* New Haven, CT: Yale University Press, 2015.

———. *The Great Awakening: A Brief History with Documents.* Boston: Bedford/St Martins, 2008.

———. *The Great Awakening: The Roots of Evangelical Christianity in Colonial America.* New Haven, CT: Yale University Press, 2009.

———. "The Very Vital Breath of Christianity: Prayer and Revival in Provincial New England." *Fides et Historia* 36 (2004) 19–33.

Kiffen, William. "Preface." In *Glimpses of Sion's Glory: Or, The Churches Beautie Specified* by Thomas Goodwin. London: William Larnar, 1641.

Kirkby, Arthur Henry. "Andrew Fuller: Evangelical Calvinist." *BQ* 15 (1954) 195–202.

———. "The Theology of Andrew Fuller and its Relation to Calvinism." PhD diss., University of Edinburgh, 1956.

Klauber, Martin I. "Transatlantic Revivalism: Popular Evangelicalism in Britain and America 1790–1865." *JETS* 50 (2007) 871–73.

Kling, David, and Douglas Sweeney, eds. *Jonathan Edwards at Home and Abroad.* Columbia, SC: University of South Carolina Press, 2003.

Knollys, Hanserd, *Christ Exalted, A Lost Sinner Sought, and Saved by Christ.* London: Jane Coe, 1646.

Kreitzer, Larry Joseph. *William Kiffin and his World.* Oxford: Regent's Park, 2011.

Kuyper, Abraham. *Lectures on Calvinism.* Grand Rapids: Eerdmans, 1961.

———. *The Work of the Holy Spirit.* Grand Rapids: Eerdmans, 1956.

Lambert, Frank. *Inventing the "Great Awakening."* Princeton, NJ: Princeton University Press, 1999.

Langford, Paul. *A Polite and Commerical People: England 1727–1783.* Oxford: Clarendon, 1989.

Langley, Arthur S. "Baptist Ministers in England about 1750 A.D." *Transactions of the Baptist Historical Society* 6 (1918) 138–62.

Laird, Michael. "William Carey and Bengal." In *The Kettering Connection—Northamptonshire Baptists and Overseas Missions*, edited by L. Greenall, 47–54. Leicester: University of Leicester, 1993.

Law, William. *A Serious Call to a Devout and Holy Life*. Peabody, MA: Hendrickson, 2012.
Laws, Gilbert. *Andrew Fuller: Pastor; Theologian, Ropeholder*. London: Carey, 1942.
———. "Andrew Fuller, 1754–1815." *BQ* 2 (1942) 76–84.
Lee, Sang Hyun. *The Philosophical Theology of Jonathan Edwards*. Princeton: Princeton University Press, 1988.
Lesser, M. X. *Jonathan Edwards: An Annotated Bibliography in Three Parts, 1729–2005*. Grand Rapids: Eerdmans, 2008.
Lewis, Donald M., ed. *Dictionary of Evangelical Biography, 1730–1860*. Peabody, MA: Hendrickson, 2004.
Lim, Paul. *In Pursuit of Purity, Unity, and Liberty: Richard Baxter's Puritan Ecclesiology in Its Seventeenth-Century Context*. Leiden: Brill, 2004.
Locke, John. *An Essay Concerning Human Understanding*. 1689. Abridged and edited by Kenneth P. Winkler. Repr. Indianapolis: Hackett, 1996.
———. *A Letter Concerning Toleration*. Edited by J. W. Gough. Repr. Mineola, NY: Dover, 2002.
Lowman, Moses. *A Paraphrase and Notes on the Revelation of St. John*. London: John Noon, 1737. Eighteen Century Collections Online. https://archive.org/details/paraphrasenotesooolowm/page/n2.
Lumpkin, William L. *Baptist Confessions of Faith*. 2nd ed. Valley Forge, PA: Judson, 1969.
MacDonald, Murdina D. "London Calvinistic Baptists 1689–1727: Tensions within a Dissenting Community under Toleration." DPhil diss., Regent's Park College, Oxford University, 1982.
Macleod, Donald. "God or god? Arianism, Ancient and Modern." *EQ* 68 (1996) 121–38.
Manning, Bernard. *Essays in Orthodox Dissent*. London: Independent, 1939.
———. *The Hymns of Wesley and Watts: Five Informal Papers*. London: Epworth, 1942.
Marsden, George. *Jonathan Edwards: A Life*. New Haven, CT: Yale University Press, 2003.
Martin, John. *Thoughts on the Duty of Man Relative to Faith in Jesus Christ In Which Mr Andrew Fuller's Leading Propositions on the Subject Are Considered*. London: W. Smith, 1788–1791.
Mather, Samuel. *The Figures or Types of the Old Testament, by which Christ and the heavenly things of the gospel were preached and shadowed to the people of God of old: explain'd and improv'd in sundry sermons*. London: Nath. Hillier, 1705.
Matthew, H. C. G., and Brian Harrison, eds. *Oxford Dictionary of National Biography*. Oxford: Oxford University Press, 2004.
Mauldin, A. Chadwick. *Fullerism as Opposed to Calvinism: A Historical and Theological Comparison of the Missiology of Andrew Fuller and John Calvin*. Eugene, OR: Wipf & Stock, 2011.
McBeth, Leon, ed. *The Baptist Heritage: Four Centuries of Baptist Witness*. Nashville: Broadman, 1987.
———. *A Sourcebook for Baptist Heritage*. Nashville: Broadman, 1990.
McClymond, Michael J. *Embodying the Spirit: New Perspectives on North American Revivalism*. Baltimore: Johns Hopkins University Press, 2004.
McClymond, Michael J., and Gerald McDermott. *The Theology of Jonathan Edwards*. New York: Oxford University Press, 2011.

McDermott, Gerald. *Jonathan Edwards Confronts the Gods: Christian Theology, Enlightenment Religion, and Non-Christian Faiths*. Oxford: Oxford University Press, 2000.
McGlothlin, W. J. *Baptist Confessions of Faith*. Philadelphia: American Baptist Publication Society, 1911.
McLoughlin, William G. *Modern Revivalism: Charles Grandison Finney to Billy Graham*. New York: Ronald, 1959.
———. *New England Dissent, 1630–1833: The Baptists and the Separation of Church and State*. Cambridge, MA: Harvard University Press, 1971.
———. *Revivals Awakenings and Reform*. Chicago: University of Chicago Press, 1978.
Middleton, Erasmus. *Biographica Evangelica*. 4 vols. London: W. Baynes, 1816.
Miller, Perry. *Errand into the Wilderness*. Repr. New York: Harper and Row, 1964.
———. *Jonathan Edwards*. New York: W. Sloane Associates, 1949.
———. "Solomon Stoddard, 1643–1729." *HTR* 34 (1941) 277–320.
Milner, Isaac. *History of the Church of Christ*. London: Longman, Brown, Green and Longman's, 1847.
Milner, J. "Andrew Fuller." *Reformation Today* 17 (1974) 18–29.
Milner, Thomas. *The Life, Times, and Correspondence of the Rev. Isaac Watts D.D.* London: Simpkin and Marshall, 1834.
Milton, Michael. "The Pastoral Predicament of Vavasor Powell (1617–1670): Eschatological Fervor and its Relationship to the Pastoral Ministry." *JETS* 43 (2000) 517–27.
Mitchell, Christopher. "Jonathan Edwards's Scottish Connection." In *Jonathan Edwards at Home and Abroad*, edited by David Kling and Douglas Sweeney, 222–47. Columbia: South Carolina University Press, 2003.
Moorhead, James H. *Princeton Seminary in American Religion and Culture*. Grand Rapids: Eerdmans, 2012.
Morden, Peter. "Andrew Fuller and the Baptist Mission Society." *BQ* 41 (2005) 134–57.
———. "Andrew Fuller: A Biographical Sketch." In *'At the Pure Fountain of Thy Word,': Andrew Fuller as an Apologist*, edited by Michael A. G. Haykin, 1–41. Milton Keynes: Paternoster, 2004.
———. "Andrew Fuller and the Birth of Fullerism." *BQ* 46 (2015) 140–52.
———. *Communion with Christ and His People: The Spirituality of C.H. Spurgeon*. Eugene, OR: Wipf & Stock, 2014.
———. "John Bunyan: A Seventeenth-Century Evangelical?" *International Congregational Journal* 15 (2016) 79–100.
———. "John Bunyan: A Seventeenth Century Evangelical?" In *Grounded in Grace: Essays to Honor Ian M. Randall and Renewal Evangelicalism*, edited by Peter J. Lalleman et al., 33–52. London: Baptist Historical Society/Spurgeon's College, 2013.
———. *The Life and Thought of Andrew Fuller 1754–1815*. Carlisle, UK: Paternoster, 2015.
———. *Offering Christ to the World: Andrew Fuller (1754–1815) and the Revival of English Particular Baptist Life*. Studies in Baptist History and Thought 8. Carlisle, UK: Paternoster, 2003.
———. "'So valuable a life...': A Biographical Sketch of Andrew Fuller (1754–1815)." *SBJT* 17 (2013) 4–14.

Morris, J. W. *Memoirs of the Life and Writings of the Rev. Andrew Fuller.* Boston: Lincoln and Edmonds, 1830.

Morris, Thomas V. *Anselmian Explorations: Essays in Philosophical Theology.* Notre Dame: Notre Dame University Press, 1987.

———. "On Duty and Divine Goodness." In *Anselmian Explorations: Essays in Philosophical Theology.* Notre Dame, IN: Notre Dame University Press, 1987.

Muller, Richard A. *After Calvin: Studies in the Development of a Theological Tradition.* Oxford: Oxford University Press, 2003.

———. *Calvin and the Reformed Tradition: On the Work of Christ and the Order of Salvation.* Grand Rapids: Baker Academic, 2012.

———. "Jonathan Edwards and the Absence of Free Choice: A Parting of the Ways in the Reformed Tradition." *Jonathan Edwards Studies* 1 (2011) 3–22. http://jestudies.yale.edu/index.php/journal/article/view/63.

———. "Philip Doddridge and the Formulation of Calvinistic Theology in an Era of Rationalism and Deconfessionalization." In *Religion, Politics, and Dissent 1660–1832,* edited by Robert Cornwall and William Gibson, 65–84. New York: Ashgate, 2010.

———. *Post-Reformation Reformed Dogmatics,* 4 vols. Grand Rapids: Baker, 2003.

Murray, Iain. *Jonathan Edwards: A New Biography.* Carlisle, PA: Banner of Truth, 1987.

———. *Pentecost Today? The Biblical Basis for Understanding Revival.* Edinburgh: Banner of Truth, 1987.

———. *The Puritan Hope: A Study in Revival and the Interpretation of Prophecy.* Carlisle, PA: Banner of Truth, 1971.

———. *Revival and Revivalism: The Making and Marring of American Evangelicalism 1750–1858.* Carlisle, PA: Banner of Truth, 1994.

Murray, Victor. "Doddridge and Education." In *Philip Doddridge: His Contribution to English Religion,* edited by Geoffrey Nuttall, 102–21. London: Independent, 1951.

Mursell, Gordon. *English Spirituality: From 1700 to the Present Day.* Louisville: Westminster John Knox, 2001.

Naylor, Peter. *Calvinism, Communion and the Baptists: A Study of English Baptists from the later 1600's to the Early 1800's.* Studies in Baptist History and Thought 7. Carlisle: Paternoster, 2003.

Nettles, Thomas J. "Andrew Fuller." In *The British Particular Baptists 1638–1910,* edited by Michael A. G. Haykin, 2:97–141. Springfield, MO: Particular Baptist, 2000.

———. "Andrew Fuller and Free Grace." *Reformation Today* 82 (1985) 6–14.

———. *The Baptists: Key People Involved in Forming a Baptist Identity.* Ross-shire, Scotland: Christian Focus, 2005.

———. *By His Grace and for His Glory: A Historical, Theological, and Practical Study of the Doctrines of Grace in Baptist Life.* Grand Rapids: Baker, 1986.

———. "Edwards and His Impact on Baptists." *Founders Journal* 53 (2003) 1–18.

———. "The Influence of Jonathan Edwards on Andrew Fuller." *Eusebeia* 9 (2008) 97–116.

———. "John Gill and the Evangelical Awakening." In *The Life and Thought of John Gill (1697–1771): A Tercentennial Appreciation,* edited by Michael A. G. Haykin. New York: Brill, 1997.

Newman, A. H. "Andrew Fuller." In *The New Schaff Herzog Encyclopedia of Religious Knowledge,* edited by Samuel Macauley Jackson, 409. New York: Funk and Wagnalls, 1929.

Nicholson, Henry. *Authentic Records Relating to the Christian Church Now Meeting in George Street and Mutley Chapels, Plymouth, 1640–1870.* London: Elliot Stock, 1904.

Nicholson, John F. V. *Vavasor Powell 1617–1670.* London: Independent, 1961.

Noll, Mark. *America's God: From Jonathan Edwards to Abraham Lincoln.* Oxford: Oxford University Press, 2005.

———. *The Rise of Evangelicalism: The Age of Edwards, Whitefield and the Wesleys.* Downers Grove, IL: InterVarsity, 2003.

Nuttall, Geoffrey F. *Calendar of the Correspondence of Philip Doddridge, DD.* London: HMSO, 1979.

———. *The Holy Spirit in Puritan Faith and Experience.* Oxford: Oxford University Press, 1947.

———. *Howell Harris 1714–1773: The Last Enthusiast.* Cardiff: University of Wales Press, 1965.

———. "Methodism and Older Dissent: Some Perspectives." *JURCHS* 2 (1981) 248–58.

———. "Northamptonshire and the Modern Question: A Turning-Point in Eighteenth-Century Dissent." *Journal of Theological Studies* 16 (1965) 100–23.

———, ed. *Philip Doddridge: His Contribution to English Religion.* London: Independent, 1951.

———. *Richard Baxter.* London: Thomas Nelson, 1965.

———. *Richard Baxter and Philip Doddridge: A Study in Tradition.* London: Dr. Williams Library, 1951.

———. "'The State of Religion in Northamptonshire' (1793) by Andrew Fuller." *BQ* 29 (1981) 177–79.

———. *The Welsh Saints: 1640–1660: Water Cradock, Vavasor Powell, Morgan LLwyd.* Cardiff: University of Wales Press, 1957.

O'Brien, Susan. *Evangelicalism Comparative Studies of Popular Protestantism in North America, the British Isles, and Beyond, 1700–1990.* Edited by Mark Noll et al. Oxford: Oxford University Press, 1994.

O'Gorman, Frank. *The Long Eighteenth Century: British Political and Social History 1688–1832.* London: Hodder Arnold, 1997.

Oliver, Robert. "The Emergence of a Strict and Particular Baptist Community Among the English Calvinistic Baptists, 1770–1850." DPhil diss., CNAA [London Bible College], 1986.

———, ed. *John Owen: The Man and His Theology.* Phillipsburg: Presbyterian and Reformed, 2002.

Orchard, Stephen. "Selina, Countess of Huntingdon" *JURCHS* 8 (2008) 77–90.

Owen, John. *The Works of John Owen.* CD-ROM. Ages Software, 2000.

———. *Communion with the Triune God.* Edited by Kelly M. Kapic and Justin Taylor. Wheaton, IL: Crossway, 2007.

———. *The Death of Death in the Death of Christ.* Edited by William H. Goold. The Works of John Owen 10. Repr. Edinburgh: Banner of Truth, 1965.

———. *Discourse on the Holy Spirit.* Edited by William H. Goold. The Works of John Owen 3. Repr. Edinburgh: Banner of Truth, 1965.

———. *The Doctrine of Justification by Faith.* Edited by William H. Goold. The Works of John Owen 5. Repr. Edinburgh: Banner of Truth, 1965.

———. *On Indwelling Sin.* Edited by William H. Goold. The Works of John Owen 6. Repr. Edinburgh: Banner of Truth, 1965.

———. *The Reason of Faith*. Edited by William H. Goold. The Works of John Owen 4. Repr. Edinburgh: Banner of Truth, 1965.

Packer, J. I. *Among God's Giants: The Puritan Vision of the Christian Life*. Eastbourne: Kingsway, 1991.

———. *A Quest for Godliness*. Wheaton, IL: Crossway, 1994.

———. "Puritanism as a Movement of Revival." *EQ* 52 (1980) 2–16.

———. "The Redemption and Restoration of Man in the Thought of Richard Baxter." DPhil diss., Oxford University, 1954.

Paul, Robert S. *The Assembly of the Lord*. Edinburgh: T. & T. Clark, 1985.

Payne, Ernest Alexander. "Abraham Booth, 1734–1806." *BQ* 26 (1975) 28–42.

———. "Andrew Fuller as Letter Writer." *BQ* 15 (1954) 290–96.

———. "Eighteenth Century English Congregationalism as Exemplified in the Life and Work of Philip Doddridge." *Review and Expositor* 48 (1951) 286–301.

———. "John Dyer's Memoir of Carey." *BQ* 22 (April 1968) 326–27.

Payne, Robert. *The Prayer Call of 1784*. London: Kingsgate, 1941.

Pelikan, Jaroslav. *Credo: Historical and Theological Guide to Creeds and Confessions of Faith in the Christian Tradition*. New Haven, CT: Yale University Press, 2003.

Pereboom, Derk. "Theological Determinism and Divine Providence." In *Molinism: The Contemporary Debate*, edited by Ken Perszyk, 262. Oxford: Oxford University Press, 2011.

Perkins, William. *The Works of That Famous and Worthy Minister. . . Mr. William Perkins, 1613, 1616*. n.d.

Perszyk, Ken, ed. *Molinism: The Contemporary Debate*. Oxford: Oxford University Press, 2011.

Piggin, Stuart. "The Expanding Knowledge of God: Jonathan Edwards's Influence on Missionary Thinking and Promotion." In *Jonathan Edwards at Home and Abroad*, edited by David Kling and Douglas Sweeney, 266–96. Columbia: South Carolina University Press, 2003.

Piper, John. *God's Passion for His Glory: Living the Vision of Jonathan Edwards*. Wheaton, IL: Crossway, 1998.

———. *Holy Faith, Worthy Gospel, World Mission*. Wheaton, IL: Crossway, 2016.

Pittsley, Jeremy. "Christ's Absolute Determination to Save: Andrew Fuller and Particular Redemption." *Eusebia* 9 (2008) 135–66.

Plantinga, Alvin. *God, Freedom, and Evil*. Grand Rapids: Eerdmans, 1977.

Pocock, John G. A. "Historiography and Enlightenment: A View of their History." *Modern Intellectual History* 5 (2008) 83–96.

Potts, E. Daniel. *British Baptist Missionaries in India 1793–1837*. Cambridge: Cambridge University Press, 1967.

———. "'I Throw Away the Guns to Preserve the Ship': A Note on the Serampore Trio." *BQ* 20 (1963) 115–17.

Powicke, F. J. *The Life of Reverend Richard Baxter (1615–1691)*. 2 vols. Boston: Houghton Mifflin, 1924–1927.

Priest, Gerald L. "Andrew Fuller's Response to the 'Modern Question'—A Reappraisal of The Gospel Worthy of All Acceptation." *Detroit Baptist Seminary Journal* 6 (2001) 45–73.

Purferoy, George A. *A History of the Sandy Creek Baptist Association, from its Organization in AD. 1759, to 1858*. 1859. Repr. New York: Arno, 1980.

Rack, Henry. *Reasonable Enthusiast: John Wesley and the Rise of Methodism.* 3rd ed. London: Epworth, 2002.

Randall, Ian M. "Christ Comes to The Heart: Moravian Influence on the Shaping of Evangelical Spirituality." *Journal of European Baptist Studies* 6 (2006) 5–23.

Rathel, David Mark. "Was John Gill a Hyper-Calvinist? Determining Gill's Theological Identity." *BQ* 48 (2017) 47–59.

Reed, Edward Allen. "A Historical Study of Three Baptist Doctrines of Atonement as Seen in the Writings of John Smyth, Thomas Helwys, John Gill and Andrew Fuller." ThM thesis, Golden Gate Baptist Theological Seminary, 1958.

Renault, James Owen. "The Changing Patterns of Separate Baptist Religious Life, 1803–1977." *Baptist History and Heritage* 14 (1979) 16–25.

Riker, D. B. *A Catholic Reformed Theologian: Federalism and Baptism in the Thought of Benjamin Keach 1640–1704.* Eugene, OR: Wipf & Stock, 2010.

Rinaldi, Frank. *The Tribe of Dan: The New Connexion of General Baptists 1770–1891: A Study in the Transition from Revival Movement to Established Denomination.* Studies in Baptist History and Thought 10. Eugene, OR: Wipf & Stock, 2008.

Rippon, John. *A Brief Memoir of the Life and Writings of the Late Rev. John Gill, D.D.* London: John Bennet, 1838. Rep. Harrisonburg, VA: Gano, 1992.

Robe, James. *A Faithful Narrative of the Extraordinary Work of the Spirit of God, at Kilsyth.* 2nd ed. London: S. Mason, 1742–1743.

Roberts, Phil. "Andrew Fuller." In *Theologians of the Baptist Tradition,* edited by Timothy George and David Dockery, 34–51. Nashville: Broadman, 1990.

Robinson, Olin C. "The Legacy of John Gill." *BQ* 24 (1971) 111–25.

Rogers, Henry. *Life and Character of John Howe.* London: William Ball, 1879.

Routley, Erik. "The Hymns of Doddridge." In *Philip Doddridge: His Contribution to English Religion,* edited by Geoffrey Nuttall, 46–78. London: Independent, 1951.

Rupp, Gordon. *Six Makers of English Religion.* New York: Harper & Brothers, 1957.

Ryland, John, Jr. *Seasonable Hints to a bereaved church; And the blessedness of the dead, who die in the Lord.* Northampton: T. Dicey and Co., 1783.

———. *The Work of Faith, the Labour of Love, and the Patience of Hope Illustrated in the Life and Death of the Rev. Andrew Fuller.* 2nd ed. London: Button and Sons, 1818.

Ryle, J. C. *Christian Leaders in the Past Century.* London: Thomas Nelson and Sons, 1869.

Saussure, Ferdinand. *Courses in General Linguistics.* Edited by Charles Bally et al. Translated by Wade Baskin. London: Fontana/Collins, 1978.

Schaff, Phillip. *Creeds of Christendom.* New York: Harper, 1877.

Schreiner, Thomas R., and Bruce A. Ware, eds. *Still Sovereign: Contemporary Perspectives on Election, Foreknowledge, and Grace.* Grand Rapids: Baker, 2000.

Schultz, Walter. "The Metaphysics of Jonathan Edwards's End of Creation." *JETS* 59 (2016) 339–59.

Secrett, A. G. "Philip Doddridge and the Eighteenth-century Revivals." *EQ* 23 (1951) 242–59.

Seeman, Erik. *Pious Persuasions: Laity and Clergy in Eighteenth-Century New England.* Baltimore: John Hopkins University Press, 1999.

Sell, Alan P. F. *Dissenting Thought and the Life of the Churches: Studies in an English Tradition.* San Francisco: Mellen Research University Press, 1990.

———. *Enlightenment, Ecumenicism, Evangel: Theological Theme and Thinkers, 1550–2000.* Milton Keynes: Paternoster, 2005.

———. *The Great Debate: Calvinism, Arminianism and Salvation*. Grand Rapids: Baker, 1983.

———. "John Howe's Eclectic Theism." *JURCHS* 2 (1980) 187–93.

———. *Testimony and Tradition: Studies in Reformed and Dissenting Thought*. New York: Ashgate, 2005.

Seymour, Aaron Crossley Hobart. *The Life and Times of Selina Countess of Huntingdon*. London: William Edward Painter, 1840.

Shaw, Ian. *High Calvinists in Action: Calvinism and the City Manchester and London c. 1810–1860*. Oxford: Oxford University Press, 2002.

Sheehan, Clint. "Great and Sovereign Grace: Andrew Fuller's Defense of the Gospel against Arminianism." In *'At the Pure Fountain of Thy Word': Andrew Fuller as Apologist*, edited by Michael A. G. Haykin, 85–87. Studies in Baptist History and Thought 6. Carlisle, UK: Paternoster, 2004.

Skepp, John. *Divine Energy or the Operations of the Spirit of God upon the soul of man in his effectual calling and conversion, state, proved, and vindicated. . .being an antidote against Pelagian Error*. London: Printed For Joseph Marshall and Aaron Ward, 1722.

Skinner, Quentin. *Visions of Politics I: Regarding Method*. Cambridge: Cambridge University Press, 2002.

Smart, Robert Davis. "Edwards's Revival Instinct and Apologetic in American Presbyterianism: Planted, Grown, and Faded." In *Pentecostal Outpourings: Revival and the Reformed Tradition*, edited by Robert Davis Smart et al., 133–63. Grand Rapids: Reformation Heritage, 2016.

Smith, A. Christopher. "The Spirit and Letter of Carey's Catalytic Watchword: A Study in the Transmission of Baptist Tradition." *BQ* 33 (1990) 226–37.

———. "William Ward, Radical Reform, and Missions in the 1790's." *ABQ* 10 (1991) 226–44.

Smith, George. *The Life of William Carey, D.D., Shoemaker and Missionary*. London: John Murray, 1885.

Smith, John E. *Jonathan Edwards: Puritan, Preacher, Philosopher*. Notre Dame: Notre Dame University Press, 1992.

Smith, John H. *The Perfect Rule of the Christian Religion: A History of Sandemanianism in the Eighteenth Century*. Albany: State University of New York Press, 2008.

Soham Baptist Church Book. Cambridge County Archive N/B—Soham, 1752–1868.

South, Thomas J. "The Response of Andrew Fuller to the Sandemanian View of Saving Faith." PhD diss., Mid-America Baptist Theological Seminary, 1993.

Spurr, John. *English Puritanism 1603–1689: Social History in Perspective*. London: MacMillan, 1998.

Stanford, Charles. *Philip Doddridge, D.D. Heroes of Christian History*. New York: A. C. Armstrong, 1881.

Stanley, Ayling. *John Wesley*. London: Abingdon, 1979.

Stanley, Brian. *The History of the Baptist Missionary Society 1792–1992*. Edinburgh: T. & T. Clark, 1992.

Starr, Edward C. *A Baptist Bibliography*. Rochester, NY: American Baptist Historical Society, 1963.

Stein, Stephen J. "The Quest for the Spiritual Sense: The Biblical Hermeneutics of Jonathan Edwards." *Harvard Theological Review* 70 (1977) 99–113.

Stewart, Kenneth J. "Did Evangelicalism Pre-Date the Eighteenth-Century? An Examination of the David Bebbington Thesis." *EQ* 77 (2005) 135–53.

———. *Ten Myths about Calvinism: Recovering the Breadth of the Reformed Tradition*. Downers Grove, IL: IVP Academic, 2011.

Stoeffler, F. Ernest. *The Rise of Evangelical Pietism*. Leiden: Brill, 1971.

Stonehouse, George. *Fullerism Defended; or Faith in Christ Asserted to be a Requirement of the Moral Law*. Cranbrook, Kent: S. Waters, 1804.

Stout, Harry S. *The Divine Dramatist: George Whitefield and the Rise of Modern Evangelicalism*. Grand Rapids: Eerdmans, 1991.

Striven, Robert. *Philip Doddridge and the Shaping of Evangelical Dissent*. Farnham, Surrey: Routelege, 2015.

Sutcliff, John. "Preface." *An Humble Attempt to Promote Explicit Agreement and Visible Union of God's People in Extraordinary Prayer for the Revival of Religion and the Advancement of Christ's Kingdom on Earth, pursuant to Scripture Promises and Prophecies concerning the Last Time*, by Jonathan Edwards. Repr. Northampton: T. Dicey and Co., 1789.

Sutherland, Martin. *Peace, Toleration and Decay: The Ecclesiology of Later Stuart Dissent*. Studies in Christian History and Thought. Eugene, OR: Wipf & Stock, 2003.

Sweeney, Douglas A., and Allen C. Guelzo. *The New England Theology: From Jonathan Edwards to Edwards Amasa Park*. Grand Rapids: Baker, 2006.

Sweet, William Warren. *Religion in the Development of American Culture 1765–1840*. New York: Charles Scribner's Sons, 1952.

Swinburne, Richard. *Mind, Brain, and Free Will*. Oxford: Oxford University Press, 2013.

Taylor, Abraham. *The Modern Question Concerning Faith and Repentance*. London: Aaron Ward, 1742.

Taylor, Daniel. *Observations of the Rev Andrew Fuller's late pamphlet entitled the Gospel Worthy of All Acceptation*. London: J. Buckland, 1788.

Tempe, Kevin. *Free Will: Sourcehood and Its Alternatives*. 2nd ed. London: Bloomsbury, 2013.

Thiselton, Anthony. *The Hermeneutics of Doctrine*. Grand Rapids: Eerdmans, 2007.

Thomas, Graham C. G. "George Whitefield and Friends: The Correspondence of Some Early Methodists." *National Library of Wales Journal* 27 (1991) 65–96.

Thompson, Philip, and Anthony Cross, eds. *Recycling the Past or Researching History?* Studies in Baptist History and Thought 8. Carlisle: Paternoster, 2005.

Tiessen, Terrance L. *Providence and Prayer: How Does God Work in the World?* Downers Grove, IL: InterVarsity, 2000.

Timpe, Kevin. *Free Will: Sourcehood and Its Alternatives*. 2nd ed. New York: Bloomsbury, 2008.

Tindall, Matthew. *Christianity as Old as the Creation, or the Gospel a republication of the Religion of Nature*. London: 1730.

Toland, John. *Christianity not Mysterious: or, A treatise shewing that there is nothing in the Gospel contrary to reason, nor above it and that no Christian doctrine can be properly call'd a mystery*. London: Sam Buckley, 1696.

Toon, Peter. *The Emergence of Hyper-Calvinism in English Nonconformity 1689–1765*. Cambridge: Burlington, 1967.

———. *God's Statesman: The Life and Work of John Owen, Pastor, Educator, Theologian*. Grand Rapids: Zondervan, 1973.

———, ed. *Puritans, the Millennium and the Future of Israel: Puritan Eschatology 1600–1660*. Cambridge: James Clarke, 1970.

Torbet, Robert G. *A History of the Baptists*. 3rd ed. Valley Forge, PA: Judson, 1963.

Torrey, Samuel. *An Exhortation unto Reformation, amplified, by a discourse concerning the parts and progress of that work, according to the word of God. Delivered in a sermon preached in the audience of the General Assembly of the Massachusetts Colony, at Boston in New-England, May 27, 1674. Being the Day of Election There.* Evans Early American Imprint Collection. https://quod.lib.umich.edu/cgi/t/text/text-idx?c=evans;idno=N00141.0001.001.

Trueman, Carl. *Histories and Fallacies: Problems Faced in the Writings of History*. Wheaton, IL: Crossway, 2008.

———. "John Owen and Andrew Fuller." *Eusebia* 9 (2008) 53–70.

———. *John Owen: Reformed Catholic, Renaissance Man*. New York: Ashgate, 2007.

———. "Puritanism as Ecumenical Theology." *Nederlands Archief Voor Kerkgeschiedenis* 81 (2001) 326–36.

———. "The Reception of Calvin: Historical Considerations." *Church History and Religious Culture* 91 (2011) 19–27.

Tudur, Geraint. *Howell Harris: From Conversion to Separation, 1735–1750*. Cardiff, UK: University of Wales Press, 2000.

Underhill, Edward Bean. *Confessions of Faith and other Public Documents Illustrative of the History of Baptist in England*. London: Haddon Brothers, 1854.

Underwood, A. C. *A History of the English Baptists*. London: Carey Kingsgate, 1947.

Van Asselt, Willem J. *The Federal Theology of Johannes Cocceius 1603–1669*. Translated by Raymond A. Blacketer. Leiden: Brill, 2001.

Van Asselt, Willem J., et al., eds. *Reformed Thought on Freedom: The Concept of Free choice in Early Modern Reformed Theology*. Grand Rapids: Baker Academic, 2010.

Van Eijnatten, Joris. *Preaching, Sermon, and Cultural Change in the Long Eighteenth Century*. Leiden: Brill, 2009.

Van Horn, Luke. "On Incorporating Middle Knowledge into Calvinism: A Theological/Metaphysical Muddle?" *JETS* 55 (2012) 807–27.

Van Inwagen, Peter. *An Essay on Free Will*. Oxford: Oxford University Press, 2002.

Vedder, Henry C. *A Short History of the Baptists*. Valley Forge, PA: Judson, 1907.

Venn, Henry. *The Complete Duty of Man: or, a system of doctrinal and practical Christianity; with prayers for families and individuals*. Glasgow: Willliam Collins, 1829.

Vihvelin, Kadri. "Arguments for Incompatibilism." *Stanford Encyclopedia of Philosophy*. http://plato.stanford.edu/entries/incompatibilism-arguments/.

Walker, Austin. *The Excellent Benjamin Keach*. Dundas, Ontario: Joshua, 2004.

Walker, R. B. "Religious Change in Cheshire 1750–1850." *Journal of Evangelical History* 17 (1966) 77–94

Walker, Wilston. *The Creeds and Platforms of Congregationalism*. Boston: Pilgrim, 1960.

Wallace, Dewey D. *Puritans and Predestination: Grace in English Protestant Theology, 1525–1695*. Chapel Hill: University of North Carolina Press, 2002.

———. *The Spirituality of the Later English Puritans: An Anthology*. Macon, GA: Mercer University Press, 1987.

Walls, Jerry. "Why No Classical Theist, Let Alone Orthodox Christian, Should Ever be a Compatibilist." *Philosophia Christi* 13 (2011) 75–104.

Walsh, John. "Origins of the Evangelical Revival." In Essays in Modern Church History edited by John Walsh et al., 132, 154. London: A. & C. Black, 1966.

Walton, Brad. *Jonathan Edwards, Religious Affections and the Puritan Analysis of True Piety, Spiritual Sensation and Heart Religion*. Lewiston, NY: Edwin Mellen, 2002.

Ware, Bruce. *God's Greater Glory: The Exalted God of Scripture and the Christian Faith*. Wheaton, IL: Crossway, 2004.

Watson, Thomas. *A Body of Divinity*. Repr. Carlisle, PA: Banner of Truth, 2011.

———. *The Doctrine of Repentance*. Repr. Carlisle, PA: Banner of Truth, 2016.

Watts, Isaac. *Divine and moral songs, attempted in easy language, for the use of children, revised and corrected and Plain and easy catechism for children, and preservative from the sins and follies of childhood and youth*. Windham, CT: Samuel Webb, 1813.

———. *Discourses of the Love of God and Its Influence on All the Passions*. New York: J. H. Turney, 1832.

———. *A Guide to Prayer*. 9th ed. Boston: J. Draper, 1739.

———. *An Humble Attempt toward the Revival of Practical Religion among Christians*. London: E. Matthews, R. Ford, and R. Hett, 1731.

———. *The Works of the Late Reverend and Learned Isaac Watts, D.D. Published by Himself, and Now Collected into Six Volumes. Revised and Corrected by D. Jennings, DD. And the Late P. Doddridge, D.D.* London: T. and T. Longman, and J. Buckland; J. Oswald; J. Waugh; and J. Ward, 1753.

Watts, Isaac. *Wattiana: Manuscript Remains of the Rev Isaac Watts, DD from the Library of Mr Joseph Parker, his amanuensis*. London: British Library.

Watts, Michael R. *The Dissenters*. Oxford: Clarendon, 1978.

Wayman, Lewis. *A Further Enquiry After Truth, wherein, is shown what faith is required of unregenerate persons*. London: J. and J. Marshall, 1738.

Webb, R. K. "The Emergence of Rational Dissent." In *Enlightenment and Religion: Rational Dissent in Eighteenth-century Britain*, edited by Knud Haakonssen, 12–41. Cambridge: Cambridge University Press, 1996.

Wellwood, Henry Moncreiff. *Account of the Life and Writings of John Erskine, D.D., Late One of the Ministers of Edinburgh*. Edinburgh: Archibald Constable and Company, 1818.

Wesley, John. *The Works of John Wesley*. Edited by Frank Baker. Oxford: Clarendon, 1982.

Wheeler, Nigel David. "Andrew Fuller's Ordination Sermons." *Eusebia* 9 (2008) 167–82.

———. "Eminent Spirituality and Eminent Usefulness: Andrew Fuller's (1754–1815) Pastoral Theology in His Ordination Sermons." PhD diss., University of Pretoria, 2009.

Whelan, Michael T., ed. *Baptist Autographs in John Ryland's University Library of Manchester, 1741–1845*. Macon, GA: Mercer University Press, 2009.

White, Anthony. "A Theological and Historical Examination of John Gill's Soteriology in Relation to Eighteenth-Century Hyper-Calvinism." PhD diss., Southern Baptist Theological Seminary, 2010.

White, B. R. *The English Separatist Tradition: from the Marian Martyrs to the Pilgrim Fathers*. Oxford: Oxford University Press, 1971.

———. *Hanserd Knollys and Radical Dissent In the 17th Century*. London: Dr. Williams's Trust, 1977.

White, Barrie R. *The English Baptists of the 17th Century*. Didioct: The Baptist Historical Society, 1996.

———. "William Kiffin—Baptist Pioneer and Citizen of London." *Baptist History and Heritage* 2 (1967) 91–103.

Whitefield, George. *Eighteen Sermons Preached by the Late Rev. George Whitefield, A.M.* Edited by Joseph Gurney. Springfield, MA: Thomas Dickman, 1808.

———. *Memoirs of the Rev. George Whitefield*. Edited by John Gillies. Middletown: Hunt & Co., 1841.

Whitley, W. T. *Calvinism and Evangelism in England*. London: Kingsgate, 1933.

———. *A History of British Baptists*. London: Charles Griffin and Company, 1923.

Wigger, John. *American Saint: Francis Asbury and the Methodists*. New York: Oxford University Press, 2009.

Williams, Gary J. "Enlightenment Epistemology and Eighteenth-Century Evangelical Doctrines of Assurance." In *The Emergence of Evangelicalism*, edited by Kenneth Steward and Michael A. G. Haykin, 345–74. Nottingham: Apollos, 2008.

Wills, Gregory A. *Democratic Religion: Freedom, Authority, and Church Discipline in the Baptist South 1785–1900*. Oxford: Oxford University Press, 1997.

———. "The Spirituality of John Gill." In *The Life and Thought of John Gill 1697–1771: A Tercentennial Appreciation*, edited by Michael A. G. Haykin, 209. Leiden: Brill, 1997.

Wingard, John C., Jr. "Confession of a Reformed Philosopher: Why I Am a Compatibilist about Determinism and Moral Responsibility." *Themelios* 42 (2017) 263–84.

Wolffe, John. *The Expansion of Evangelicalism: The Age of Wilberforce, More Chalmers and Finney*. Downers Grove, IL: InterVarsity, 2007.

Woolrych, Austin. *Britain in Revolution: 1625–1660*. Oxford: Oxford University Press, 2004.

Worth, R. N. *History of Plymouth From the Earliest Period to the Present Time*. Plymouth: William Brendon, 1890.

Woznicki, Christopher. "Is Prayer Redundant? Calvin and the Early Reformers on the Problem of Petitionary Prayer." *JETS* 60 (2017) 333–48.

Yeager, Jonathan, ed. *Early Evangelicalism*. New York: Oxford University Press, 2013.

———. *Enlightened Evangelicalism: The Life and Thought of John Erskine*. Oxford: Oxford University Press, 2011.

———. "The Letters of John Erskine to the Rylands." *Eusebia* 9 (2008) 183–95.

Yong, Jeremy Yuen Ming. "Tending to Love—'The Plant of Paradise': Andrew Fuller on Love and its Role in Local Church Revival." DMin thesis, Southern Baptist Theological Seminary, 2015.

Young, Doyle. "Andrew Fuller and the Modern Missionary Movement." *Baptist History and Heritage* 17 (1982) 17–27.

———. "The Place of Andrew Fuller in the Developing Modern Missions Movement." PhD diss., Southwestern Baptist Theological Seminary, 1981.

www.ingramcontent.com/pod-product-compliance
Lightning Source LLC
Chambersburg PA
CBHW051743230426

43670CB00012B/2135